D0754315

Continued on back

HYPNOSIS
AND RELAXATION

HYPNOSIS
AND RELAXATION
MODERN VERIFICATION
OF AN OLD EQUATION

William E. Edmonston, Jr.
Colgate University

A Wiley-Interscience Publication

John Wiley & Sons, New York • Chichester • Brisbane • Toronto

Library of Congress Cataloging in Publication Data:

Edmonston, William E
  Hypnosis and relaxation.

  (Wiley series on personality processes)
  "A Wiley-Interscience publication."
  Includes index.
  1. Hypnotism. 2. Relaxation. I. Title.
[DNLM: 1. Hypnosis. 2. Relaxation. WM415
E24h]
BF1152.E35   154.7'7   80-22506
ISBN 0-471-05903-X

Printed in the United States of America

10 9 8 7 6 5 4 3 2 1

To
Nellie, Kathy, Beckie, and Owen

Series Preface

This series of books is addressed to behavioral scientists interested in the nature of human personality. Its scope should prove pertinent to personality theorists and researchers as well as to clinicians concerned with applying an understanding of personality processes to the amelioration of emotional difficulties in living. To this end, the series provides a scholarly integration of theoretical formulations, empirical data, and practical recommendations.

Six major aspects of studying and learning about human personality can be designated: personality theory, personality structure and dynamics, personality development, personality assessment, personality change, and personality adjustment. In exploring these aspects of personality, the books in the series discuss a number of distinct but related subject areas: the nature and implications of various theories of personality; personality characteristics that account for consistencies and variations in human behavior; the emergence of personality processes in children and adolescents; the use of interviewing and testing procedures to evaluate individual differences in personality; efforts to modify personality styles through psychotherapy, counseling, behavior therapy, and other methods of influence; and patterns of abnormal personality functioning that impair individual competence.

IRVING B. WEINER

University of Denver
Denver, Colorado

Preface

Hypnosis and Relaxation evolved out of a growing awareness that in the field of experimental hypnosis, responses of subjects to a variety of stimuli while under hypnosis did not differ from their responses while simply relaxed. This realization was slow in developing. Like many young investigators, my initial concern was with finding some response, some behavior that signaled hypnosis as a unique state, similar to many other conditions but singular nonetheless. Toward this goal I carefully measured several behavioral and physiological responses, and in the course of seeking more refined experimental control in my studies I utilized a group instructed to relax but not to be hypnotized.

Even then I was shackled by my history, for I continued to search for the unique response, claiming, each time a response did not differ between hypnosis and my new-found control group of relaxed subjects, that this or that response did not constitute a signal marker of the state of hypnosis. It was in the refutation of slow eye movements (SEMs) as a response unique to hypnosis that the more important meaning of my data began to become clear. As I indicate herein, it was not so much that SEMs or any other responses were not unique to hypnosis, but that none of these responses were *different* in hypnosis when compared to the same responses in nonhypnotic relaxation. This one salient reorientation set me on a course of exploring the entire field of hypnosis for other indications of similarities between hypnosis, as traditionally understood, and states of relaxation. I found the relationship astounding in its breadth and clarity, so much so that I decided it was time that researchers stop and review with me the potential meaning of this apparent symbiosis. Thus I proceeded to write *Hypnosis and Relaxation*.

Writing this book has been an education in itself, and I highly recommend book writing to anyone truly interested in understanding an area of investigation. It is a delightful excursion into the unknown, not only the unknown of literature with which you were unfamiliar but into the unknown of your own inner self and of a world of ideas and new and different perspectives that you never suspected existed, much less within yourself. Many were the days that the morning's writing began at one point and ended at another that was never consciously considered at the outset. In a frighteningly real sense the book wrote itself, leading me through vast fields of ideas that I neither knew I possessed nor knew I was capable of birthing. At times the flood of ideas was too rapid for my fingers to capture before they had once again faded back into that nether land of neurons and glia. There were moments of severe frustration, when all of those "brilliant" cognitions were again obscured from revelation, never (or so I thought) to be inked into history. Fascinatingly, they did return when I did two things: *relaxed* and assumed the same physical position I was in when the integration of the old with the new had originally taken place.

I do not wish to leave the reader with the impression that writing this book was some sort of ethereal combination of unconscious ferment in a sea of relaxation, effortlessly recorded on an old IBM. It was downright hard work. And worrisome too. The hard work, of course, lay in the gathering together of the vast number of books, papers, articles, and studies that formed the empirical base for justifying the ideas put forward, and the melting of all of these ores into some sort of cohesive, flowing synthesis. The cause of worry, however, was something different: It was the concern that what I had to say was not really important, or worse yet, that it should not be said at all, because even if predominantly accurate it might slow rather than speed the progress of the field. Many was the time I gave serious consideration to suspending work on the manuscript permanently. No doubt some of the readers will conclude that that is exactly what I should have done, but I found through the months that there was a simple elixir for the doldrums of self-doubt. That was to re-review some of the articles that formed the book's data base, to re-review some of the reanalyses I had made of other's works, and, more important, to reread my own writings and interpretations. Yes, writing a book *is* an author's ego-trip, but more than that, it is an exposure of one's ego, one's ideas, one's thoughts to the entire literate world for comment, positive or negative. Yet how else can we continue to grow in our understanding without the marketplace of ideas and the presentation of viewpoints contrary to those most prevalent in a given era?

But a book is never the effort of one person alone, and this work is no exception. I owe my greatest debt of gratitude to Daniel Wunderman, whose casual remark made during a therapy supervisory session launched my career in hypnosis investigation. At the time I was an upper-level graduate student at the University of Kentucky, faced with the problem of proposing an appropriate dissertation topic to my committee. Dr. Wunderman conjectured that hypnosis might be worth exploring because Frank A. Pattie was a member of the Psychology Department. This remark, two brief exposures to hypnosis by Milton H. Erickson through the Seminars on Hypnosis, and the support of Dr. Pattie as my dissertation advisor led me into the study of hypnosis. From this almost inadvertent beginning, the encouragement of Dr. Pattie, the friendship of Dr. Erickson, and the editorship of the *American Journal of Clinical Hypnosis* mushroomed my career in the field. A debt is owed to all three of these men and to the many colleagues I have come to know along the way.

Debts of a different sort are owed to those individuals whose talents played in the mechanics of the manuscript preparation: to the typists. Shelly E. Sykes, Lynn Leindecker, Prudence Y. Potter: to the indexers, Laurie I. Greene, Enid A. Kelly and Annette Nielsen; to the draftsperson, Julie Meyerson; and to the members of the Colgate University Research Council who deemed my work worthy of financial support. Finally, a special note to those to whom the book is dedicated, my wife and family, who through it all tolerated my "growling bear" disposition with alacrity and affection.

WILLIAM E. EDMONSTON, JR.

Hamilton, New York
October 1980

Contents

HYPNOSIS
AND RELAXATION

CHAPTER 1

History: Twenty-Four Centuries of Hypnosis as Sleep

It would be redundant to begin this book with a protracted history of hypnosis. Such summaries already exist. Rather, the history contained herein will be selective, touching on but a few of the many lives associated with the significant events that took place in the history of hypnosis. Each of the individuals discussed below is noted for his scientific and/or clinical contributions to the study of hypnosis. More important, a common thread runs through all their work—that the fundamental, basic fundamental, basic foundation of neutral hypnosis is the relaxation that lays the fertile groundwork for eliciting the various phenomena associated with the term hypnosis. At times relaxation is to be found in the induction procedures used, at times in the individual's particular theoretical orientation to hypnosis. Whichever it is, relaxation is a pervasive aspect of neutral hypnosis both in its history and, as we shall see later, in the more recent experimental investigations.

Before we begin, a word about neutral hypnosis is in order. By far the most avid interest in hypnosis has been in the phenomena of hypnosis (age-regression, amnesias, catalepsies, anaglesias, time distortion, etc.) and the use of such phenomena for treatment purposes (psychotherapy, wart removal, tension and stress relief, asthma, etc.) and the alleviation of pain (dental, surgical, headaches, etc.). From the observations on the uses to which hypnosis and hypnotic phenomena have been put, various theories concerning the fundamentals of hypnosis have developed. Modern viewpoints of hypnotic phenomenology have formed, and the literature is replete with theoretical sorties into the battlefields of state versus nonstate, credulous versus incredulous, task-motivation versus simulator models, and the like. Recently (Hilgard, 1977) Janet's old dissociation hypothesis, which had its antecedents in Braid's observations, has been resurrected in modern garb, derived primarily from data on the effectiveness of a hypnotic phenomenon (analgesia); that is, observations of individuals who had had instructions to be both hypnotized *and* to be analgesic for the particular pain stimulus administered.

As we will see in the ensuing chapters, relatively few investigations of hypnosis have tackled the problem of understanding it from a fundamentally

1

neutral base; that is, from the presentation of hypnotic induction instructions *without* the confound of additional instructions suggesting either the hypnotic phenomena or that hypnosis would be effective in alleviating this or that disorder, worry, or distress. As history has demonstrated, extrapolating to the fundamentals of hypnosis from observations of the effectiveness of hypnotic phenomena (as opposed to neutral hypnosis alone) is a valid endeavor, but what it makes up in life-like complexity, it gives up in the clarity of simplicity. By introducing instructions beyond those necessary to induce neutral hypnosis, propensities for both a broader viewpoint and a confounded viewpoint are entertained. Viewing hypnosis from the less complex, less confounded stance of neutral hypnosis may lead us to insights that have been overlooked in the complexity of the data base of most investigations.

Throughout our historical search one point must be realized: that more often than not the relationship between relaxation and hypnosis was denoted by the words sleep or somnambulism. The emphasis on relaxation as a state or as a technique for influencing bodily functions is more modern. Although investigators from the past were inclined to describe individuals who were hypnotized (or mesmerized) as being in a trance, as being somnambulistic, or as having dissociated themselves from their bodies, the word most often used to effect these descriptions was *sleep*.

Modern investigators have abhorred the use of the word sleep, primarily because of the series of studies undertaken by Hull and his students (1933) to explore the sleep-hypnosis relationship. As we will see in chapter 2, the concept of sleep is not unitary, and the assumption that we should abandon consideration of a sleep-hypnosis relationship if one can demonstrate that hypnosis does not resemble sleep in every way has led us away from, rather than toward, the fundamental principle underlying hypnosis.

So pervasive have been the results of these "hypnosis is not sleep" studies that modern investigators and clinicians alike scrupulously avoid the use of the word sleep in induction procedures, substituting for it the word relax or relaxation. But more about modern induction procedures later.

ANCIENT HISTORY

It is not fortuitous that the fifth century B.C. Egyptian temples of healing are referred to as sleep temples. According to summary accounts, individuals came to these temples of the healing goddess, Isis, for an incubation period of nine days, during which they would sleep and be cured of their afflictions through the intervention of gods in their dreams.

So influential were the Egyptian sleep temples that by the fourth century B.C. Trikka, Greece, became the site of the Temple of Asklepios. Satellite temples were soon spawned throughout the countryside, and Greece was caught up in the sleep cult. As with their Egyptian predecessors, the Grecian seekers of solence gained entrance to the sacred sleep room by cleansing themselves physically (by bathing), spiritually (by giving valuable objects to the temple), and by serving a series of probationary periods of prayer and education by the priests. Once in the Abaton, the sleep cure took place, often with the priests serving as inter-mediaries, making suggestions and performing "minor miracles." The latter were often a combination of religious rites and medical and surgical procedures. So dramatic and numerous were the cures of the sleep temples that their fame spread throughout what was then western civilization, and they gained a major foothold in the Roman Empire, particularly on Tibur Island, in the form of the Temple of Aesculapius (the Roman counterpart of Asklepios).

The striking resemblance of the activities outlined above to what in later time has been successively labeled "mesmerism" and hypnosis led Charcot (1893) to write of the "faith-cure" and to attribute the cures described in these ancient temples to autosuggestion. More modern writers (Rogers, 1947; Ludwig, 1964) have described these antecedents to modern hypnosis apparently without recog-nizing the full import of the notion of sleep in the procedures described. In the temple cures sleep was the prerequisite for all that followed (once the neophyte had gained entrance through sacrifice and cleansing). Sleep was fundamental to the cure, for it was while the sufferer was in the sleep that the curative rituals and suggestions were offered and carried out. Sleep and hypnosis are long-time bedfellows.

THE EIGHTEENTH CENTURY

Mesmer did not capitalize on the relationship between sleep (relaxation) and hypnosis. Theoretically, his emphasis was on the prevalent notions of his time of a universal vital fluid and the use of magnets to redirect this fluid in the service of his patients. His rather dramatic cures centered not on the sleep (coma) that followed the hysteroform crises but on the fits and crises themselves. In fact, when the Marquis de Puységur entertained the idea of somnambulism or sleep as fundamental to the mesmeric state, Mesmer opposed such an interpretation, opining that the somnambulism de Puységur noted in Victor Race was merely one form of the magnetic crisis, which was generally evident by the patient going into "convulsions and disorderly movements" (Ellenberger, 1965a, p. 138).

Little did the Marquis Armand-Marc-Jacques de Chastenet, Marquis de Puységur (1751-1825), realize when he wrote a member of the Society of Harmony of his discovery of "artificial somnambulism" that he was redirecting the mainstream of mesmeric thought back to the ancient sleep-hypnosis relation-ship, away from the notions of a universal vital fluid and eventually toward the present relaxation-hypnosis hypothesis. As was the wont of the aristocrats of his day, this eldest of three brothers dabbled in the physics experiments of the time at his leisure on the family estate in Buzancy. His original intent was not to contest for centerstage with his teacher, Mesmer, but to reduce what he perceived to be the dangerous aspects of the violent crises that were considered the *sine qua non* of magnetism. His attepmts to do so were striking with one of his very first patients—Victor Race, a 24-year-old peasant living in a cottage near the estate. Not only did de Puységur reduce the violence of the crisis, but he produced several phenomena. First, and foremost, Victor appeared asleep, lethargic, and relaxed. Yet when spoken to, he responded, which was all the more startling because he was ordinarily a very quiet individual, shy, perhaps withdrawn. Not only was he able to speak and engage in complex movements, but he appeared to have acquired a new intelligence, seeming to divine the magnetist's thoughts, and showed—the Marquis thought—clear signs of clairvoyant powers. (The latter observation led de Puységur and his followers on the tangential pursuit of individuals with special powers to diagnose and prescribe for the ill, a practice that did not subside until the 1840s and has never really become extinct.) De Puységur described his own surprise at the events that look place when he first worked with Victor:

These small successes (with other individuals) made me attempt to be of use to a peasant, a man of four-and-twenty, much reduced by an inflammation of the chest of four days' standing. I went to see him, and found him much weakened by fever. Having desired him to rise, I mesmerised him, and what was my surprise at the end of eight minutes, to see this man sleeping quietly in my arms quite free of pain. I continued to act upon him, which produced delirium; he spoke aloud, and occupied himself about his affairs. When I thought his ideas were becoming disagreeable, I arrested them, and sought to inspire him with more pleasant ones. It was not difficult to do so, and then I saw him become happy, imagining that he was shooting for a prize or dancing at a *fête*. I encouraged these ideas, and obliged him to move about in his chair, as if keeping time to an air, which, by singing mentally, I made him sing aloud. By these measures, I produced an abundant sweat in the patient that day. After an hour, I calmed him, and they brought him bread and soup, which I made him eat, and this he had not done for five days before. He slept the whole of that night and next day, remembering nothing of what had happened last evening; he informed me that he was much better. (Esdaile, 1852, pp. 72−73)

Although it is contended that Mesmer himself suppressed knowledge of somnambulism and that the Chevalier de Barbarin had produced it prior to de Puységur, it is the Marquis who has received credit "for the first clear recognition of the pivotal importance of mesmerically-induced sleepwalking" (Shor, 1972, p. 21) and to whom most general histories of hypnosis point in discussions of the relationship of sleep and hypnosis. But how does one account for de Puységur's observation, which so few before him had noted? Pattie (1967) attributes it to the Marquis' keen sense of observation, demonstrated by the lengthy, involved reports he wrote of his patients and experiments, an attribute in which Mesmer seemed to be lacking.

Ellenberger (1965a), on the other hand, attributes de Puységur's findings to the social context in which he performed his experiments, particularly in contrast with that of Mesmer. The latter, Ellenberger opines, practiced in sophisticated Paris, among the aristocracy, to whom hysteria and hysterical seizures were well known and, if not prevalent, at least expected. Many of Mesmer's patients were of this stock, and many knew what was expected at the mesmeric *baquet*. On the other hand, Ellenberger notes, de Puységur was working among peasants. Since he was an aristocrat whose family had been known to the surrounding villagers and their kin for centuries, Ellenberger is little surprised that the villagers would be deferent, eager to please, and especially tuned to the subtly, and not so subtly, conveyed desires of the Marquis that they remain calm and relaxed during the magnetic sleep. The natural relationship of landowner to tenant was carried forth in the mesmeric relationship. In more modern jargon, the "demand characteristics" of the situation dictated the strikingly different outcomes achieved by Mesmere and de Puységur. But if so, why and how did the ancients recognize early on the curative balm of sleep and relaxation? And why did Mesmer himself feel compelled to suppress notation of the "lucid sleep?" Perhaps, beyond the characteristic limitations of a particular situation, there is an overriding, pervasive essence.

THE NINETEENTH CENTURY

In the early 1800s a Portuguese priest, José Custódio de Faria (the Abbé Faria) came to Paris and subsisted by offering demonstrations of animal magnetism. Although discredited by a simple stage actor, his insights into the phenomena of magnetism, presented in his posthumously published book (Faria, 1819), had a profound bearing on the future directions pursued by other practitioners.

Taught by de Puységur, the Abbé Faria continued to obtain a "lucid sleep" or somnambulism in his subjects. For him, the processes involved in the production of trances were the same as those involved in producing natural sleep, to the point that he thought the two—natural sleep and somnambulism—to be the same. His method of induction reflected this viewpoint. Once the subject was comfortably seated in a chair, with eyes closed, he announced: "Sleep," thus producing the lucid sleep he perceived as fundamental to the trance. In addition, he made use of a fatiguing eye-fixation induction procedure, a technique Braid was to use to advantage later.

So extensive was Faria's recognition of the sleep-magnetism relationship that he selected his subjects on the basis of their ability to fall easily into a natural sleep. In a real sense the Abbé anticipated modern scales of the capacity for hypnosis, which generally begin with the subject demonstrating his or her ability to become "naturally" relaxed. Faria even attempted to change—unsuccessfully, we now know—the terminology of his time. He preferred the terms concentration and lucid sleep to animal magnetism and somnambulism, respectively.

The curious thing about present-day historians of hypnosis (e.g., Pattie, 1967; Shor, 1972) is that they dwell not on Faria's belief and demonstrations that sleep and "concentration" were intimately related but on the Abbé's shift in emphasis from the magnetizer to the subject. Granted the Abbé Faria was the first practitioner to speculate that the subject's lucid sleep was the product of the subject characteristics, Pattie refers to them as "the liquidity of the blood and a certain 'psychic impressionability' (suggestibility)" (1967, p. 25); while Shor calls them "heightened expectations and receptive attitude" (1972, p. 26). But what is most important, it seems to me, is the *presence* of the lucid sleep rather than its theoretical *raison d'être*. In their drive to demonstrate hypnosis to be heightened suggestibility, subjective expectations, imagination and/or the perceived presses of the hypnotic situation, many current authors have lost sight of the fact that the sleeplike characteristics of hypnosis are there—and have been for centuries—no matter how we strive to understand them. Even Moll, in his classic historical review in which he discussed the Abbé Faria, continued this overtone of interpretation while unconsciously acknowledging the fundamental: "This is the main principle of hypnotism and of suggestion (subjectivity), of which Faria even then made use in *inducing sleep*" (Moll, 1889, p. 10, italics added).

In 1823, Bertrand published his *Traité du Somnambulisme* that, while recognizing the presence of somnambulism, persisted in the older, mesmeric explanations, that: (a) the presence of life forces unites all animal bodies in the world and (b) somnambulism is but one of the crises of animal magnetism. Despite the latter idea, he did outline four types of somnambulism: (a) essential, which is seen in individuals with a particular nervous predisposition; (b) symptomatic, which occurs as a symptom of certain diseases; (c) ecstatic, such as occurs in moral or religious ecstasies; and (d) artificial, which is seen in animal magnetism. Despite these Mesmerlike interpretations, Bertrand continued the earlier reports of somnambulism (as a basic ingredient in animal magnetism) that had reached epidemic proportions since de Puységur's letter of 1784.

The work of Bertrand and the writings of such individuals as General Noizet drew the attention of the Academy of Medicine (Royal Society of Medicine). According to Binet and Fére (1888), Foissac urged the Academy to investigate the process. This was done through a commission that included Itard, Leroux, Magendie, and Husson, who presented the report of five-year's investigation in 1831. The commission recommended that the Academy encourage investigations of animal magnetism, but more important for the thesis being expounded here, the report contained the following paragraph:

"We have constantly observed that natural sleep, which is the repose of the organs of the senses, of the intellectual faculties, and of voluntary movements, *precedes and terminates* the state of somnambulism" (Teste, 1843, p. 26, italics added).

Although six years later a second commission offered the Academy the opposite opinion with respect to encouraging animal magnetism, references to the "sleep" condition of the subject remained. In this one point the two reports concurred.

Braid

The English successor to the Abbé Faria was James Braid (1795—1860). Braid extended the Abbé's observation that the phenomena of magnetism were due to forces and events within the subject, not the operator; and that there were no fluids passing between the operator and the subject. Something going on in the subject accounted for the apparent changes taking place in the subject. In addition, Braid's introduction of a new nomenclature signaled his debt to Faria. His *Neurypnology* (1843) introduced not only his physiological theories but the term hypnotism (once the prefix neuro- had been dropped) or nervous sleep, from the Greek *hypnos,* "to sleep."

The account of Braid's introduction to the mesmerism of his day is instructive in understanding why he initially followed the Abbé Faria's lead in recognizing the central importance of sleep (relaxation) to hypnosis and hypnotic phenomena. According to Williamson's account (Bramwell, 1903) Braid, along with a Dr. Wilson, first observed a demonstration of clairvoyance in the city where he had his practice (Manchester, Scotland). Braid and Wilson denounced the whole affair when the Frenchman who was giving the demonstration (M. Lafontaine) announced that his female subject was "in a state of sound sleep." Their denunciation was short-lived, as Williamson related:

I at once raised her eyelids, and found the pupils contracted to two small points. I called Wilson's attention to this evidence of sound sleep, and he at once gave me a look and a low whistle, conscious that he was in a mess. Braid then tested the girl by forcing a pin between one of her nails and the end of her finger. She did not exhibit the slightest indication of feeling pain, and Braid soon arrived at the conclusion that it was not all "Bog" (humbug). (Bramwell, 1903, p. 465)

Braid's first method of inducing hypnosis was an obvious counterpart of the sleep hypothesis contained in his choice of the word hypnosis and his early physiological viewpoint. By creating fatigue in the eyes through the fixation of visual attention, a general fatigue ensued that eventually affected the activity level of the nervous system and produced the nervous sleep. However, Braid soon found that the attention need not be fixed through physical means (eye fixation) only, but could be accomplished through mental fixation on a particular thought or idea suggested verbally. To demonstrate the latter, he hypnotized sighted subjects in the dark and blind individuals. These experiments paralleled the changes taking place in Braid's theory as to the processes underlying hypnosis. Fixing the gaze or mental concentration both lead to the same end. Thus Braid shifted his emphasis from physical fatigue to mental fatigue, although the phenomena produced and often the general appearance of the subjects remained the same.

By this time Braid had developed his later theoretical position, or, as his biographers interpret it, he had moved from the physiological to the psychological. As Braid cultivated his notions of monoideism (a single dominant idea) and the attention-arresting characteristics of monoideism, he wished to substitute yet another new vocabulary for his own, still fetal, nomenclature. During the later period of his experimentation he made two suggestions that anticipated some of the more modern theorists (e.g., Hilgard, 1977): (a) that the term hypnosis be reserved for that condition in which artificial sleep appeared, accompanied by state-limited amnesia (capable of being removed in subsequent trances), and (b) that there appeared to be a second consciousness in hypnotic subjects through which they could attend to more than one thing at a time.

Neither of these points, however, obviated the observation that the induced condition—hypnosis—whether induced by physical (eye fixation) or mental (monoideistic) means, must be present as a prerequisite to the elicitation of the various phenomena of hypnosis, including curative manipulations. Although Braid was quick to point out that natural sleep and artificial sleep were not the same, such a clarification did not deter him from continuing to subsume them under the same rubric, sleep, even in his later writings. It was not until 1847 that he declared that sleep was not a basis of hypnotism but rather a symptom. However, this shift of emphasis may have been premature and not of the importance that historians to date have attributed to it. That Braid himself continued to recognize the sleep-hypnosis relationship can be seen in his attempt to retain the term hypnotism but restrict it to the amnesia that accompanied the artificial sleep of somnambulance.

The way in which Braid distinguished one from the other is highly reminiscent of the current notions of "alert" and "passive" trance, which we will explore in Chapter 8 and which he himself also anticipated when he wrote of the "alert" and "deep" conditions of hypnosis. For Braid natural sleep was more passive than artificial sleep in that the mind could not focus upon a single idea and was only aroused to dreaming if an operator offered verbal suggestions. During hypnosis, however, verbal suggestions were acted upon and the mind focused on the suggested tasks. Pavlov, as we shall see in Chapter 2, took both of these conditions into account in proposing a wakefulness—deep sleep continuum. But the point is that while Braid did mention that some subjects (about one tenth) could respond to hypnotic suggestions without passing through an apparent sleep stage, his descriptions of hypnosis as a sleeplike condition persisted.

Esdaile

Just as Braid had used the physical method of blowing on his patients' eyes to arouse them from hypnosis, so too did James Esdaile in distant India. Esdaile, working about the same time as Braid, used the same stroking and passes to induce hypnosis that had been in vogue in the early days of mesmerism. These passes, issued in a darkened room, were accompanied with verbal urgings to go to sleep. So effective were these procedures that Esdaile and his native assistants were able to perform hundreds of major surgical procedures without appreciable pain in the patient, and with a greatly reduced mortality rate (see Table 1.1 for a list of surgeries).

Throughout his books, *Mesmerism in India* and *Natural and Mesmeric Clairvoyance,* he and his patients alike refer to the mesmeric condition as sleep, a reduced, or lack of, awareness of the events taking place between the time Esdaile's assistants began the passes and when Esdaile blew on the patients' eyes. For example, in tracing the history of magnetism, Esdaile reports an example of the apparent relationship between magnetism and sleep. He comments on a document from the Archbishop of Lausanne and Geneva, addressed to the Sacred Penitentiary at Rome in May, 1841. It read in part:

A magnetised person, who is generally of the female sex, enters into that state of sleep called *Magnetic Somnambulism* so deeply, that not even the greatest noise at her ears, nor any violence of iron or fire, is capable of raising her from it. She is brought into this kind of ecstasy by the magnetiser alone, to whom she had given consent (for consent is necessary), either by various touches or gesticulations . . . (Esdaile, 1846, p. 36)

Dupotet, to whom John Elliotson, a rather vigorous, energetic physician of North London Hospital, owed his start in his rather tempestuous involvement with mesmerism, also noted the remarkable resemblance of mesmerism to natural sleep. Although intermixing phenomena occurring in the trance with statements referring to the trance itself, he observed: "Sometimes, however, there is said to supervene a state of coma; at others, exaltation, depression, or some anomalous modification of sensibility; and occasionally, a state somewhat approaching to that of reverie. . . . In this peculiar state of sleep . . ." And finally, "yet so profound is the physical state of lethargy, that the sleeper will remain undisturbed and insensible to tortures, which in the waking state, would be intolerable" (Esdaile, 1846, p. 62).

Esdaile points out that a Dr. Passavant of Frankfort also noted the relationship of the mesmeric trance to that of natural sleep.

Table 1.1   Surgeries Performed in the Government Hospitals of Hooghly and Calcutta

Amputation of thigh	2
Amputation of leg	1
Amputation of arm	2
Amputation of breast (one of 7 lbs., another of 10 lbs. weight)	4
Amputation of thumb	1
Amputation of great toe	1
Amputation of penis	3
Amputation of one testis	3
Amputation of two testes	2
Amputation of enlarged nymphea and clitoris	1
Amputation of scrotal tumours of all sizes, from 10 lbs. to 103 lbs.	200
Cancer of cheek extirpated	1
Cancer of eyeball	1
Cancer of scrotum	2
Cartilaginous tumours on ears removed	2
Cataracts operated on	3
End of bone in compound fracture sawn off	1
End of thumb cut off	1
Great toe nails cut out by the roots	5
Gum cut away	1
Heels flayed	3
Hypertrophy of penis removed	3
Hypertrophy of prepuce	1
Lithotomy	1
Lithotrity	1
Piles, suppurating, cut out	1
Prolapsus the size of a child's head reduced in the trance	1
Strangulated hernia reduced in trance	3
Straitened contracted knees	3
Straitened contracted arms	3
Tumour in groin removed (a fungoid undescended testis)	1
Tumour in Antrum Maxillare removed	1
Tumour on leg removed	1
Total	261

(From Esdaile, 1852, pp. 168–69)

As an especial effect of the power of animal magnetism, results the magnetic sleep. This is mostly deeper than ordinary sleep, the mediation of the senses is yet more decidedly suspended. The sensibility can so have vanished in a moment, that the loudest sound, the brightest light, even bodily injuries, are not perceived in this sleep. (Esdaile, 1846, p. 63)

Esdaile himself calls attention to the sleep relationship from his own practice.

Mesmeric sleep.—This simulates, perfectly, sound natural sleep, and is more refreshing, even if it has been resorted to for soothing pain, or disturbance of the system, and can be had recourse to when it would be improper or useless to administer common narcotics;—over which it had the advantage of not inducing a disagreeable constitutional derangement, after the specific influence has ceased. The restorative powers of mesmeric sleep seem to depend upon an actual infusion of nervous vigour into the body, and when induced as a remedial agent, this may account for its superiority over common sleep. (Esdaile, 1846, pp. 63–64)

Thus, the trance is akin but not identical to natural sleep.

Although Esdaile certainly had his detractors, he faired much better than his countryman, Elliotson, in England, for he was eventually granted a small hospital in which to carry on his experimental treatments. At least part of the reason, no doubt, was the fact that trance induction (induced by passes, laying on of hands, and breathing on the patient) for the purposes of curing individuals of various ills was already a part of the Indian culture. The process of *jar-phoonk* practiced by the conjurors of the time, the *jadoowalla,* derived its name from the Hindustani *jarna,* meaning to stroke, and *phoonkna,* meaning to breathe. Esdaile describes his observation of a woman cured of "epilepsy and insanity"* by a *jadoowalla:* Following the passes, breathing, and laying on of hands, "she soon became drowsy, and appeared to sleep. . . ." Upon follow-up, the woman's mother reported "this man not only put her to sleep whenever he came, but made her speak during that sleep . . ." (Esdaile, 1852, pp. 54–55).

As with his observations of *jar-phoonk,* Esdaile's own cases were reported in terms of sleep. In the extended case report of Mrs. McKenzie (Esdaile, 1852), he continually spoke of her being "asleep." In fact, like Braid he indicated that the mesmeric coma (sleep) is not the same as natural sleep: "I had substituted *mesmeric* for *natural* coma" (p. 97, italics added); and, like Pavlov, he commented on degrees of sleep: "she was mesmerized on the spur of the moment, when not merely asleep, but in a state of *intense* natural coma . . ." (p. 103, italics added). His patients, too, described the trance as sleep; one shouted out: "don't cut me—don't cut me—put me to sleep," while in describing his medical cases Esdaile himself spoke of the "refreshment from sleep" and the "sedative influence of the trance" (pp. 196–197).

Esdaile's very induction technique both capitalized on and promoted the sleep-hypnosis relationship he and others had noted in their patients. The patient was placed on a bed in a darkened room and the passes begun, *without anyone suggesting the idea of sleep* verbally. Esdaile felt the supine position to be superior to the European technique of having the patient seated upright, because it enhanced the achievement of the coma. In fact, he noted: "My patients seemed to escape the first stimulating effects of Mesmerism (the somnambulistic stage), and to plunge at once into the coma" (Esdaile, 1852, p. 142). It is curious to note that the progression from alert condition to coma was the opposite of which Braid spoke when he indicated that some patients could enter the active somnambulistic stage without passing through a condition similar to sleep. Thus, in Esdaile's

---

*Whether or not these terms fit the modern definitions of the disorders is a matter of conjecture.

hands, as in Braid's and others, de Puységur's rediscovery of the ancient association of sleep (coma, relaxation) and hypnosis (trance) was further developed.

While Esdaile is mainly noted for his contributions to the history of hypnosis as a practitioner, demonstrating to the world of the nineteenth century that medical and surgical treatments could be effected during hypnosis, he also advocated a theoretical position. He argued very strenuously against those who would attribute the phenomena of trances to suggestion and imagination:

If all this [Dr. Kean's use of mesmerism in a lunatic asylum] is not sufficient to give the *coup de grace* to the theory of *suggestion* and *imagination* as explanatory of the results obtained in my practice of Mesmerism, I will adduce instances of people being entranced from another room without their having the least suspicion of my intentions, and of a blind man being reduced on the first attempt to the most intense degree of mesmeric coma. (Esdaile, 1852, p. 226).

The surgeon of India held very strongly to the notion of a vital force or fluid that passed from the operator to the patient, affecting the latter's nervous system. Thus, Esdaile took his place as did Elliotson, with the physical theorists, eschewing a psychological or suggestive explanation of hypnosis.

Liébeault

It was not until after the death of both Esdaile and Braid that Ambroise Auguste Liébeault began in earnest his use of hypnosis. Although virtually unheard of until Bernheim's association with him in the 1880s, Liébeault is credited by Bramwell (1903, p. 32) with the "development of modern hypnotism". Generally presented as a quiet country doctor who plied hypnosis with the French peasants around Nancy (see Pattie, 1967, for a different view), he was influenced by Braid's early viewpoints and further developed and used the Abbé Faria's sleep techniques of hypnotic induction.

Moll pointed out that "Liébeault, Bernheim, Brullard and Forel (Zurich) consider hypnosis an ordinary sleep" (1889, p. 192), and that the only difference between hypnosis and sleep was the object of rapport in each case. The person asleep is in rapport with him- or herself, while the person in hypnosis is in rapport with the operator. This orientation of Liébeault toward hypnosis and sleep is often lost in biographers' accounts because of the heavy emphasis on the "doctrine of suggestion" that Liébeault and Bernheim developed and contested with Charcot at the Salpêtriére in Paris. But as Shor noted: "Hypnosis was seen as an extension of suggestibility that *began by having the subject focus on the idea of sleep*" (1972, p. 29, italics added).

Bramwell's description of his visit with Liébeault in the summer of 1889 is particularly instructive with respect both to method and to where the notion of suggestion fits into the therapeutic procedures. He was struck by the air of gentleness and calm that pervaded the overflowing waiting rooms. There was none of the "morbid excitement" reported at the Salpêtrière, nor none of the hysterical chaotic anticipation surrounding, one suspects, Mesmer's *baquet*. But here is the telling point: "The patients told to go *to sleep* apparently fell at once into a quiet slumber, *then* received their dose of curative suggestions . . ." (Bramwell, 1903, p. 31). They received their dose of curative suggestions *after* instructions to go to sleep. For Liébeault, hypnosis (sleep) preceded the suggestions intended to assist his patients. The two events, hypnosis and curative suggestions, were perceived and casually reported by Bramwell as separate and distinct events. It was only later that the idea of sleep was blended with the suggestive therapeutics (to borrow a phrase from Bernheim) to incorporate the entire process under the doctrine of suggestibility, which eventually had widespread influence on both sides of the Atlantic (see, e.g., Hull, 1933).

Allow yet another of Bramwell's observations:

Two little girls, about six or seven years of age, no doubt brought in the first instance by friends, walked in and sat down on a sofa behind the doctor. He [Liébeault], stopping for a moment in his work made a pass in the direction of one of them, and said: "Sleep, my little kitten," repeated the same for the other, and in an instant they were both asleep. He rapidly gave them their dose of suggestion and then evidently forgot all about them." (Bramwell, 1903, p. 32).

Liébeault induced what to a trained observer of his time appeared to be sleep, and then proceeded to treat the patients.

In all fairness it should be noted that Bramwell (1903) argued against the analogy of sleep with hypnosis, but like others before and after him, his argument seemed based on absolutism—that hypnosis and natural sleep are not *identical*. There is no argument here; they are not identical, but there are points of similarity. And these points did not begin with Pavlov (see Chapter 2), but have been the common thread in the history of hypnosis.

Bernheim

Although a latecomer to Liébeault's views, Hippolyte Marie Bernheim also believed that the fixation of attention on the idea of sleep was the basis of both natural and hypnotic sleep. As indicated above, the difference between these two sleeps was the object of the subject's rapport: "In ordinary sleep, as soon as consciousness is lost, the subject is only in relationship with himself. In *induced sleep* his mind retains the memory of the person who put him to sleep . . ." (Bramwell, 1903, p. 342).

In addition to being the counterpart of Liébeault at the Nancy School, Bernheim's other note of fame was his apparent prowess as a hypnotic operator, achieving, it is reported, a success rate of 85% with over 10,000 patients (Bramwell, 1903). His success, often contrasted to that of Freud, who attempted to dominate his patients through the singular directive, "Sleep!" (shades of Liébeault), could probably be attributed to his method as much as to his patients' or his own personality characteristics. Following a brief allaying of the patients' fears, he said: "Look at me and think of nothing but sleep; your eyelids begin to feel heavy, your eyes are tired; they begin to blink, they are getting moist, you cannot see distinctly. They are closed" (Bernheim, 1888, p. 42). As with Liébeault and with Braid before, the emphasis of the induction was on sleep, tiredness, heaviness, and the like. It was only when some patients did not respond with signs of drowsiness and sleep that Bernheim suggested that sleep was unessential for hypnotic treatment. It is reasonable to assume that such patients were among the 15% considered unsuccessful in treatment.

For Bernheim, as with his predecessor and colleague, the presence or absence of hypnosis preceded the curative suggestions, and once again we see this constantly present, but little noted, separation between hypnosis and the treatment occurring within its context. First Bernheim hypnotized his patients ("induced sleep"), then he offered curative suggestions. If hypnosis did not ensue, he proceeded with the treatment suggestions anyway. The doctrine of suggestion applied to *both* the induction of hypnosis *and* to treatment *during* hypnosis, in that the suggestions of sleep-induced hypnosis and the treatment suggestions effected a cure. The point to be emphasized is that regardless of the basis, hypnosis was not considered to be present unless there was the appearance of sleep and drowsiness on the part of the patient. It is curious that historians and the individuals about whom they wrote could collectively miss this point, which was present in their very own writings.

Charcot

For an individual so completely intolerant of the views of others, who, according to Pattie (1967), never hypnotized anyone, and who worked with a limited number of hysterical women, Jean-Martin Charcot (1825–1893) holds an unusually revered position in the history of hypnosis as the individual who refocused interest in hypnosis and achieved its recognition by the scientific community (Chertok, 1967). No doubt part of this fame was the halo effect generated from his earlier successes in pulmonary and kidney diseases and the scleroses and ataxias (Ellenberger, 1965b). The rest derived from the well-documented controversy between his Paris School and that at Nancy in the late 1800s, and the importance of his concern with scientific rigor, which was not fully appreciated until this century (Shor, 1972).

Charcot's position that hypnosis was basically an experimental neurosis could have been anticipated easily had he paid more attention to the details of the backgrounds of the patients through whom he offered his demonstrations. But whether he and Broca sided with the physiological and physical viewpoint or not is not as cogent to the thesis of this book as the fact that his observations led him to propose three stages of hypnosis: lethargic, cataleptic, and somnambulistic.

Although his explanations of the mechanisms underlying the three stages are physiological, his methods of inducing each bordered on the mystical (see Chapter 3).

The first stage—lethargy—repeats the basic observation of those who preceded him. Lethargy, sleep, drowsiness, relaxation distinguish hypnosis for the observer, *after which* additional states, conditions, and experiences are elicited. For example, Ellenberger (1965b), establishing the role of the patient and the patient's background in the phenomena demonstrated, describes Jules Janet's (Pierre's brother) work with Blanche Wittmann, probably Charcot's most renowned subject.

After achieving the "first stage of hypnosis," that is, lethargy, Jules Janet modified the usual technique [for achieving the later stages] and saw the patient in a quite new condition: a new personality, "Blanche II," emerged, showing herself much more balanced than "Blanche I." The new personality disclosed that she had been permanently present and conscious, hidden behind "Blanche I," and that she was always aware of everything which occurred during the many demonstrations when she had acted out the "three stages of hypnosis" and was supposed to be unconscious. (Ellenberger, 1965b, p. 263)

Here we have not only a direct anticipation of a "hidden observer" (Hilgard, 1977) in the form of multiple personality, but a subtle statement of the separation of hypnosis as a condition resembling sleep and the later second personality emergence. While Blanche II was reported to have been everpresent, it was through the sleeplike-appearing hypnosis that she was brought forth and eventually rid of her hysterical symptomatology.

According to Chertok (1967) the battle between the Paris and Nancy schools was the main feature of the First International Congress of Experimental and Therapeutic Hypnotism, with Babinski uncompromisingly defending the need for "clearly defined physical signs in the hypnotic state" (Chertok, 1967, p. 190).

Moll

In that same year, 1889, Albert Moll published his now-classic *The Study of Hypnosis,* in which he also recognized the sleep-hypnosis relationship. Noting the Liébeault-Bernheim distinction between sleep and hypnosis with respect to the object of rapport in each, Moll considered two conditions of hypnosis—light and deep. While light hypnosis was distinguished from sleep in that the former is an inhibition of will affecting movements and not memory, deep hypnosis was viewed as comparable to sleep with respect to dreaming and movement. The only difference between the dreams in deep hypnosis and sleep, Moll related, was that the former are due to suggestions and the latter to some nonsuggestive external stimulus.

Although Moll appeared to follow the viewpoint of the Nancy School very closely, his attempts to differentiate natural sleep from hypnosis on the basis of voluntary muscle involvement (or impairment) followed leads put forth by such investigators as Heidenhain and Charcot. He viewed hypnosis and sleep as basically the same, the one distinguishing feature being that in hypnosis movement was easy and in sleep, difficult.

Consequently, the movements of subjects in [deep] hypnosis do not offer a fundamental contrast to sleep, especially when they are caused by suggested delusions of sense. . . . To my mind the dividing line between sleep and hypnosis is merely a quantitative difference in movements. (Moll, 1889, p. 201)

To his mind there also appeared to be two different types of hypnosis, an active and a passive. While a more thorough discussion of this particular viewpoint of hypnosis follows in Chapter 8, it is interesting to note that even the notation of two apparently disparate forms of hypnosis did not undercut a common thread underlying both: "Hypnosis often shows itself as passive at the beginning: as soon as the eyes are closed the head droops forward or backward, because the supporting muscles of the neck are relaxed" (Moll, 1889, p. 78). The relaxation-hypnosis relationship remained.

But, as these remarks imply, Moll did not subscribe to a strict sleep-hypnosis equation. He repeatedly described similarities between the two conditions while maintaining their differences. He was adamant that just because the same method may be used to induce the two states, there was no reason therefore to assume their identity. "But we should never conclude an identity of states from the identity of their causes. We should observe whether the symptoms are identical" (Moll, 1889, p. 203). He concluded that the symptoms were not identical, but neither were the two conditions totally different. Thus Moll kept alive the consideration of the hypnosis-sleep relationship, and, as we shall see in Chapter 2, anticipated the continuum viewpoint of wakefulness and sleep within which hypnosis takes its place. Needless to say, Moll rejected the idea that hypnosis was a form of mental disorder.

CONCLUSION

Following the controversy between the Nancy and Paris schools, hypnosis once again bowed from centerstage. Bernheim and his colleagues seemed to have prevailed, not so much in the unstated—and often blatantly denied—inclusion of a sleep-hypnosis relationship, but in placing the emphasis on suggestion as the *sine qua non* of the hypnotic condition. It was Charcot who had gotten the scientific community to reexamine hypnosis and hypnotic phenomena in the first place by raising it from the psychological mire of imagination perpetrated originally by Mesmer. However, since his and Babinski's physiological viewpoint had lost the day, established science moved on to other things.

It was left to Janet to keep interest alive through his own work on dissociation, and by arousing the interest of other practitioners. Freud, mainly through the influence of Bernheim, became interested for a while, but soon turned to the development and elaboration of psychoanalysis. His concept of transference owed a major debt to what Bernheim had only partially alluded to—the relationship between the hypnotist and the patient/subject.

A number of other well-known physicians of the late nineteenth and early twentieth centuries involved themselves in hypnosis, but only in passing. One, Krafft-Ebing, did make a major contribution to hypnotic phenomena with his notation of hypnotic age-regression (Krafft-Ebing, 1889), but relatively little happened with respect to theory until Pavlov and Hull began their investigations into hypnosis.

No doubt some readers will fault the present work at this point, saying that the sleep-hypnosis controversy was settled long ago with Braid's second and third look at hypnosis. Or, if not then, certainly Bernheim laid the whole issue to rest with his observation that hypnotic phenomena can be obtained without first inducing sleep. Others will point out that if the sleep-hypnosis relationship was not doomed in the 1840s and 1890s, it certainly has been relegated to the archives of the unimportant by Sarbin's role theory or Orne's social psychology or Barber's task-motivation explanations.

However, it was not my attempt to prove a relationship by historical precedent, but simply to demonstrate that no matter what period one chooses in the history of hypnosis, the sleep-relaxation-hypnosis relationship is a part of the literature. This brief historical survey is admittedly selective, only to show the very point just made. No matter what additional observations have been made in no matter what historical period, the concern with the relationship between hypnosis and sleep-relaxation persists. To say that is not to say that persistence is proof, for we all know how slowly the myths of mankind fade. What it is saying, however, is that through the centuries virtually everyone connected with hypnosis has taken note of the sleeplike, relaxed appearance of most hypnotic subjects, even if they later ignored their own initial observations (e.g., Braid). Such a pervasive observation should not go unnoticed historically or empirically. The empirical and experimental evidence for the relaxation-sleep-hypnosis relationship will be presented in the chapters to follow.

CHAPTER 2

Pavlov: Hypnosis as Partial Sleep

Ivan Petrovitch Pavlov was an extraordinary man whose interests were as diverse as his talents. The first son of a poor priest in Ryazan, born on September 26, 1849, he was endowed with a tenacity of purpose that served him well as he ferreted out the secrets of the circulatory, digestive, and central nervous systems (Pavlov, 1928*a*, pp. 11−31). His professional career was a series of logical steps, beginning with his early university studies inspired by Tsyon. His technique of the chronic fistula, coupled with his interests in the neural aspects of gastrointestinal secretions, won him a Nobel Prize in 1904 and led to the elaboration of the concept of conditioned responses. In order to account for such responses, he developed a general theory of neural activity and inhibition and applied it to all behavior. It was from this generalized theory, his growing interest in the problems of psychiatry, and his observations of aberrant behavior in his dogs that, in his eighth decade, Pavlov's theory of hypnotic behavior developed.

In this chapter I will try to capture the flavor of his theory and present much of the data that support the theory. In this way the historical progression begun in the first chapter will move another step along the way to our understanding neutral hypnosis as relaxation, for Pavlov's theory, though couched in terms of sleep and inhibition, is a theory of hypnotic relaxation.

To understand Pavlov's views of hypnosis is to understand his views of sleep, which in turn is to understand central nervous system (CNS) activity in terms of the two contrapuntal forces in living tissue—excitation and inhibition. For Pavlov, the organism had no interim state between degrees of excitation and degrees of inhibition. All cells, and most particularly those in the central nervous system, are capable of excitation and inhibition, and thus the general condition of the neurons determines the overall state of the organism.

On this logical ground alone, Pavlov argued against a sleep center in the hypothalamus—or anywhere else in the CNS, for that matter. Sleep was not localized but a general inhibition irradiated over the cerebral hemispheres and down into the subcortical areas. Thus the more cells in inhibition the more profound the sleep, with different forms of sleep (and hypnosis) depending on the degree of cellular inhibition measured in the quantity of inhibited cells. Although much later data have indicated that it may not be so much that neurons are capable of both excitation and inhibition but that synapses between cells are specialized with respect to giving rise to excitatory or inhibitory postsynaptic potentials, the effect on Pavlov's views is merely a shift of emphasis from the number of cells in the inhibitory state to the number of inhibitory synapses activated at a given moment.

Pavlov explained all of the behavior of organisms by noting that throughout the nervous system individual cells and groups of cells are in varying degrees of excitation or inhibition. When an individual acts, groups of cells in the motor-related areas enter an excitation phase, while other cells, both immediately surrounding the excited cells and in distant areas, are in a state of inhibition. Thus Pavlov outlined a phenomenon he labeled negative induction, indicating that excitatory foci induce inhibition (negative) in areas not directly involved in the behavior at hand. An opposite relationship also obtained when an inhibitory stimulus is applied to the animal or human (e.g., a continuous, monotonous stimulus or a time delay between the conditioned stimulus—CS—and the uncon-ditioned stimulus—US); that is, that the areas surrounding the foci of inhibition are in a state of increased excitation. This condition Pavlov called positive induction. Two purposes are thereby served: (a) the focus of excitability or inhibition is heightened by contrast, and (b) the potential for interference by other cellular areas is reduced.

Attesting to Pavlov's genius for extrapolation from his observations is the fact that it has only been in the last few decades of this century that positive and negative induction have been experimentally demonstrated. Kuffler (1953), for example, discovered that the center and periphery of the visual field in the retina are mutually antagonistic, one being excited with the onset of stimulation and the other with its cessation. The notion of mutual antagonism, which Pavlov used so extensively in his interpretation of his data, is the cornerstone of his notions with respect to sleep and hypnosis.

SLEEP

"Sleep . . . is an inhibition which has spread over a great section of the cere-brum, over the entire hemispheres and even into the lower lying midbrain. Inhibition spreads and sleep sets in, or the inhibition is limited and sleep disap-pears" (Pavlov, 1928b, p. 311). This was the conclusion Pavlov reached after more than ten years of research and the consideration (and subsequent rejection) of five or six other hypotheses.

Pavlov's interest in sleep was the outgrowth of his work on conditioned re-sponses. Sleep and its precurser, inhibition, were viewed as difficulties arising in the sequence of events leading to the establishment of conditioned salivary and leg flexion responses. He and his coworkers noted that if the US (the reinforcing agent) was delayed by as much as 30 seconds in the process of elaborating conditioned responses (CRs), the dogs tended to fall into a passive state, only to become alert again in the moments just preceding the onset of the US. Pavlov attributed this tendency of the animal to slip into a profoundly passive state in the midst of a situation that ordinarily would call for alert action, whether motoric or gastronomic, to *internal inhibition,* through which conditioned inhibition, differential inhibition, and extinction take place. Whereas sleep was defined as above, inhibition was considered "a strictly localized sleep, confined within definite boundaries under the influence of the opposing process—that of excitation" (Pavlov, 1928*b,* p. 311).

Once again we note Pavlov's concern with the two opposing life forces, inhibition and excitation. As with positive and negative induction—concepts that, as we will see, are highly important for the understanding of hypnosis— Pavlov opined the simultaneous occurrence of both throughout the structures of the nervous system. Thus, as his dogs approached the excitation state attending the emitting of a conditioned response, there appears an apparent paradoxical burst of inhibition just prior to the onset of salivation or leg flexion. The opposite—a burst of excitation in the midst of inhibition, or approaching inhibition—is a familiar experience we have all shared. As the excitation of wakefulness dissolves into the inhibition of sleep, there is often a burst of excitement just preceding the onset of sleep. Occasionally this excitation—often noted externally by a motoric and vocal startle response—is of sufficient magnitude to recall the would-be sleeper to wakefulness. More often it is the spouse who finds her or his late-evening reading distributed by this last outcry against the irradiating inhibition.

The relationship between excitation and inhibition is quantitative and inverse, one leading to wakefulness and the other to sleep. In its simplest form:

$$Sl = fI$$

where

$$I = 1/E$$

with Sl representing sleep, I inhibition, and E excitation (Edmonston, 1967, p. 353). Thus, as total sleep occurs, I approaches infinity and E zero. The opposite occurs—E approaches infinity and I zero—as wakefulness emerges.

Since the changes from sleep to wakefulness to sleep and vice-versa are not abrupt but occur gradually and at different rates for different individuals, Pavlov needed to account for the different stages of sleep (see below) at a cellular level. Here the physiology of his day was of little help, and he could only theorize about the underlying mechanisms. As he saw it, the inactivity of a cell is transmitted to adjoining cells through a "special process or substance . . ." (Pavlov, 1928b, p. 308), which eventually elaborates the irradiating inhibition over both hemispheres and the subcortical regions. While present-day neurophysiology would suggest that the mechanisms of shifting from wakefulness to sleep (and vice-versa) may depend on neurotransmitters residing in the synaptic vesicles, the precise understanding of the underlying processes has yet to be realized. However, what Pavlov was able to specify, from the strength of data, was the external mechanism of producing increasing inhibition and eventual sleep.

Any monotonous, repetitive stimulation, unaccompanied by other external stimulation, eventually leads to inhibition and sleep. Thus the continual presentation of a CS to a dog without the subsequent presentation of the US leads not only to the eventual extinction of the conditioned response but to drowsiness and sleep. This phenomenon was noted regardless of the noxiousness of the CS. Whether the CS was a potent electric shock or a gentle stroking of the dog's skin, the inhibitory response was elicited to its repetitious presentation.

In this manner then we may understand why most hypnotic induction techniques involve repetitive stimulation—passes and strokes in the last century and words in the present. So also may we begin to understand how it is that some hypnotists can shout their patients into hypnosis, while others depend on slow, quiet words of assurance and relaxation. Just as Pavlov's dogs habituated to the repetitious stimulation and their central nervous system entered an inhibitory phase, so too do human subjects enter neutral hypnosis through repetitious external stimulation. Monotony, relaxation, inhibition, and hypnosis are of the same process.

By the same token, Pavlov explained the phenomenon of habituation, wherein the orienting response (OR) slowly habituates or ceases to be elicited by a novel stimulus upon its repeated presentation. Habituation of the OR was but a waystation on the road to sleep, in that, in the absence of a change in external stimulation, the animal proceeded to lapse into drowsiness and sleep.

Stages of Sleep

It was quite clear to Pavlov that as we attend to different stimuli in our environments (external and internal), corresponding areas of the nervous system, particularly the cerebral hemispheres, must become alternately excited and inhibited. As we attend to one aspect of environmental interaction, those portions of the CNS charged with relating to other aspects must perforce be less active, hence inhibited. Consequently, the cortex (and to some extent the subcortical areas) is a mosaic of cells in phases of excitation and inhibition. While wakefulness and profound sleep are the extreme endpoints on the continuum from excitation to inhibition, there is a plethora of intermediate stages. Pavlov noted three phases on the basis of his animal studies and the reactions of his dogs to the experimental situation.

Pavlov's dogs were trained both to salivate and to take food when presented.

Thus, two responses, one secretory and the other motoric, were elaborated in the experimental situation. In wakefulness both responses were evident. However, if the animal were allowed to stand in the experimental harness a short while before the experiments began, the first phase of sleep became apparent by the disappearance of the secretory response, but not the motoric (Pavlov, 1928b). If, on the other hand, the beginning of the experiment was delayed still further, a second phase of sleep was attained in which the response pattern was reversed; that is, the secretory response was present, but the motoric, absent. Finally, a prolonged delay resulted in both responses being eliminated in the third phase.

Even more striking is the fact that if the animal were gradually awakened, the exact *reverse* response-appearance sequence occurs. First the secretory response returned without the motoric, then the motoric was apparent without the secretory, and finally, both were elicited.

These three phases noted by Pavlov in his experimental animals very closely resemble the three categories of sleep outlined by Platonov (1959): "broken-up, partial and total sleep." "Broken-up" sleep most closely resembles wakefulness and is akin to the first phase outlined above. During this phase there is a "complex mobile mosaic" (Platonov, 1959, p. 27) of cells in excitatory and inhibitory stages. Thus, CRs that were last elaborated (secretory, in the case of Pavlov's work) are temporarily lost, while the motoric are retained. Such a phenomenon, according to Pavlov, is paralleled by cellular inhibition in the alimentary centers but not in the motor centers.

In partial sleep (the second phase) there is increasing inhibition spread over the cortex; however, there remain, to greater and lesser degrees, foci of excitation so that there continues to be commerce with the external world. One phase of partial sleep is conditioned-response sleep, or the inhibition of first-signal system responses.

In conditioned-response sleep, stimuli that had in the past been associated with sleep now effected sleep, even when fatigue was not evident in the animal. Thus Pavlov explained the observation that the dogs became lethargic and sleepy upon being placed in the experimental situation, before any experimental stimuli were presented. The general stimuli of the surrounding experimental environment had become conditioned, by association, to elicit inhibition. (One is reminded of the "quick induction" signals used by many clinicians.) In addition, the acquisition of conditioned-response sleep is related to both ontogenetic development and the relative involvement of different muscle groups. For example, those responses most directly involved with the response being conditioned, in both effort and time relationship, are lost first.

Thus we see in the experimental animal the elimination of the conditioned motor response: The dog no longer takes food but does salivate. This apparent paradox in the progression of response elimination can be attributed to the passage of the cortical motor cells into a state of inhibition, along with those cortical cells involved in the elaboration of the secretory response. However, both the subcortical areas relating to the unconditioned aspects of these two responses have been unaffected by the elaborating inhibition and are still capable of having their influence. While the animal no longer has the conditioned motor response, it maintains its posture. By the same token, the conditioned secretory response is now replaced by unconditional salivation controlled subcortically, and possibly misinterpreted as a conditioned secretory response.

Finally, at the stage of total sleep (phase three), the animal loses both responses and may hang limply in the harness. Here the cortex is in complete inhibitory repose, and inhibition has spread to selected subcortical areas, notably the midbrain.

Phases of Inhibition

Pavlov made several other observations of his animals that are relevant to my discussion of human hypnosis. As inhibition increased, he noted other changes in the dogs' responses to a variety of stimuli. First there occurred a phase in which both weak and strong stimuli were capable of eliciting a response. In other

Table 2.1.   Schematic Presentation of Pavlov's Theory

State of Organism	Phase	Degree of Inhibition
Wakefulness		Minimal $(E \rightarrow \infty; I \rightarrow 0)$
"Broken-up" sleep		
Partial sleep		
Natural partial sleep		
Hypnotic sleep		
(1st-signal system) – CR sleep		
Suggested sleep		
(2nd-signal system)		
First stage		
First degree		
Second degree		
Third degree		
Second stage		
First degree		
Second degree		
Third degree	Equalization	
Third stage		
First degree		
Second degree		
Third degree	Paradoxical	
	Ultraparadoxical	
Total sleep	Complete inhibition	$(E \rightarrow 0; I \rightarrow \infty)$ Maximum

(Decreasing cortical excitation / Increasing cortical inhibition)

(From Edmonston, 1967)

words, the apparent linear response between stimulus amplitude and response elicitation was abrogated. This phase of partial sleep he called the *equalization phase,* because stimuli of different strengths were equipotential.

As inhibition continues to overwhelm cortical excitation, a *paradoxical phase* is entered, when the magnitude of the effect and the strength of the stimulus enter an inverse relationship. Now weak stimuli are more potent than strong stimuli, and paradoxically, a weak stimulus elicits the response that cannot be aroused by a strong one.

Finally, just preceding complete cortical inhibition (total sleep), an *ultraparadoxical phase* is attained in which formerly excitatory stimuli act as inhibitors and inhibitory stimuli elicit excitation. This phase is related to the phenomena noted above, wherein in the midst of excitation inhibition ensues and in the midst of inhibition (going to sleep, for example) there is a final burst of excitation before sleep.

Table 2.1 summarizes Pavlov's theory with respect to sleep, wakefulness, inhibition, and excitation. Here we see the progressive states of the organism from full wakefulness to total sleep, with the concomitant degrees of inhibition noted. The degree of differentiation of partial sleep gives some clue to the importance this particular stage held for Pavlov. It was here that much of his observations on dogs was elaborated into an understanding of hypnosis in humans.

HYPNOSIS

Hypnosis, like sleep, is a struggle between two life forces, excitation and inhibition. In fact, for Pavlov: "Inhibition, ordinary sleep and hypnosis are one and the same process" (Pavlov, 1923, p. 604). As noted above, it is within the category of partial sleep that we find hypnosis, both animal and human, described.

Animal Hypnosis

Pavlov described two types of animal hypnosis. The first ensued when a sudden, catastrophic environmental stimulus occurred. For example, if the animal is suddenly inverted and laid on its back, a catalepsy occurs in which the animal is completely immobile and may be placed in a variety of unnatural postures. Pavlov called this naturally occurring response "a self-protecting reflex of an inhibitory character" (Pavlov, 1955, p. 352). Such innate behavior has been described in detail in a variety of species by Ratner (1967), and there is some general agreement that "freezing" cataleptic responses do serve the animal in times of extreme environmental threat. That this particular form of animal hypnosis is directly related to human hypnosis is not indicated in Pavlov's writings and is certainly not supported in the current literature.

What initially fascinated Pavlov was the second type of animal hypnosis—hypnotic sleep (first-signal system)—CR sleep (see Table 2.1). Pavlov used the term hypnotic sleep to refer to nonverbally induced partial sleep, which can occur in either animals or humans. (The term suggested sleep was reserved for human hypnosis alone, as we shall see below.) "The basic condition required for the development of this state is a prolonged action of monotonous stimuli, which finally bring the corresponding cortical cells to a state of inhibition" (Pavlov, 1955, p. 354). Initially Pavlov attributed the "sleeping hypnotic state" in his dogs (Bek, John and Brains) to the general monotony of the experimental situation. Little by little he and his coworkers became aware, first, that the time delay between the presentations of the CS and the US was critical to the induction of certain sleeplike behaviors and then, more important, that stimuli deliberately presented by the experimenter could also create a partially inhibitory state in which certain responses (primarily motoric) were apparently no longer available to the animal. Noting the difference between this form of sleep and the usual, Pavlov noted that there was a relaxation of the skeletal musculature (eye closure, drooping head) that indicated "an absence of the normal function of the cortex" (1927, p. 265).

The sequence of response of the dogs was as follows. Ordinarily, when CSs were followed shortly by the US (food), the animal yielded an alimentary response (salivation) and a motor response (taking the food), and remained standing in the harness. If, however, there was a delay in the presentation of the US, the animal gave only the alimentary response, without its motor component. With even further delay, salivation also disappeared and the dog slumped in the harness, fast asleep—even snoring.

For Pavlov there could be but one explanation. Cortical inhibition spread slowly over the hemispheres, first affecting the motor areas. As the inhibition continued to develop, it eventually descended to the subcortical areas, abrogating the conditioned alimentary response also, as the animal drifted into total sleep. Prior to the stage of total sleep,

we are dealing with a complete inhibition confined exclusively to the cortex, without a concurrent descent of the inhibition into the centres regulating equilibrium and maintenance of posture. . . . In this form of sleep the plane of demarcation between the inhibited regions of the brain and the regions which are free from inhibition seems to pass just beneath the cerebral cortex. (Pavlov, 1927, p. 266)

Thus, with this early work on dogs, Pavlov firmly established cortical inhibition as the neuroanatomical substrate of hypnosis. Heidenhain, one of Pavlov's early mentors, held the same view: "the cause of the phenomena of hypnotism lies in the inhibition of the activity of the ganglion-cells of the cerebral cortex . . ." (Heidenhain, 1888, p. 46).

In accounting for both hypnotic sleep behaviors and behavior in general, Pavlov assumed the presence of analyzers within the central nervous system, relating to various sensory, motor, and visceral functions. Thus, in the case of the conditioned alimentary and motor responses, the inhibition of the latter during hypnotic sleep was through the inhibition of the motor analyzer, the alimentary analyzer (and thus the alimentary response) being untouched by the spreading partial inhibition. Figure 2.1 indicates schematically the relationships among the analyzers, the response centers, and hypnotic sleep (and, as we will see, suggested sleep—human hypnosis).

In Figure 2.1A a conditioned environmental stimulus excites a visual auditory analyzer, which, in turn, arouses the motor (2) and alimentary (4) analyzers. These latter analyzers excite their respective response centers, and the animal acts appropriately (salivates and takes food). If, however, there is a delay in the presentation of the food (US), hypnotic sleep ensues with the concomitant inhibition of the motor analyzer and subsequent motor response. The alimentary analyzer, and thus salivation, continues in its usual state of excitation, continuing the conditioned alimentary response.

As in the case of approaching sleep, "hypnotization" affects the motor (voluntary) components in a progressive fashion, which is dependent upon the original sequence of acquisition, the degree of involvement of differing musculature, and ontogenetic considerations. "During the repeated act of eating the maxillary muscles and tongue were most exercised, then the neck muscles and lastly the trunk, and inhibition follows in that same sequence" (Pavlov, 1941, p. 81). The dogs, when presented with food following a long delay (4−5 minutes), would turn to it but not take it into their mouths and masticate. With further delays the animals would no longer even turn to the food (using the neck muscles), and finally, as hypnotized sleep deepened, even the postural responses of the trunk were lost.

Although he noted very important differences between hypnotic sleep (animal

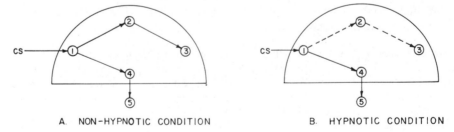

A. NON-HYPNOTIC CONDITION   B. HYPNOTIC CONDITION

1. VISUAL AUDITORY ANALYZERS
2. MOTOR ANALYZER
3. MOTOR RESPONSE CENTER
4. ALIMENTARY ANALYZER
5. ALIMENTARY RESPONSE CENTER

Figure 2.1. Schematic presentation of Pavlov's theory of the effects of hypnosis on the cerebral cortex. (From Edmonston, 1979, p. 416)

hypnosis) and suggested sleep (human hypnosis), Pavlov felt that the fundamentals of both were the same. For example, both were induced by monotonous environmental stimuli, both involved a partial sleep brought about by a spreading cortical inhibition, and both were noted by a progressive loss of response patterns. Thus, Figure 2.1 is a depiction of the fundamentals of both hypnotic and suggested sleep.

Suggested Sleep

As seen in Table 2.1, suggested sleep, hypnosis in the human, is the most elaborate and complex of the various stages of sleep. Although still working from his data on dogs, Pavlov noted an aspect of cortical inhibition that pertains even more dramatically to the human animal than the dog. "A similar demarcation of excitable areas from areas which have undergone complete inhibition may exist also between different large areas of the cortex itself, producing what may be called a localized sleep" (Pavlov, 1927, p. 266). While differential inhibition of portions of the cortex occurred in dogs, in humans it was the nature of what is differentiated—the second-signal system—that solidly establishes suggested sleep as human hypnosis.

In humans responses are progressively lost in the process of "hypnotization" in accord with the progression noted above, but both phylogeny and ontogeny play greater roles in people than in the dog. It is the speech analyzer that is first inhibited in humans (phylogeny), and it is inhibited in accord with ontogeny. "The more complex and ontogenetically later conditioned bonds of the speech-motor analyzer are inhibited first as the subject lapses into a state of suggested sleep and are disinhibited last as the subject awakens from this state" (Platonov, 1959, p. 75).

Signal Systems

"Words, words, words, I'm so sick of words," cried Eliza Doolittle, not realizing she was abhoring the very characteristic that distinguished her from the dumb beasts. For humans symbolize, and symbolize verbally more than any other way. And these verbal symbols of ours are just as real as any other stimuli we encounter.

Thus it was not difficult for Pavlov to observe that speech provides the most obvious, the most natural conditioned stimuli in people's repertory of responsivity. And it was through speech primarily that the monotonous stimuli necessary for the induction of suggested sleep were achieved.

The method of inducing hypnosis in man involves conditions entirely analogous to those which produce it in our dogs. The classical method consisted in the performance of so-called "passes"—weak, monotonously repeated tactile and visual stimuli, just as in our experiments upon animals. At present the more usual method consists in the repetition of some form of words, describing sleep, articulated in a flat and monotonous tone of voice. (Pavlov, 1927, p. 404).

Pavlov attributed this heavy involvement of speech in hypnosis to his notation of a second-signal system, which refers to the verbal or inferential capacities of human beings, the ability to engage in abstract thought. This latter function "is achieved because the image of objects and actions expressed in words and ideas replaces their concrete effect on the organism" (Platonov, 1959, p. 16). The concrete effect is the function of the first-signal system. So that to the extent that animals (and humans) engage in concrete imagery, and that imagery has an effect (elicits a response of some sort, motoric or visceral) on the organism, we are dealing with what Pavlov called the first-signal system. The dog and the person may both salivate to a morsel of food, but only the person will salivate to the word food. This most significant contribution of Pavlov—hypothesizing two distinct signaling systems—became the cornerstone of differentiating hypnotic (animal) and suggested (human) sleep.

Rapport Zones

Although both the outward signs and the basic format of the internal inhibition in hypnosis were viewed as similar by Pavlov, it is the rapport zones that further differentiated hypnotic and suggested sleep. As early as 1851, Wood made the same distinction:

I think one great difference between natural sleep and that produced in magnetism is this—in the former, *all* nervous centres are tired out, and *all* repose; in the latter, those of sensations and volition are chiefly affected—and they being lulled to rest, the others retain their wonted activity. (Wood, 1851, p. 433)

Cortical inhibition is incomplete in both the animal and the human during partial sleep, so that there is the mosaic of excited and inhibited cell groups. However, in the case of the animals, the excited areas are first-signal system phenomena only; in human beings, they are both first- and second-signal related. Rapport zones are second-signal system cortical areas in the excited phase.

It is through the rapport zones that the relationship with the hypnotist is both established and maintained. As the monotonous verbal instructions for hypnotic induction are presented, second-signal system zones are excited. These zones, through the process of negative induction, initiate and enhance the spread of inhibition over the other areas of the cotex, thus inducing hypnosis. "The *rapport zone* produced in the sleeper by verbal suggestions is a more or less confined centre of concentrated excitation isolated from the remaining regions of the cortex . . ." (Platonov, 1959, p. 43). This then is the manner of hypnotic induction, internal inhibition produced by negative induction through circumscribed excitation zones established by monotonous verbal patter.

But the rapport zones serve more of a function than merely making induction possible. It is through these zones that the hypnotist maintains the capability of eliciting further hypnotic phenomena by additional verbal suggestions. Kubie and Margolin (1944) echoed this same point, although they extended it into a psychoanalytic interpretation of the dissolution of the boundaries of the ego:

It is characteristic of the onset of the hypnotic state that the subject appears to lapse into "sleep" while maintaining at least one sensori-motor contact with the outside world, and further that by the gradual elimination of other sensori-motor relationships the hypnotist becomes for a time the sole representative of or bridge to the outer world. . . . According to this description, the onset of the hypnotic state can be defined as a condition of partial sleep, in which one or two open channels of sensori-motor communication are maintained between the subject and the outside world. (p. 612)

As the verbal instructions (e.g., for an arm catalepsy or a sensory distortion) are presented, excitation spreads from the rapport centers to other portions of the cortex needed to carry out the content of the instruction. Thus the rapport zone is not fixed but is dynamic, and thereby may form excitatory bonds with different areas of the cortex at different times. It is important to take particular note of the fact that the induction of suggested sleep (human hypnosis) is a *process of inhibition* (manifested as relaxation), while the subsequent elicitation of hypnotic phenomena is a *process of disinhibition*. Thus hypnosis is at least a two-step process, the first step one of relaxation and inhibition and the second, one of disinhibition through excitation. This first step serves as the major focus of this book.

Having established that the rapport zone concept is a second-signal system, and therefore a human phenomenon, we should take note that humans are not restricted to rapport zones. People can also, and do, have foci of excitation that are related to the first-signal system. Such "sentry posts" are exemplified by the sleeping parent who awakens instantly to any unusual change in his or her infant's breathing, while the nonparent continues blissfully in repose. Such responses to nonverbal stimuli are akin to the foci of excitation in the dog during hypnotic (CR) sleep.

In fact, in the human there is often a mixing of first- and second-signal system foci of excitation. While the initial induction of hypnosis is usually through monotonous verbal instructions, later established "quick induction" signals are not, or at least are a combination of verbal and nonverbal manipulation. Consider some of the nonverbal techniques—a quick focusing of the eyes on an object, which is then lowered with a concurrent closing of the eyelids; tactile pressure on the shoulder applied by the hypnotist; an agreed-upon sound presented by the hypnotist. All of these signals qualify as conditioned stimuli in that they now have the power to induce that with which they have only previously been contiguously associated.

Words take on a dual function in the context of quick induction signals in that they are responded to as if they were, in fact, first-signal system stimuli. Through the association of a single word such as "sleep" or "relax" with the hypnotic condition, these words assume the property of rapidly inducing that condition. "Such words are, of course, conditioned stimuli which have become associated with the state of sleep. In this manner any stimulus which has coincided several times with the development of sleep can now, by itself, initiate sleep or a hypnotic state" (Pavlov, 1927, p. 404).

Thus Pavlov viewed the verbal suggestion as the simplest form of a conditioned reflex in humans. The suggestion concentrates cortical excitation in narrow foci, and, as indicated above, intensifies inhibition in the surrounding areas through negative induction. The negative induction abolishes other foci of excitation relating to contemporary or past stimuli, which allow the verbal suggestion to become regnant. Pavlov dealt with posthypnotic phenomena in this manner also. Since the rapport zone is, by virtue of the negative induction procedure, isolated from the rest of the cortex, it remains so upon awakening, in the absence of instructions to the contrary. Thus this focus of excitation resides within the individual, acting and directing behavior, and so detached from other cortical areas that the individual cannot readily alter its influence. That posthypnotic suggestions are retained for periods of days to years is attested to in the literature (Erickson and Erickson, 1941; Kellogg, 1929; Wells, 1947; Weitzenhoffer, 1950). The length of effectiveness is probably dependent upon a number of variables, not the least of which are the natural differences among individuals, a phenomenon Pavlov also noted in his dogs' capacity for hypnotic sleep.

Finally, should the rapport zone itself be overcome with inhibition the subject is not doomed to a perpetual existence in a state of hypnosis, but moves naturally and effortlessly into natural total sleep. Thus even in his delineation of the rapport zone, Pavlov kept reminding the reader that hypnosis and sleep are but points on the same continuum, as depicted in Table 2.1.

Katkov's Scheme

Just as hypnosis, wakefulness, and sleep are points on a continuum, so too are there a number of progressively inhibitory steps in the initiation and deepening of suggested sleep. As seen in Table 2.1, suggested sleep is divided into three stages, each of which is further subdivided into three degrees. This portion of the table incorporates the work of Katkov (1941), who took as his starting point earlier work by Bechterev. Basically, nine degrees of hypnotic depth are presented, with their corresponding physiological indices and each with its particular balance of cortical excitation and inhibition, which depicts the interaction between the two signal systems and the various analyzers. Such a scheme allows the investigator to fractionate hypnotic depth behaviorally.

Since Katkov's scheme is presented in detail in Platonov (1959, pp. 425–428), the following is a brief summary, showing the progression of hypnotic depth through increased irradiated cortical inhibition.

First Stage, First Degree. This degree has been called the prehypnoidal state, in which cortical tone is weakening and the subject reports pleasant sensations of restfulness. All sensibility is retained and the subject can be easily awakened. Although the eyes are generally closed, they need not be.

First Stage, Second Degree. With the progressive drop in cortical tone there is now an inhibition of the "kinesthetic system" and a growing feeling of heaviness. The eyes are closed, and although the subject still retains usual sensitivity to his environment and can easily awaken, the latency of motor reactions lengthens.

First Stage, Third Degree. Cortical tone and kinesthetic system activity drop off dramatically, and the subject now exhibits a pronounced increase in verbal, as well as motor response, latency. Although the subject reports that he could have terminated the hypnosis or resisted the hypnotist's suggestion if he wanted to, "he just did not feel like it."

Second Stage, First Degree. As before, there is continued inhibition across the cortex and in the kinesthetic analyzer. Inhibition of the second-signal system is more pronounced, and there now appear the symptoms of catalepsy. The subject is now very "sleepy," motor latencies are prolonged, the breathing is regular, and interest in environmental sounds is lost.

Second Stage, Second Degree. By this time the kinesthetic system is totally inhibited and the cutaneous analyzer is beginning to show the effects of deepening. Although spontaneous analgesias are noted, suggested illusions are not yet available.

Second Stage, Third Degree. As increasing inhibition of the second-signal system continues, some suggested illusions begin to be effective, provided the subject's eyes remain closed. In particular, negative olfactory illusions can be elicited. The subject reports that his own thoughts have receded to the background and only the verbal suggestions of the hypnotist retain importance.

Third Stage, First Degree. By this point, the subject is operating mainly on the first-signal system (excluding the rapport zone, of course). Consequently, motor latencies to suggestions are shorter than in previous degrees. Illusions, with the eyes closed, are now easily evoked in all spheres except visual and auditory. Auditory illusions can be elicited with difficulty, yet there is no spontaneous amnesia.

Third Stage, Second Degree. With the exception of the rapport zone, the subject's spontaneous use of his second-signal system is obliterated, and positive hallucinations in all senses can be effected. However, the subject's eyes are still closed during hallucinations; opening them destroys the illusion and often initiates awakening. Partial spontaneous amnesias appear in this next-to-last degree of suggested sleep.

Thrid Stage, Third Degree. Only the rapport zone of the second-signal system remains; the unified work of the cortex is now fragmented, awaiting the suggestions of the hypnotist. It is during this degree of suggested sleep that all of the phenomena usually associated with "deep trance" are manifested—positive and negative hallucinations, total spontaneous amnesias, age regression, and the like. For Katkov, and for the Pavlovian scheme, this degree is what others have labeled somnambulism, the plenary trance, or simply deep hypnosis (Erickson, 1952).

Katkov's accounting not only shows us the progressive irradiation of inhibition over the cortex, with its concomitant behavioral manifestations, but also relates certain phenomena noted by Pavlov in his dogs to the human behaviors. As described above, Pavlov noted phase changes in the animals' responsiveness to stimuli of varying intensities. These phase changes also occur during suggested sleep (see Table 2.1).

During the third degree of the second stage of suggested sleep, the human subjects (as did Pavlov's dogs) attain an equalization phase of responsiveness, in which either the word or the actual stimulus calls forth the illusion, in much the same manner that both a weak and a strong stimulus were equally capable of eliciting a response to the dog. Thus the "weak" stimulus (the word) attains equalization with the "strong" (the actual event).

The paradoxical phase, in which weaker stimuli—words in the case of the human—achieve regnancy over stronger, is highly significant for the understanding of many deep-trance phenomena. This phase appears in the third degree of the third stage of suggested sleep, in which hallucinatory, amnesic, and regressive behaviors are elicited. Thus, in the human, the capability of words to call forth negative hallucinations in the face of impinging environmental stimuli to the contrary may be viewed as an example of a universal phenomenon across species. The only basic difference between Pavlov's dogs and humans in the paradoxical phase is that the latter are responding to second-signal stimuli (words) and the former to first-signal stimuli. The same is noted even more so in the ultraparadoxical phase, in which negative stimuli now take on positive characteristics, or as Pavlov noted in the dogs, a stimulus that previously inhibited the conditioned response began to elicit the response; i.e., takes on positive characteristics. Should the cortical inhibition in the human continue to increase in the paradoxical stage, the ultraparadoxical and, finally, the total inhibition phases ensue.

While it is readily apparent from the more recent work on hypnotic depth scaling, as seen in the development of hypnotic susceptibility scales (e.g., see Hilgard, 1965, and Chapter 3), that the progression of events is not as orderly as Table 2.1 and the description above would have us believe, Katkov's suggested sleep hierarchy follows closely the behavioral manifestations of Pavlov's notions of the variations between excitation and inhibition occurring in hypnosis. Individual differences (Hilgard, 1965) obviously will invert some of the steps in the degrees of hypnotic depth, but by and large this schema is commensurate with the observations of both clinical and experimental investigators, and represents, in terms of inhibition (relaxation), yet another historical antecedent to the data supporting the proposition that neutral hypnosis is relaxation.

EXPERIMENTAL DATA

Having outlined Pavlov's general theory of hypnosis as irradiating cortical inhibition, it is appropriate to review some of the more modern experimentation related to the theory. These data fall into two categories: (a) studies having to do with the relationship between hypnosis and sleep, and (b) studies investigating the fate of certain conditioned responses during "hypnotization."

Hypnosis and Sleep

One of the most prevalent errors in attempts to evaluate Pavlov's theory experimentally has come from authors who misinterpreted Pavlov as equating hypnosis with sleep. "It has never been claimed by Pavlov or Pavlovians that hypnosis is sleep" (Das, 1958, p. 85). Platonov's review (1959, pp. 52–66) of the Russian literature pertaining to the physiology of suggested sleep makes it very clear that total sleep and suggested sleep (hypnosis) are quite different, although both reside on the same continuum of inhibition and are fundamentally the same process. That hypnosis may appear at times to be more similar to wakefulness than to total sleep does not disprove Pavlov's notions, but serves to point out that most of the early investigators, in the words of Marenina, "did not study hypnosis dynamically" (1959, p. 647). In other words, the stages (depth) of hypnosis must be taken into account when looking for sleep similarities.

Bass's (1931) work on the patellar reflex is pivotal for the early evaluations of Pavlov's theory. Bass assumed that if a simple response, the knee jerk, which is known to diminish in amplitude during total sleep, could be shown not to diminish during hypnosis, then the theory would be weakened. He further assumed that "if the 'suggested sleep differs in no respect from ordinary sleep,' we should expect the knee jerk to disappear at once" (p. 386). Seven male college students were tested for the patellar reflex and a voluntary button-pushing response during sleep, hypnosis, and wakefulness. The apparatus delivered a blow to the patellar tendon approximately once every nine seconds in each state for 100 trials.

Bass's findings were simply that the knee jerk response did not diminish during hypnosis and wakefulness, but did during sleep. The voluntary response showed a slight tendency to be weaker in hypnosis than in waking, a point well worth noting. On the basis of these data, Bass concluded: "It is difficult to come to any other conclusion than that sleep is not hypnosis and that hypnosis is neither suggested sleep nor a modified sleep nor anything between sleep and the normal waking state" (p. 398). This rather overgeneralized conclusion became central to Hull's (1933) arguments against a sleep-hypnosis identity and to several decades of ignoring not only Pavlov's views but the Russian literature in general. Pity that more had not read Pavlov more carefully.

It is not difficult to criticize an investigator's work *post hoc,* and particularly after some 40 years have passed. Modern authors might fault Bass for a lack of objective criteria of hypnosis, but in his day statistically developed depth scales did not exist; and besides, he did report that all of his subjects had partial or total amnesia for the experience, easily placing them in the third degree of stage 3 of suggested sleep. Even by modern technology, Bass's study is well done, but the latter part of his conclusion above leaves the reader a bit startled. That "sleep is not hypnosis" is an appropriate interpretation of the data, and one with which neither Pavlov nor more recent Russian investigators would quarrel. That it is not "anything between sleep and the normal waking state" is more problematic for several reasons. First, that interpretation is based solely on the patellar reflex data, which assumes Bass expected the knee jerk to be diminished somewhat in hypnosis, but not as much as in sleep. Second, the weakened voluntary response seems to be ignored at this point, and it may have been crucial to potential error in the latter portion of his interpretation. A diminution of a voluntary response during hypnosis, but not to the extent of that in sleep, is precisely what would have been predicted by Pavlov. Also, since the patellar reflex is a visceral (involuntary) response, there is no reason to assume that it would disappear or diminish during hypnosis. In fact, if any response should *not* diminish during hypnosis, the patellar reflex is a prime example. Remember that the knee jerk is a spinal reflex, and Pavlov was very clear in emphasizing hypnosis as a *cortical* inhibition, not affecting the subcortical areas (e.g., spinal reflexes) until it had progressed into total, natural sleep. The patellar reflex is just not an appropriate response on which to base a counterargument to Pavlov's theory. As will be seen below, the same kind of error was made in the interpretations of early data regarding the fate of conditioned responses during hypnosis (Scott, 1930; Hull, 1933). In the meantime it is important to understand that Bass's data do not run counter to Pavlov's theory, but rather are suggestive of support for it, because of the nature of the responses measured. Koster (1954), in fact, claimed to have refuted Bass in a clinical study of six patients. His data showed a 39% reduction of the waking knee jerk response in both sleep and hypnosis, which by Pavlov's interpretation would have indicated either extremely deep hypnosis or natural sleep.

Another approach to the sleep-hypnosis question has been taken by Dittborn. Instead of attacking the question directly by measuring a response that changes during sleep, Dittborn took an indirect approach. He hypothesized that if hypnosis and sleep are related, individuals who are quite facile at hypnosis (highly susceptible) should also be quite facile at going to sleep. He developed a technique of presenting a low-intensity stimulus (a quarter-watt light or a buzzer) every 9 to 12 seconds to a subject, who, in turn, responded with a softly spoken word or telegraph key depression. During this stimulus-response interaction sleep was suggested to the subjects. In one study Dittborn found that subjects entered "behavioral sleep," noted by the cessation of subject response (Dittborn et al., 1960); in another, electroencephalogram (EEG) changes similar to "normal nocturnal sleep" occurred (Borlone et al., 1960). Subjects in this latter study who fell asleep also had partial or total amnesia, an indication that results similar to those obtained with hypnotic inductions were being obtained.

In a third study, hypnotic susceptibility, measured on a one-to-five rating scale from "no response" to "amnesia and posthypnotic response," was compared to behavioral and physiological sleep in 52 subjects. The latter were measured by cessation or reduction of subject response and a self-rating scale and EEG patterns, respectively. While the direct comparison between physiological sleep and hypnotizability yielded nonsignificant results, two findings with respect to behavioral sleep are of interest. First, the five subjects who did not enter physiological sleep but did demonstrate behavioral sleep were the only five highly hypnotizable subjects in that group. In other words, while their EEGs were not sleeplike, their behavior was, so that the behavioral concomitants of sleep are elicited in the most susceptible subjects.

Second, and this is most curious, 10 of the 17 subjects who yielded more than a minute and a half of EEG sleep (Stage 1) continued to respond to the signal! These 10 were not particularly more or less hynpotizable, but this finding does suggest that there is not a one-to-one correspondence between what happens physiologically and what happens behaviorally when an individual is "asleep." It may seem, therefore, somewhat premature to dismiss a sleep-hypnosis relationship, for we still seem to be able to demonstrate or refute such a relationship on the basis of criteria selection.

One final point is worth mentioning, because it will come up again in Chapter

3. The set of instructions given to the subjects by Dittborn very closely resemble, in their basic elements, those used for standard hypnotic inductions:

While the buzzer is sounding regularly and you are responding, you will remain relaxed with your eyes closed. As you continue to press the telegraph key, you will become more and more sleepy. Just let this feeling grow; do not concern yourself with anything else. It doesn't matter if you actually fall asleep and stop responding to the buzzer. Do not try to resist this feeling of sleepiness, but also do not try to bring it about. Simply allow yourself to develop the feeling of sleepiness, letting it come about naturally. This is the procedure I told you about which helps people to enter sleep. Remember, do not try either to resist the feeling of sleepiness or to bring it about while answering the buzzer by pressing the telegraph key. Just let yourself go. (Dittborn and O'Connell, 1967, p. 184)

Compare these instructions with the various forms of hypnotic inductions mentioned in Chapter 3. Particularly compare the elements of being passive to the process and of "letting oneself go" to these same elements in the elicitation of the "relaxation response" discussed in Chapter 4.

Electroencephalogram

Obviously, one of the major difficulties in interpreting the relationships between hypnosis and total sleep has been the choice of the responses to be measured. As in Bass's study, most investigators have attempted to use some "involuntary" response or set of responses. By far the major interest has been in potential EEG changes during hypnosis.

Citing primarily Loomis et al. (1936), Blake and Gerard (1937), Blake et al. (1939), Davis et al. (1938), Dynes (1947), and Ford and Yeager (1948), reviewers of studies of physiological responses to hypnosis (Gorton, 1949a, 1949b; Weitzenhoffer, 1953; Sarbin, 1956; Crasilneck and Hall, 1959; Barber, 1961; and Evans, 1972) have concluded, with Chertok and Kramarz (1959), that: "Electroencephalographic investigations, in the present state of this technique, cannot furnish irrefutable proof regarding the question of similarity or dissimilarity between the hypnotic state and sleep" (Chertok and Kramarz, 1959, p. 237).

Evans's conclusions of his review of the EEG literature (1979) does not fault the technique as much as it points to the methodological inadequacies of our ability to present independent criteria of hypnosis and whatever stage of sleep may be relevant for comparison. Evans also reviewed the literature on EEG alpha activity and hypnosis, which has grown since Kamiya's (1969) claim that alpha density can be brought under voluntary control by operant techniques. Evans found no relationships between the capacity for hypnosis and waking alpha production and stated that: "merely being in a hypnotic trance does not alter frequency, amplitude, or density of alpha" (Evans, 1979, p. 156).

Although it will be dealt with in more detail in Chapter 6, it is appropriate to note that one study has directly compared alpha density between groups of subjects, one instructed in hypnosis and one instructed to be relaxed but not hypnotized (Edmonston and Grotevant, 1975). Briefly, it was found that the alpha densities did not differ between the two groups, which did not necessarily indicate that hypnosis did not alter alpha production but rather that it did not alter it in any different manner than did instructions to relax, a particular instructional set that may also place the individual in some stage between wakefulness and total sleep.

It is also well kept in mind that some studies present data indicating that there are EEG changes commensurate with hypnosis. Spindle and slow delta activity have been reported in the EEGs of hypnotized subjects (Barker and Burgwin, 1948, 1949; Schwarz et al., 1955; Marenina, 1959) as well as EEG similarities between "light sleep" and hypnosis (Chertok and Kramarz, 1959).

In the case of the Barker and Burgwin studies (1948, 1949), EEG activity paralleled organism-environmental relationships during hypnosis in much the same manner as nonhypnotic relationships. Using students, physicians, and epileptic patients, the authors tested a number of suggestions (sleep, removal of symptoms, sensory activity, etc.) and found that EEG activity that would have appropriately accompanied these same activities normally took place during hypnosis. For example, during hypnosis the suggestion of sleep and its concomitant muscular relaxation was accomplished by a decrease of alpha production and an increase in slow low-voltage waveforms. Although the mere induction of hypnosis did not bring about any consistent changes in the ongoing alpha patterns, the authors concluded: "Hypnosis and sleep are special forms of organism-environment integration characterized by reduction of the integrative activity of the central nervous system" (Barker and Burgwin, 1949, p. 420). In addition, they noted Pavlov's foci of excitation: "Hypnosis involves the reduction of organism-environment integration to a thin line of interpersonal communication" (p. 418).

According to Marenina (1959) both suggested and natural sleep show similar EEG characteristics. In fact, she reported a progressive quieting and appearance of sleeplike waves, as her subjects moved through the three stages of suggested sleep. Even their EEG response to an irritating stimulus (100-watt light bulb) diminished as hypnosis deepened. Unlike wakefulness, in which there is a delayed recovery of a prestimulus pattern, the removal of the light in the second stage elicited no such delayed recovery response. By the third stage, "this same light irritant ceased to have almost any effect at all on the curve of cerebral potentials" (Marenina, 1959, p. 648). Similar results were also reported to tone stimulation by Shpil'berg (1959). Thus Platonov (1959), from his review of the Russian literature on this topic, concluded that "the electric activity of the cerebral cortex coincides both in suggested sleep and natural sleep" (p. 61).

Unanimity with respect to EEG evaluations of the relationship between hypnosis and natural sleep is certainly not apparent as yet, and my earlier admonition

(Edmonston, 1967) to suspend judgment seems as reasonable now as it did then. At this juncture, it is more important to recognize that, despite the methodological difficulties Evans (1979) noted, some EEG data have suggested that while hypnosis is not total sleep, it may reside on an EEG continuum between wakefulness and total sleep. Pavlov's theory does not lead us to the conclusion that the two phenomena of hypnosis and sleep are identical, and we should be cautious not to make the same error in the interpretation of EEG records that Hull and Bass made with respect to the patellar reflex.

Other Physiological Systems

As with the EEG findings, reviewers of the literature with respect to other physiological measures have also concluded that hypnotic induction does not affect blood pressure, pulse rate, respiratory rate, and gastric secretions (Gorton, 1949a, 1949b; Crasilneck and Hall, 1959, 1960; Barber, 1961). Again the general conclusion belies the particulars.

As early as 1924, Luckhardt and Johnston, using a single male subject, discovered a significant rise in gastric acidity upon the induction of hypnosis alone. Although their study was intended to demonstrate the effect of suggested food intake during hypnosis, a rise in acidity was noted at each induction. This abrupt rise was of such magnitude that the investigators had to wait as much as an hour or two for it to subside before proceeding with the original study. The finding was consistent over a number of inductions. The authors "attributed the abrupt rise resulting from the induction of the hypnotic state to removal of cortical inhibition" (Luckhardt and Johnston, 1924, p. 179). In Pavlovian terms, the irradiating cortical inhibition of hypnosis functionally ablated the normal cortical inhibition on gastric secretions, allowing an increased flow of free and total acidities.

On the other hand, Eichhorn and Tracktir (1955) reported opposite findings. Using 24 medical and dental students, they assessed the effects of hypnosis alone on gastric secretions by measuring volume, bile, consistency, free acid, total acid, and pepsin before, during, and after inducing hypnosis through suggestions of relaxation, drowsiness, and sleep. Free acid, total acid, volume, and pepsin significantly decreased with the induction of hypnosis. With the exception of pepsin, the measures increased back to near prehypnotic levels upon the termination of hypnosis.

The Russian literature also indicates that induction is accompanied by diminished gastric secretion and that the general and free acid curves during hypnosis approximate (but are not identical to) those in total sleep (Platonov, 1959). Tsinkin (1930b, 1930c) demonstrated a slowing of both the pulse and respiratory rates and a drop in arterial blood pressure during suggested sleep. More rhythmic breathing has been reported in both the Russian literature and the clinical reports in the United States. In fact, suggestions to that effect are inherent in many of the modern induction procedures, as we will see in Chapter 3. For the present, we should take note of Platonov's conclusion from his review of the Russian studies: "the arterial pressure and the depth of respiration are in inverse proportion to the depth of suggested sleep, and the slower the falling asleep, the slower the drop in arterial pressure" (Platonov, 1959, p. 61).

Earlier, Lovett Doust (1953) reported a reduction in arterial oxygen saturation during hypnotic induction. In the context of studying the influence of hypnotically suggested emotions (joy, ecstasy, rage, depression, anxiety) and pain tolerance during hypnosis, the author noted that arterial oxygen saturation (measured peripherally from a finger) dropped significantly upon induction. In his four patients (three hysterics; one psychopathic personality) oximetric values dropped from an average of 96% to 88% when a progressive relaxation induction procedure was presented. "The extent of the anoxaemia resembles the results obtained by similar oximetric methods in reverie, natural sleep, and other (e.g., psychotic) states in which comparable dreamlike states of consciousness are seen" (Lovett Doust, 1953, p. 123).

In a more clinical vein Strosberg and Vics (1962), through the microscopic observation of the eyes of 10 patients before and after induction, noted a reduced vascular supply and other changes following hypnotic induction. While the report suffers from the lack of observations of an adequate control group (e.g., relaxed but not hypnotized) and the potential confounding of experimenter bias (The observer knew the state of the patient when making the observations.), the findings are suggestive, and, to date, have not been followed up.

The increasing inhibition of bodily functions as suggested sleep deepens was also noted in progressive changes in motor chronaxie (Maiorov, 1948), and a progressive decrease in skin perspiration as subjects move through the stages of suggested sleep toward total sleep (Marenina, 1952). Western studies also are beginning to show consistent findings with respect to skin potentials. Ravitz (1950, 1951a, 1951b, 1962), for example, has demonstrated a consistent smoothing of direct current potentials during hypnotic induction, and a number of studies of spontaneous fluctuations in the electrodermal response (EDR) have presented data suggesting that there is a marked difference in this sort of bodily activity between wakefulness and hypnosis, the latter residing somewhere between the former and total sleep. The EDR studies will be presented in more detail in Chapter 6.

Hypnosis and Conditioned Responses

Just as Hull argued against the Pavlovian position on the basis of Bass's patellar reflex study, so did he on the basis of a conditioned response (CR) study by Scott (1930). Since Scott was able to form a conditioned finger withdrawal response during hypnosis, he and Hull concluded that Pavlov's notions were inaccurate, because if hypnosis were inhibition, then the difficulty of establishing CRs should increase with both induction and deepening.

Pavlov's theory (and Platonov's restatement of it) makes clear that changes in establishing new CRs and changes in CRs already present should occur in suggested sleep. The degree and type of changes are highly dependent on the stage of hypnosis, the individual subjects, and the nature of the CR. For example, considering just the two analyzers posited by Pavlov and presented schematically in Figure 2.1—the alimentary and the motor—alimentary CRs should be the last effected (and the most difficult to establish) and the motor, the first (and easiest to establish). Thus what Pavlov implied was that we should see increasing interference with both the degree and the kind of CRs as hypnosis developed.

Korotkin and Suslova's long series of studies (1951, 1953, 1955a, 1955b, 1955c, 1959, 1960, 1962) offered evidence of the above. Not only did they demonstrate a progressive diminution of unconditioned responses and cognitive abilities (arithmetic reasoning), but they found it increasingly difficult to establish a conditioned eyelid response as hypnosis progressed through the three stages, until, finally, in the third degree of the third stage, it could not be formed at all. While it could always be argued that the subjects at that point had slipped into total sleep, it is of little consequence considering the progressive aspects of response detriment that Korotkin and Suslova have shown.

In other parts of his argument against Pavlov's theory, Hull assumed that if it could be demonstrated that there was no discontinuity between events (CRs) in the hypnotized and nonhypnotized states, then the notions of hypnosis as "sleep" (inhibition) would be weakened (see Hull, 1933). Pavlov never indicated that a clearcut discontinuity of functioning should be expected, but rather that there is a progression of decreasing function as hypnosis is induced and deepened, and that different responses would be affected differently. For example, if one were looking for the lack of discontinuity to "disprove" Pavlov, then the Livshits (1959) study would serve well. Using a differential vascular dilation and contraction conditioned response, he showed that "conditioned reflexes elaborated in the waking state were preserved in the state of hypnosis" (p. 752). However, an accurate understanding of Pavlov's position makes it clear that there should not be a discontinuity with respect to this vascular response, because of its "involuntary" nature. The induction of hypnosis alone should not affect the visceral analyzers. Humanity's predilection for clearly bounded categories must always be tempered with the reality that nature operates in fluid continua.

That the influence of hypnosis on CRs is also dependent on the depth of the trance is suggested by the findings of McCranie and Crasilneck (1955), who reported the loss of a conditioned hand-withdrawal response following the addition of age-regression suggestions to hypnotic induction. In addition, the authors found that a less voluntary response (eyelid) was unaffected by the additional instructions. The interpretation suggested here is that the age-regression instructions served to deepen the trance and thus influence the hand withdrawal in a manner commensurate with Pavlov's predictions.

Thus there are two distinct aspects to the supposed relationship between hypnosis and the stages of hypnosis and conditioned responses: (a) that a given response will be affected (inhibited) progressively as the hypnosis progresses from wakefulness to total sleep, and (b) that the effect of hypnosis on a given response will begin at a different point on the wakefulness-total sleep continuum and have a different inhibition time course depending on the nature of the response (e.g., motor versus visceral). It was not until recently that the latter proposition was subjected to a series of experimental evaluations.

Although these studies, carried out at Washington University and Colgate University during 1964–1968, have been reported in detail elsewhere (Edmonston, 1979), a brief summary will show the sort of influence hypnosis has on a graded ("voluntary" to "involuntary") series of CRs. In the first of the series (Plapp and Edmonston, 1965) a finger-withdrawal response was conditioned to a criterion in 12 subjects. Following hypnotic induction instructions or control instructions to remain quiet, each to half of the group, 12 extinction trials were presented. A second set of extinction trials followed the countermanding of the instructions for each subgroup. The results appear in Figure 2.2, which makes

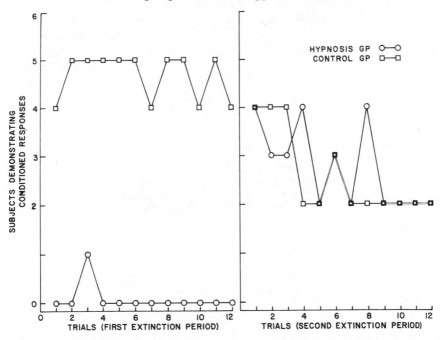

Figure 2.2. The number of subjects giving CRs on each extinction trial. (From Plapp and Edmonston, 1965, p. 380)

clear the fact that during hypnosis the CR was obliterated but returned after the termination of hypnosis. Pavlov's idea that the motor analyzer, and hence motor (voluntary) behavior, would be more easily affected by hypnosis appeared to receive a modicum of support.

The second study in the series (Plapp, 1967), involved eyelid conditioning, a response that Korotkin and Suslova (1951) had increasing difficulty achieving as hypnosis deepened. In his investigation Plapp, attempting to rectify what he saw as the inadequacies of control conditions in previous studies, employed several groups, one of which was treated in the same manner as subjects in the finger-withdrawal study—CR acquisition trials, hypnotic induction, CR extinction trials, termination of hypnosis, CR extinction trials (second series). The extinction trials for Plapp's work are shown in Figure 2.3 and interpreted by him as follows:

Only Group 2 Ss, hypnotized prior to the first extinction period, gave a significantly reduced number of eyeblink CRs on the first extinction as compared with that of the last acquisition trial. . . . The number of CRs given by Group 2 Ss decreases more rapidly and remains at a lower level during the first exteninction period. (Plapp, 1967, p. 71)

The reversal of this effect noted in our finger-withdrawal study during the second extinction period was not, however, as conclusive in Plapp's eyelid conditioning series. Subtle changes between two responses such as these serve only to call attention to the degree of "voluntariness" inherent in the two responses, since, as Marquis and Hilgard (1936) pointed out, the eyelid response is not totally dependent upon cortical connections. The fact that it is affected by hypnosis in a slightly different manner from the finger-withdrawal response is no surprise to the Pavlovian view. Unless there were marked differences in the depth of the hypnosis employed, the two responses should have been affected differently, and in exactly the lessening degree noted, the finger-withdrawal being influenced more blatantly. Thus the progressive interference with these two responses is precisely as would have been predicted by Pavlov.

In addition to measuring the eyelid response, Plapp also recorded EDRs, plethysmographic orienting responses, and reaction times in his subjects. Although his procedures generally failed to influence the physiological responses, two other findings should be noted: (a) there was a significant negative correlation between electrodermal spontaneous fluctuations (EDSFs) and the capacity for hypnosis, and (b) the reaction time measure increased significantly for Group 2 following hypnotic induction. These findings will be mentioned in Chapters 6 and 7, respectively, because they relate directly to the general thesis of this book—that neutral hypnosis is relaxation—but Plapp's conclusion regarding increased reaction time is worth noting here. "The effects of hypnosis may go beyond the primarily voluntary kind of response to also depress responses which are not directly under voluntary control and are not obviously subject to

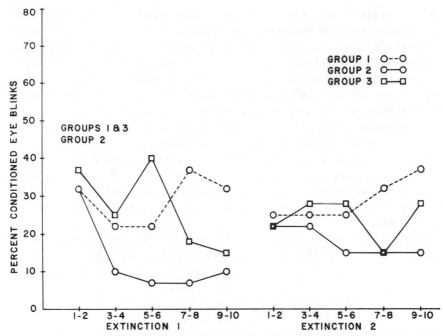

Figure 2.3.   Percent conditioned eyeblinks over two series of extinction trials. (From Plapp, 1967, p. 39)

S-expectations regarding hypnotic effects'' (Plapp, 1967, p. 67). As one explores the influence of hypnosis on CRs (and other behaviors as well), it must be kept in mind that there are varying degrees and stages of hypnotic depth that will dictate the kind of response affected at any given moment. The visceral analyzers, and thus less "voluntary" responses, can be influenced, but only as depth increases.

Next in this series of investigations to assess the influence of hypnosis on CRs varying along the voluntary-involuntary continuum were four studies using the conditioned EDR. As we will see in Chapter 6, a number of investigators were interested in EDR changes during hypnosis, but none had directly investigated conditioned EDRs. Following the same experimental format of introducing hypnotic instructions after the CR had been established (and before extinction trials), the studies, conducted at the Colgate University laboratories, involved a total of 69 adult subjects.

Anyone who has worked with the electrodermal response is fully aware of the difficulties inherent in such work. In the first place, it is difficult to justify the phrase "conditioned EDR" because there is virtually no stimulus that does not elicit an EDR, making the establishment of a CS elusive at best and mythical at worst. What one generally does, then, is to use a stimulus that leads to an EDR and habituate the EDR to that stimulus. Once the organism is habituated to the stimulus, then that same stimulus is paired with a second stimulus to which the organism has not been habituated, and this pair is used as the CS-US complex. It becomes even more confusing when one considers whether this pair is not to be used, in toto, as an unhabituated stimulus or as a conditioning model in the classical sense. By such pairing, is the first (habituated) stimulus of the pair now to be considered a dishabituated stimulus and no longer worthy of the title CS? Or do we maintain that it has retained its habituated properties, despite the change—sometimes rather dramatic—in the entire stimulus complex? If the former, how can we claim that a CR has been established? If the latter, how do we assess the assumption, since it is now being presented with a second EDR-eliciting stimulus? As you can see, EDR conditioning is not without its own set of experimental Gordian knots.

In order not to be compromised by the inherent logical difficulties with the response itself, the data for the groups of subjects in these studies—(a) hypnosis instructed, (b) relaxation instructed without hypnosis instructions, (c) no instructions, and (d) hypnosis instructed plus knowledge of the experimental hypothesis—and for individual subjects who by a standard conditioning criterion did, in fact, emit conditioned EDRs were assessed.

Whether we looked at group or individual data, the result was the same. Hypnosis instructions did not affect conditioned EDRs, thus suggesting that as the response to which we attend is farther and farther removed from the subject's voluntary control (is more under the various visceral analyzers), hypnosis has less and less influence—as Pavlov's theory would predict.

For example, the data of individual subjects who had met a conditioning criterion (four conditioned EDRs out of five consecutive conditioning trials) and who had received a particular instructional set (hypnosis, relaxation without hypnosis, or no instructions) following conditioning and prior to the first extinction trials were examined. What was discovered was that between 65% and 70% of the subjects in *each* group yielded conditioned EDRs during the first five extinction trials, demonstrating that the hypnosis instructions were no more effective than the instructions given to the two control groups. In other words, the introduction of hypnosis did not differentially affect a less voluntary, visceral response.

Of the last two studies in the series, little of substance can be said. Our attempts to assess the influence of hypnosis on a conditioned heart-rate response were at best only suggestive. If one thinks that conditioning the EDR poses difficulties, one should try heart-rate (HR) conditioning. In the first place, the very nature of what is to be called a ''response'' (acceleration or deceleration) and what is not is in apparent disarray and dependent on the particular set of experimental variables used. Second, the HR response is extremely adaptable, and habituates to novel stimuli within 10 to 15 trials, making a stable conditioned response very difficult, if not impossible, to establish.

It was in this series of studies that I introduced the notion of using a control group instructed to "Let yourself become very deeply relaxed, but do not allow yourself to enter hypnosis; allow yourself to become deeply relaxed, but do not become hypnotized." Such a control group led, as will be seen, to the major . thesis of this work.

CONCLUSION

Thus whether investigators assess the fate of a single CR through the degrees and stages of hypnosis as outlined by Katkov—for example, the Korokin and Suslova series—or a number of responses differing on a voluntary-involuntary (motor-visceral) continuum—for example, Plapp and my series—the conclusion reached is the same. Pavlov's cortical inhibition theory of hypnosis appears to make consistent predictions of behavioral changes in conditioned responses.

Both the data on sleep and those on CRs firmly establish Pavlov, his theory, and the work of his followers in the historical stream that was developed in the first chapter. The history of hypnosis is a history replete with associations of the term with ideas of sleep, inhibition, and relaxation. This association has been and is the dominant theme in the history of hypnosis, and Pavlov's work is no exception to the trend. In fact, Pavlov has been a major contributor to this thesis, because to the previous speculations, clinical reports, and quasi-experimental attempts to understand hypnosis, he added the rigors of the experimental laboratory, the elegance of the controlled experiment, and the replication of data by other investigators in diverse settings.

However, our historical trek is not over. Yet one more arena of history needs exploration—the hypnotic induction procedures themselves. The instructions offered to the subject or patient are the link to the historical symbiosis of relaxation and hypnosis, for the stimuli to hypnosis are the induction instructions. Subjects and patients do what they are told. And hypnotic instructions tell them not only to relax, but that to relax is to be hypnotized. If they are told not to relax, as we will see, they are not hypnotized.

CHAPTER 3

Inductions and Susceptibility: The Role of Relaxation

It is not only in the general history of hypnosis that we find the pervasiveness of the relaxation-sleep-hypnosis idea, but in the details of the history of hypnosis. In particular, the way in which hypnosis is achieved—the hypnotic induction—has reflected the connection between relaxation and hypnosis, as has the continuum known as the stages or depth of hypnosis. The hypothesized stages of hypnosis are inseparable from the early studies of hypnotic susceptibility and, by historical extension, from the scales of hypnotic susceptibility in use today. Both mirror the central role played by relaxation in hypnotic inductions, old and new.

INDUCTION PROCEDURES

Often the manipulations and rituals people perpetuate yield clues as to the nature of the phenomena they are attempting to produce. A teacher goes through certain operations to create the atmosphere in which learning can take place in his or her students. Some rituals, such as the genuine display of enthusiasm and enjoyment of learning, the utter fascination with expanding one's knowledge, lead the student, often without awareness, to those behaviors that indicate that learning has taken place. Other rituals, such as the threats of grades, the demand for attendance, the degradation of the student for not "knowing the right answer," may actually act as deterrents to the emergence of the very process they are supposed to encourage. Is the subtle technique of suggesting that learning is fun, pleasurable, unlike the subtle, almost out-of-awareness suggestions offered by Erickson to his patients? Is the more direct "If you do not learn I will fail you" technique unlike Freud's attempted authoritarian domination of his patients with a single word: "Sleep"? I suspect not, in both instances. Each teacher and each hypnotic operator is going through rituals intended to produce the desired phenomenon. Actually, both teaching procedures will produce learning in some students and both hypnotic procedures will produce hypnosis in some subjects. Thus it may appear that the crucial factor in determining the outcome is the subject's (student's) expectations.

46

From this viewpoint theorists advocating a social, situational characteristics explanation of hypnosis (and learning) would seem to have won the day. Not so, because the expectations brought to the hypnotic situation by the subject are only a part of a very complex situation and are, more important, often determined by behaviors emitted by the operator in the first place. Operators tell subjects what is expected of them, either directly or indirectly, and the manner in which this is done is itself determined by the belief system of the operator. Such communication is called the hypnotic induction procedure. Now this is a very important point: What operators believe hypnosis to be determines what they do to develop hypnosis in a given subject. By definition then a circular, self-fulfilling prophecy occurs, and the operators manipulate the situation to maximize the emergence of what they already believed hypnosis to be.

Are we dealing then with a sham, an imposture? Certainly not, any more than the teacher's rituals are a sham to produce learning. We do not fault a construction engineer for proceeding with those operations that will produce an end product, of which he had a great many preconceived ideas at the outset. Why should we fault the operator for creating the atmosphere intended to enhance the development of his or her final product? And at the same time, let us not get so entangled in the apparent circularity of social belief systems that we miss the reality of the product and, in particular, what makes up the pervasive and continuing reality of the product. Yes, operators use operations (induction procedures) that will communicate their belief systems to subjects and fulfill these systems in behavioral consequences. Such a system of behaviors and reactive behaviors does not self-fulfill some mythology created by the operator. To understand this point, we must explore the antecedents of the operators' belief systems themselves.

Granted our belief systems often blind us to some of the realities of our observations, tend to pass out of "style" only with great difficulty, and are intimately intertwined with the professional social milieu of our times; but one of the basic tenets intended to reduce observational error and bias is the replication of observations by different indiviudals in different locales. "Modern" hypnosis and hypnotic induction procedures have been in use now for almost two centuries in such diverse western and eastern cultures as France, Germany, England, the United States, and India. We have seen the belief systems develop from the magnetism of Mesmer's time (in tune, as we know, with the general "scientific" atmosphere of the eighteenth century); through the sleep emphasis of de Puységur, Braid, and others; the suggestion doctrine of Braid, Bernheim, and others; the mental disorder interpretation of Charcot; the dissociation of Janet; to the social demands and task motivation of Orne and Barber; the social role theory of Sarbin and Coe; and lately, the reassertion of dissociation by Hilgard. All of these changes have been in tune with the scientific or professional milieu of the times in which they emerged. For example, one of the vital interests of the intellectuals of the middle 1700s was the "new" physics, the fascination with magnets and the concern with the influence of planets and stars on human behavior. Hence Mesmer's beliefs extended magnetic properties to living organisms and "explained" changes in behavior by an appeal to a universal fluid. The same sort of contextual influence on the emergence of given belief systems is found today. The emphasis on social theory and the social context in which mankind lives gave rise—naturally, we say—to the emphasis on social and role theories of hypnotic behavior. Even more recently, the reemphasis of consciousness and, if the behaviorists will forgive, "the mind," no doubt had an impact on Hilgard's resurrection of Braid, Bernheim, and Janet's dissociation hypothesis. However, as has been pointed out in Chapter 1, the one pervasive theme transcending all of the social context explanations of hypnosis has been the sleep-relaxation observation. Regardless of the particular emphasis of a particular era, the relaxation-hypnosis relationship has been continually observed and reported. In the face of both historical vagaries and experimental investigations, this relationship is unique in its tenacity.

But tenacity alone does not demonstrate veridicality. Old belief systems are slow to dissolve, and many readers will simply reduce the continuation of the hypnosis-relaxation notation in the literature to our inability to profit from past errors. After all, did not the idea of a magnetic fluid predominate for a century or more? As a matter of fact, the belief in such unseen and independently immeasurable forces still pervades the nonprofessional public and even has its adherents in professional ranks (e.g., extrasensory perception). The antecedents of operator's belief systems are themselves complex, but several items in the history of hypnosis are enlightening.

In the case of Mesmer, his magnetic fluid belief system apparently did, in fact, blind him to a phenomenon present in his mesmerism. It was noted in Chapter 1 that he considered the coma that followed the crisis to be at best inconsequential and at worst an interference with the cure he intended. Here is an example of tunnel vision borne of a preconceived notion. The same is not the case with de Puységur. His induction method was in part dependent upon his belief that the crisis should be reduced in severity. But what is important about his experience is that he was *surprised* by his results. In spite of the orientation of the belief system he had learned from his mentor, Mesmer, he observed something he did not expect—sleep, drowsiness, relaxation. Ellenberger (1965) explains de Puységur's results by the nature of his subjects (the subject variable again)— peasants who naturally deferred to landed aristocracy; others will interpret his results by pointing to the nature of the "suggestions" he gave his subject, Victor Race. But whether Victor naturally deferred to de Puységur (He did not, in fact, in hypnosis.) or de Puységur suggested the outcome does not detract from the fact that he did not expect the outcome he obtained. De Puységur's belief system at that time dictated one outcome; when he received another, he was not so deferent to his mentor and his belief system that he could not note and appreciate what he observed.

Thus, relaxation-sleep made its reappearance in the history of hypnosis unexpectedly, in contrast to what the belief systems of the time would have predicted. Such turning points in the history of a phenomenon, when coupled with the pervasive nature of the phenomenon once rediscovered, dictate further exploration of that phenomenon, regardless of the tenor of the times. Although neither surprise nor tenacity are sufficient in and of themselves, they do indicate that we should swim upstream a bit farther and explore the headwaters of induction procedures.

Mesmer

I have already pointed out that Mesmer's induction technique took its form from the nature of his interpretation of animal magnetism. Not only did the fluid have to pass from the operator to the subject, but that fluid had to be distributed within the subject to those parts where it could do the most good. When working with individual subjects, such as Misses Oesterline and Paradis, Mesmer began with his hands on the subject's shoulders and moved them slowly down the arms to the fingertips, maintaining bodily contact all the while. At the end of each "pass," he held onto the thumbs of the subject momentarily before repeating the procedure (Bramwell, 1903). The bodily contact, particularly with female patients, as part of the induction and, later, the specific treatment, caused some moral concerns on the part of the commission that investigated Mesmer's claims (Bailly et al., 1784). Although some felt that actual contact with the patient was unnecessary, the practice of induction through passes (at a distance or in contact) persisted well into the nineteenth century.

de Puységur

Like those of his mentor, de Puységur's induction techniques were dominated by physical passes:

Suppose that you wish to magnetise a patient; sit opposite to him, take hold of his thumbs, and look steadily at him, with a permanent attention and intention, or *will* to produce the desired effect. After four or five minutes, when his thumbs have acquired the same temperature with yours, place your hands on his shoulders, let them remain there two or three minutes, then draw them very slowly along the arms, and take hold again of the thumbs; do this three or four times in succession; then, place your hands on his stomach, in such a manner that your thumbs may be in the centre, and your fingers on the sides; when you feel a communication of heat, slowly draw your hand down to his feet; then place them over his head, and slowly draw them again down to the feet, and continue in the same manner, taking care in raising your hands to his head, to turn them outwards, and extend them to both sides. The precaution never to magnetise upwards, and to separate your hands when you raised them, is recommended as essential. Touch slightly and slowly, keeping your hands a few inches from the face, and scarcely even touching the clothes; use no muscular effort; let your motions be easy and supple; your hand must not be stiff; let your fingers be a little bent, and occasionally united, for it is from the end of the fingers that the fluid flows or radiates; do not be impatient of producing effects; give yourself up entirely to feelings of sympathy, and to the wish to relieve your patient. If he feels pain in particular parts, hold your hand some time on that part; continue your operation, for about half an hour. As it is necessary that your attention should be permanent, a longer time would be fatiguing. In finishing the operation, make several long *passes,* and one across the eyes, to disseminate equally the fluid.

The *relation* once well established, contact is not necessary; the action *at a distance* is often more beneficial and salutary, than that produced by immediate contact. (de Puységur, 1837, pp. 74−75)

His approach apparently had a much more soothing, gentle, and less dominating quality to it, no doubt borne of his concern with the violence of the crises and his own shyness with respect to public display. From his writings we can infer that, in addition to the passes, he was prone at times to gather his subjects up in his arms, thus, we might opine, providing the patient with the physical warmth and closeness through which de Puységur gentled the individual into a mesmeric trance. Note, for example, de Puységur's comment on his first encounter with Victor Race: "what was my surprise to see this man sleeping quietly in my arms . . ." (Esdaile, 1846). Consider also his report to the Abbé de Poulouzat of September 20, 1784. In this letter he describes aiding one of the officers of his regiment who had had an apoplectic fit, and concluded: "I have the satisfaction of feeling him coming back alive in my arms . . ." (de Puységur, 1784; in Tinterow, 1970, p. 59).

If we are right to surmise that when de Puységur wrote "in my arms" he meant that quite literally (and also that his French did not suffer too greatly in translation), then he may have unwittingly constructed his induction technique to enhance the regressive, parent-child relationship that psychoanalysts perceive in the subject-operator relationship. Like the parent lulling the child to sleep in his or her arms, de Puységur mesmerized his patients.

Abbé Faria

The Abbé Faria's view of magnetism as a "lucid sleep" was reflected quite strongly in his induction techniques. As outlined briefly in chapter 1, he used several methods, singly or in combination. In one, the subject was instructed to sit comfortably in a chair and to close his or her eyes. After a period, during which the Abbé observed the subject to ascertain the degree of quietude attained, Faria announced "Sleep" in an emphatic, commanding tone. His technique was as follows:

He placed the patient in an arm chair, and after telling him to shut his eyes, and collect himself, suddenly pronounced, in a strong voice and imperative tone, the word "dormez," which generally produced on the individual an impression sufficiently strong to give a slight shock, and occasion warmth, transpiration, and *sometimes* somnambulism. (Braid, 1843, p. 7)

If this method was not initially successful, it was repeated several more times.

In a second method, in which he antedated Braid, Faria used eye-fixation on the operator's hand until the eyes became fatigued (denoted by increased blinking) and closed. Finally, Faria also utilized a touching method, in which he would touch the patient in various places (temples, knees, feet, forehead), thus developing the "lucid sleep."

Deleuze

Deleuze (1825) also gave elaborate instructions for magnetizing by passes, instructions that owe much to the techniques of Mesmer and de Puységur. Placing the patient in a sitting position, with his or her knees firmly between the operator's, the thumbs of the patient were held by the operator. Then the operator moved his hands to the patient's head in a circular motion and drew them down the arms to the fingertips four or five times. Following these passes, others were made—this time at a distance—down the ventral aspect of the face and body to the pit of the stomach, where the hands remained for a brief period. The anterior to posterior progression was thought to be particularly important, as descending movements were considered magnetic (and ascending were not) in that they moved the fluid from the head region to the extremities. Much emphasis was placed on the thumbs, for it was believed that the fluid escapes through the digits. All of this was directed to the goal of establishing "harmony" in the system (see Teste, 1843, pp. 151−153).

While the technique Deleuze described hardly seems related to the sleep and relaxation inductions that developed later, his *Practical Instructions in Animal Magnetism* (1846) contained passages illustrating that the relationship did not go unnoted: "the magnetized feels the necessity of closing the eyes; his eyes are so sealed that he cannot open them; he experiences a calm, a feeling of comfort; he becomes drowsy; he is put to sleep" (Esdaile, 1846, p. 62−63).

What is most noteworthy in this form of induction is not the physical passes but the setting in which operators were instructed to use them. Mesmer generally worked in a darkened room accompanied, in the case of the *baquet* by soothing music. Deleuze advised no additional witnesses, lest they disturb the patient; a moderate temperature; and precautions to avoid interruptions during the process. Historians have made note of the dramatic aspects of the environment Mesmer created, (the hysterical provoking aspects); but even when a number of patients were present at one sitting (at the *baquet*) a certain serenity, a reduction of extraneous stimuli was also created. Deleuze made this reduced sensory input explicit, and while some readers may interpret these manipulations as an attempt to focus the patient's attention on the operator and thus enhance the potency of the suggestions offered, it cannot be denied that reduced sensory input also encourages relaxation, drowsiness, and sleep. Although Mesmer denied the value of the coma, his techniques, and those directly descended from them, provided some of the environmental circumstances conducive to its production.

Braid

As we have seen, Braid's original notions on magnetism and especially his very changing of the word to hypnotism signaled his concern with the sleeplike countenance of the subjects. Brief mention was made earlier of his initial induction technique of eye-fixation. In his own words:

Take any bright object (I generally use my lancet case) between the thumb and fore and middle fingers of the left hand; hold it from about eight to fifteen inches from the eyes, at such position above the forehead as may be necessary to produce the greatest possible strain upon the eyes and eylids, and enable the patient to maintain a steady fixed stare at the object. The patient must be made to understand that he is to keep the eyes steadily fixed on the object, and the mind riveted on the idea of that one object. [Once the pupils have dilated] if the fore and middle fingers of the right hand, extended and a little separated, are carried from the object towards the eyes, most probably the eyelids will close involuntarily, with a vibratory motion. (Braid, 1843, p. 27–28)

According to Bramwell (1903), Braid later abandoned the prolonged gaze and merely instructed his patients to close their eyes early on. Once he had abandoned his physical theory, he utilized direct verbal suggestion to concentrate the attention.

While Braid's initial induction procedures did not reflect directly the relaxation-hypnosis components, they were certainly implied in the creation of physical fatigue, the dilation of the pupils, and the closing of the eyes. Few individuals sleep with their eyes open. Closing the eyes also reduces sensory input, another of the general themes running through the induction techniques of days past and present. In Braid's verbal suggestions the importance of relaxation and sleeplike behavior is also clear.

In his later works (Braid, 1855) Braid restricted the use of the term hypnosis to that state in which the subject-patient retains no memory of the events that transpired. The word hypnotic was also used to describe an even deeper state in which memory was also obliterated but could not be rearoused even with the reintroduction of hypnosis. Despite this restricted use of the term, Braid continued to speak of this "true hypnosis" in terms of sleep.

Let the term *hynpotism* be restricted to those cases alone in which, by certain artifical processes, oblivious sleep takes place, in which the subject has no remembrance on awaking of what occurred during his sleep, but of which he shall have the most perfect recollection on passing into a similar stage of hypnotism thereafter. In this mode, *hypnotism* will comprise those cases only in which what has hitherto been called the double-conscious state occurs; and let the term *hypnotic coma* denote that still *deeper* stage of the sleep in which the patient seems to be quite unconscious at the time of all external impressions, and devoid of voluntary power, and in whom no idea of what had been said or done by others during the said state of *hypnotic coma* can be remembered by the patient on awaking, or at *any* stage of *subsequent* hypnotic operations. (Braid, 1855; in Tinterow, 1970, pp. 370–371).

Esdaile

As did Braid, Esdaile made explicit use of reduced sensory input to enhance the induction procedures. Generally the patients were seen in a darkened room in which they reclined on a bed with the operator seated behind the head of the bed. However, in his first attempt at mesmerism, Esdaile sat facing his patient:

I placed his knees between mine, and began to pass my hands slowly over his face, at the distance of an inch, and carried them down to the pit of his stomach. This was continued for half an hour before he was spoken to. . . . [Later] I . . . breathed on his head, and carried my hands from the back of his head over his face and down the Epigastrium, where I pressed them united. . . . The same process was persevered in, and in about an hour he began to gape, said he must sleep, that his senses were gone. . . . (Esdaile, 1846, pp. 43–44)

Esdaile proceeded then to operate on the man's hydrocele.

As his practices became more uniform, the following became his mode of mesmerizing (carried out most often by his native assistants):

Desire the patient to lie down, and compose himself to sleep, taking care, if you wish to operate, that he does not know your intention; this object may be gained by saying it is only a trial; for fear and expectation are destructive to the physical impression required. Bring the crown of the patient's head to the end of the bed, and seat yourself so as to be able to bring your face into contact with his, and extend your hands to the pit of the stomach, when it is wished; make the room dark, enjoin quiet, and then shutting your patient's eyes, begin to pass both your hands, in the shape of claws, slowly, within an inch of the surface, from the back of the head to the pit of the stomach; dwelling for several minutes over the eyes, nose, and mouth, and then passing down each side of the neck, go downwards to the pit of the stomach, keeping your hands suspended there for some time. Repeat this process steadily for a quarter of an hour, breathing gently on the head and eyes all the time. The longitudinal passes may then be advantageously terminated, by placing both hands gently, but firmly, on the pit of the stomach and sides. . . . (Esdaile, 1846, pp. 145–146)

While this induction continued the physical passes of the past, it made maximum use of reduced sensory input: dark room, "enjoining" quiet, closing the patient's eyes, and having the patient lie down. (Both patients and operators were usually naked from the waist up.) All of these procedures enhance the relaxation-sleep connotations of the situation and create the physical prerequisites for relaxation. It is also easy to see from Esdaile's description why the general public has the hovering, dominating, Svengalian image of the hypnotist that still persists today; for example, "hands, in the shape of claws."

Elliotson too made use of passes over the patient's body coupled with breathing on the patient's forehead. All of this was done, as Esdaile did, in a darkened room. Apparently Elliotson's techniques were more rapid than those of Esdaile, for Marmer (1959) tells us that the former's induction took about one hour, whereas Esdaile was known to continue his passes for upwards of eight hours. What subject would not have gone to sleep after eight hours of induction?

Liébeault

Liébeault's concern with the sleep aspects of hypnosis has already been well established. His technique combined Faria's verbal suggestions to relax and become drowsy with Braid's eye-fixation. Not only did he use verbal suggestion for induction, but, according to Bernheim, he "conceived the idea of *applying the same vocal suggestions to therapeutics*" (Bernheim, 1884, p. 206). Bramwell's description of Liébeault's method, which he witnessed at Nancy, is instructive:

The patient was first placed in an armchair, then told to think of nothing and to look steadily at the operator. This fixation of the gaze was not maintained long enough to produce any fatigue of the eyes, and appeared to be simply an artifice for arresting attention. [Note: This was not considered primary but merely arresting, so that the affective part of the induction, verbal suggestions to relax, could be more effective.] If the eyes did not close spontaneously, Liébeault requested the patient to shut them, and then proceeded to make the following suggestions, or others resembling them—"Your eyelids are getting heavy, your limbs feel numb, you are becoming more and more drowsy," etc. This was continued for a minute or two. . . . (Bramwell, 1903, pp. 41−42)

Bernheim

Of those involved in the controversies in the latter part of the nineteenth century, Bernheim gives us the clearest picture of an induction technique that is founded on the sleep-relaxation-hypnosis equation, although the author denied such to be the case.

Following a discussion with the patient explaining "suggestive therapeutics" and indicating that "it is an *ordinary sleep,*" he said:

Look at me and think of nothing but sleep. Your eyelids begin to feel heavy, your eyes tired. [Note again the Braid emphasis on eye fatigue.] They begin to wink, they are getting moist, you cannot see distinctly. They are closed. . . . Your lids are closing, you cannot open them again. Your arms feel heavy, so do your legs. You cannot feel anything. Your hands are motionless. You see nothing, you are going to sleep. . . . Your lids are stuck together; you cannot open them. The need of sleep becomes greater and greater, you can no longer resist. . . . Sleep. (Bernheim, 1884, pp. 1−2)

This induction illustrates my general point: No matter where we look in the earlier history of hypnosis, we find the dominant theme of relaxation and sleep in the induction procedures.The question must be raised: If sleep was unnecessary for success in hypnotic therapeutics (as Bernheim told his patients who did not go "to sleep") and all that was needed was the extreme concentration on one idea (Braid's monoideism), why did even the proponents of these ideas persist in using induction procedures couched in the vocabulary of sleep and relaxation? Was it habit? Was it some sort of unconscious concern that perhaps there really was some fundamental connection between sleep, relaxation, and hypnosis? We do not know, but we do know that the same vocabulary pervades the hypnotic induction procedures of our own time.

Modern Inductions

Just as Chapter 1 was not intended to be an exhaustive history of hypnosis and the above survey was not a complete catalogue of induction procedures of the last two centuries, what follows is not a compendium of twentieth century inductions. Many of the verbatim accounts of inductions are already available in other works (e.g., Wolberg, 1948; Marmer, 1959; Heron, 1971; Crasilneck and Hall, 1975). Here, as before, my intention is to highlight the point that the induction procedures in common use verbally acknowledge the continuing concern of investigators and practitioners alike with the relaxation and sleep components of what we commonly understand to be hypnosis.

The only major change to have taken place in the development of hypnotic induction procedures in the past 80 years is that the procedures, while retaining the same vocabulary, have moved from a direct, forceful, dominant mode to an indirect, overtly humble, persuasive mode of presentation. Seldom do we find the professional operator commanding his patients to "Sleep!" Seldom do we find the operator staring his patient "down" into a trance. The autocratic, authoritation method is passe. Now the suggestions are couched in such phrases as "Perhaps your eyes are feeling tired. Perhaps your arms are beginning to feel heavy. It may be that you will have trouble opening your eyes, if you were to try." Direct challenges have been dramatically modified, and the whole mood of the hypnotic setting is client-centered.

Probably the finest examples of this latter point are the "utilization techniques" of Milton Erickson (1959) in which the imperatives of the suggestions offered to the patient are so subtle as to take effect virtually without the patient's awareness. For example, Erickson reports on a patient who had been in psychotherapy for three years and hypotherapy for one with little progress and a frustrating inability to enter a trance. Erickson proceeded as follows (His words are in italics.):

You really can't conceive of what a trance is—no, I can't, what is it?—*yes, what is it?*—a psychological state, I suppose—*A psychological state you suppose, what else?*—I don't know—*You really don't know*—no, I don't—*you don't, you wonder, you think*—think what—*yes, what do you think, feel, sense?*—(pause)—I don't know—*but you can wonder*—do you go to sleep?—*no, tired, relaxed, sleepy*—really tired—*so very tired and relaxed, what else?*—I'm puzzled—*puzzles you, you wonder, you think, you feel, what do you feel?*—my eyes—*yes, your eyes, how?*—they seem blurred—*blurred, closing*—(pause)—they are closing—*closing, breathing deeper*—(pause)—*tired and relaxed what else?*—(pause)—*sleep, tired, relaxed, sleep, breathing deeper*—(pause)—*what else?*—I feel funny—*funny, so comfortable, really learning*—(pause)—*learning, yes, learning more and more*—(pause)—*eyes closed, breathing deeply, relaxed, comfortable, so very comfortable, what else?*—(pause)—I don't know—*you really don't know, but really learning to go deeper and deeper*—(pause)—too tired to talk, just sleep—*maybe a word or two*—I don't know (spoken laboriously)—*breathing deeper and you really don't know, just going deeper, sleeping soundly, more and more soundly, not caring, just learning, continuing ever deeper and deeper and learning more and more with your unconscious mind.* (Erickson, 1959, pp. 6–7)

Erickson's induction is subtle, lethargically dramatic, effective, and yet it emphasizes throughout the ideas of relaxation and sleep. As Erickson notes elsewhere: "[There] is the need to recognize that trance induction is one thing, and trance utilization is another (even as surgical preparation and anesthesia are one thing, and the surgery is another)" (1952, p. 83). It is the former that concerns us—the hypnosis rather than its utilization. First we must define the basic characteristics of hypnosis, then we will be better able to understand the various phenomena reported to occur in hypnosis. As we have seen, and will see, investigators have combined the events elicited during hypnosis with the hypnosis *per se*. This confusion of the state and the phenomena in the state is nowhere more apparent than in attempts to outline various stages (depths) of hypnosis through behavioral signs and in the outgrowth of this categorization of the stages of hypnosis—hypnotic susceptibility scales.

STAGES, DEPTH, AND SUSCEPTIBILITY

Stages and Depths of Hypnosis

The concepts of stages of hypnosis, depth of hypnosis, and the capacity for hypnosis (susceptibility) are historically and conceptually intertwined. During the 1700s and 1800s each of the major theorists developed his own descriptive categories of the various behaviors observed during the induction and period of the trance. Even Mesmer, who, as pointed out above, was concerned with the curative powers of the crisis, recognized that there was at least one additional stage of the mesmeric condition—the coma. Thus he described his magnetism in two stages: the crisis, which resembled the hysterical convulsions of his and the following century, and the coma or apparent unconsciousness and insensitivity to external stimuli. As I have pointed out, Mesmer saw little value to the latter, but it is important to note that even with his expectations pointed toward the crisis, the latter coma or sleeplike phase emerged.

De Puységur, like his teacher, described two basic stages of the magnetism:

first, one of relaxation and apparent sleep, followed, second, by a phase in which the subject could carry out suggestions motorically and engage in verbal intercourse with the operator or whoever the operator might designate. While the latter phase was of particular interest to de Puységur because during it he could affect the behavior of his subjects and assist them with their ills, it was the former that serves as further evidence of the historical precedent for a sleep-relaxation-hypnosis relationship. (Whether the reverse—the appearance of the relaxed stupor before the curative phase—of what Mesmer reported had sociological implications, as Ellenberger (1965) suggested, or whether it may have been more Mesmer's tunnel vision in not acknowledging this fundamental relaxation phase cannot be determined conclusively.)

Braid too described various stages of hypnosis. Although in *Neurypnology* (1843) he outlined two stages of hypnosis, the "prodigiously exalted" stage, followed by "a state of depression, far greater than the torpor of natural sleep," (p. 29), Bramwell (1903) attributes a number of stages to him. According to Bramwell, Braid divided the many stages into three major categories: (a) slight hypnosis, (b) deep hypnosis, and (c) hypnotic coma. Braid, like Pavlov later, viewed hypnosis as a continuum of stages, each running into the other. During Braid's deep hypnosis occurred the two stages he noted in *Neurypnology*: the alert and then the deep, or sleeplike, phase. He warned that he did not consider it appropriate to attempt the hypnotic coma during the first session with a patient; it should be used only after the patient had had experience with the earlier stages. The hypnotic coma was apparently similar to what others have labeled somnambulism. However, it is both in Braid's notation of the lethargic stage following the alert and in Bramwell's description of Braid's "slight hypnosis" that we see the continuing recognition of a sleeplike, relaxation aspect of the patients in hypnosis.

As I have noted several times above, Liébeault's "lucid sleep" was the first "modern" notation of the sleep-hypnosis relationship. Since he was so concerned with this relationship, his descriptive terms for the stages of hypnosis were couched in sleep and sleep-related terms. Essentially, there were six stages of hypnosis, as seen in Table 3.1. Each of the first four stages was accompanied by behavioral signs through which the operator could gauge the stage of hypnosis. For example, during drowsiness there was said to be heaviness of the head and difficulty opening the eyes. As the individual progressed through the second drowsiness stage and the light sleep phases, such behaviors as catalepsy and,

Table 3.1.   Liébeault's Stages of Hypnosis (1889)

1. Drowsiness	4. Deep Sleep
2. Drowsiness (catalepsies possible)	5. Light Somnambulism
3. Light Sleep	6. Deep Somnambulism

finally, the inability to focus attention on other than the hypnotist appeared. Like Charcot (see below), Liébeault observed the relaxation and drowsiness *before* the catalepsy, so that even the conceptual differences between the Nancy and Paris schools did not obviate the recognition of the persistent relaxation behaviors. This alone should indicate how dominant the relaxation component is in hypnosis, in that even the observers most blinded by other theoretical orientations continue—into the present—to acknowledge the presence of a sleeplike relaxation phase of hypnosis, most often the initial phase.

Both of Liébeault's somnambulistic stages (light and deep) were marked by total amnesia upon "waking," but in the latter the degree of hallucinatory potential was broader and the submission to the hypnotist more profound. Basically this phase is just a continuation of the progression of relaxation-sleep that, from his observations of patients, Liébeault felt to be linear. (We now know the progression is not totally and absolutely linear.)

Liébeault's later coworker, Bernheim, also developed an essentially linear scale of the stages of hypnosis, consisting of nine steps, which Hilgard et al. (1961) have collated into two major stages—one in which memory is retained and one in which it is not. As in the previous scales, Bernheim's first degree consists of drowsiness coupled with various bodily sensations—warmth, numbness. As the subject moves progressively through the degrees, a linear progression of what we have come to accept as hypnotic behaviors ensues, ending with posthypnotic hallucinations. See Table 3.2 for an outline of Bernheim's degrees of hypnosis.

One last representative of the Nancy School, Forel, offered a three-stage description of hypnosis: (a) drowsiness, in which suggestions are not uniformly effective; (b) hypotaxy, in which catalepsies appear; and (c) somnambulism, in which amnesia for events during hypnosis is featured.

In the Paris School we also see the heavy emphasis on sleep and sleeplike

Table 3.2. Depth of Hypnosis According to Bernheim (1891)

Memory retained on waking

1st degree.	Torpor, drowsiness, or various suggested sensations such as warmth, numbness
2nd degree.	Inability to open the eyes if challenged to do so
3rd degree.	Catalepsy suggested by the hypnotist and bound up with the passive condition of the subject, but may be counteracted by the subject
4th degree.	Catalepsy and rotary automatism that cannot be counteracted by the subject
5th degree.	Involuntary contractures and analgesia as suggested by the hypnotist
6th degree.	Automatic obedience; subject behaves like an automaton.

Amnesia on waking

7th degree.	Amnesia on waking. No hallucinations
8th degree.	Able to experience hallucinations during sleep
9th degree.	Able to experience hallucinations during sleep and post-hypnotically

(From Hilgard et al., 1961. Copyright 1961 by the American Psychological Association. Reprinted by permission.)

appearances in Charcot's (1882) three stages of hypnosis. Hypnosis began with either the stage of "catelepsy" or the stage of "lethargy." (Bernheim [1884] credited lethargy as the first stage, followed by catalepsy, but this is not in total agreement with Charcot's own writing.) The "lethargy," produced primarily by a fixed gaze at a distant object, or the succeeding catalepsy upon closing the eyes, reflected again the prevalent emphasis of relaxation and sleep. The subject appears asleep. "He then becomes flaccid, as if plunged in deep sleep" (Binet and Féré, 1888, p. 157). If the limbs are raised, they immediately fall heavily to their resting position upon release. For all intents and purposes the individual is in a state of utter and complete relaxation, although still responsive to the words of the operator. As the trance progresses, the stage of "catalepsy" appears in which the subject's limbs could be placed and kept in various unnatural positions. Finally the "somnambulism" phase appears, in which, as de Puységur and Liébeault noted earlier, the subject is lucid and capable of interacting with the operator and the environment.

Bramwell (1903) also reported a somnambulistic stage. He added this stage to Max Dessoir's two-part classification of (a) slight hypnosis, in which only the voluntary musculature could be affected, and (b) deep hypnosis, in which the special senses were affected. Dessoir's classification makes note of a progression similar to that proposed later by Pavlov (see Chapter 2). Branwell used amnesia as the behavioral sign of somnambulism and pointed out that this stage was the one in which the subjects were "alert" in the sense that they could carry out suggestions of movement and other overt behavior. This particular view of "alert trance" will be considered in Chapter 8.

Hilgard (1965) credits Richet (1884) with recognizing the fact that the common thread in the older stages of hypnosis and later depth of hypnosis catalogues was the analogy of hypnosis with sleep. In Richet's *torpor, excitation,* and *stupor* degrees, Hilgard saw the beginnings of depth scales of hypnosis. Certainly in Bernheim's categories we see the detailed forerunner of present-day depth-susceptibility scales.

Curiously, from the time of Braid on, the heavy behavioral emphasis of hypnotic operators was the amnesia said to appear spontaneously and become more profound as the individual progressed through the stages outlined. For most of the older practitioners in the field, magnetism or hypnosis was not considered to have occurred unless the subject was amnesic for events that went on in the trance. This emphasis persisted despite Braid's, Bernheim's, and others' insistence that the "sleep," although of profound assistance, was not absolutely necessary for therapeutic benefit to occur. Without the "sleep" there was no amnesia, yet this one behavior persisted as the *sine qua non* of hypnosis. Perhaps it was the operators' desire to be able to point to a dramatic event to gain acceptance for their peculiar form of treatment and to convince the scientific world that indeed something beyond chicanery was taking place. We cannot be certain, but we do know that the number of reported spontaneous amnesias is very small today. In fact, when they do occur, more often than not the operator is surprised by them, because these behaviors now are among those suggested by—rather than discovered by—the operator. Like the St. Vitus dance of old, spontaneous amnesias have moved into the realm of medical history.

What has remained, however, is the relaxation-sleeplike quality of hypnosis. As seen above, it is common to all of the older theorists' stages of hypnosis, and, as we will see, it has been retained in present-day susceptibility scales.

Susceptibility Scales

The transition from depth scales—formats for measuring what particular stage of hypnosis a subject had achieved—to quantitative susceptibility scales began in the 1930s. It was one thing to be able to state after the fact what stage of trance the subject had achieved; it was quite another to be able to predict the future and gauge beforehand what stage a given individual *might* achieve. Certainly for the practitioner who felt the need to have his or her patients in a particular stage of hypnosis before offering therapeutic suggestions, knowing beforehand how well the patient was going to respond was of value. Naturally, then, a scale that could successfully predict the future was desirable. Also, as Hilgard (1965) has made clear, such depth scales were a basic measurement necessity for studying the variables underlying the observation that some individuals respond more profoundly to hypnotic inductions and suggestions than others. This has been particularly true as our quest for knowledge in this and other fields has become increasingly quantitative.

Thus scales originally intended to tell the practitioner the stage of hypnosis his or her patient was in were converted for predictive use. Basically the early scales were the same and involved, first, putting the subject through an induction procedure—usually a relaxation eye-closure technique—and then offering a series of challenges that the subject may or may not meet. Once the general progression of difficulty of the challenges was established, a numerical value was given to various stages (depths) of hypnosis. As we will see, the last development was to quantify the stability of the assumed linearity among the various challenges, to include the induction itself as a challenge, and to produce a predictive score. These scores were then used to assign subjects to various experimental and control groups and/or to give the practitioner some idea of what hypnotic phenomena could or could not be expected in subsequent therapeutic sessions. The scales themselves all acknowledge the observation of relaxation-sleep as a fundamental and usually initial observation associated with hypnosis.

M. M. White's (1930) original scale involved a series of challenges (suggestions) to which the subject's behavior was noted and assigned a number. The challenges were: (a) stiff fingers, (b) inability to say the number three and the letter *d*, (c) visual and auditory hallucinations, (d) hand anesthesia, (e) inability to write "vowels," (f) adding columns of figures during auditory distraction, and

(g) a posthypnotic suggestion. Each item was assigned a weighted score. Prior to the issuing of these challenges an eye-fixation technique (not further specified), accompanied by verbal suggestions, was presented to each subject.

Shortly thereafter followed the Davis and Husband (1931) and the Barry, MacKinnon, and Murray (1931) scales. The former, presented in Table 3.3, is very clearly a series of gradated challenges given to the subjects and scaled from 0 to 30. It also *began* with an eye-fixation induction technique fashioned after Braid's method, progressed through four major categories of trance (hypnoidal, light, medium, and somnambulistic), and ended with negative visual hallucinations. Probably because of its apparent linear simplicity, this scale was used more than any others until the advent of the Stanford individual scales and the Harvard group scale (see below). Two aspects of the Davis and Husband scale have persisted to the present: the use of an eye-fixation induction procedure and the notation of progressive relaxation as initiating the trance and becoming increasingly profound as the trance progresses. Even Hull (1933), who did not develop a

Table 3.3. Hypnotic Susceptibility Scoring System

Debt (sic)	Score	Objective Symptoms
Insusceptible	0	
	1	
	2	Relaxation
Hypnoidal	3	Fluttering of lids
	4	Closing of eyes
	5	Complete physical relaxation
	6	Catalepsy of eyes
Light trance	7	Limb catalepsies
	10	Rigid catalepsy
	11	Anaesthesia (glove)
	13	Partial amnesia
	15	Post-hypnotic anaesthesia
Medium trance	17	Personality changes
	18	Simple post-hypnotic suggestions
	20	Kinaesthetic delusions; complete amnesia
	21	Ability to open eyes without affecting trance
	23	Bizarre post-hypnotic suggestions
	25	Complete somnambulism
Somnambulistic	26	Positive visual hallucinations, post-hypnotic
trance	27	Positive auditory hallucinations, post-hypnotic
	28	Systematized post-hypnotic amnesias
	29	Negative auditory hallucinations
	30	Negative visual hallucinations; hyperaesthesias

(From Davis and Husband, 1931. Copyright 1931 by the American Psychological Association. Reprinted by permission.)

depth-susceptibility scale per se, used the time necessary for the eyes to close with continued suggestions of eye fatigue, drowsiness, and lid fluttering as an indicator of hypnotizability. As we will see, modern scales use eye-closure as one of the scored items. In the main, eye-closure suggestions *precede* all others.

In the same year that Davis and Husband presented their scale, Barry, MacKinnon, and Murray (1931) published their study of hypnotizability as a personality trait. Their Hypnotic Index, which had possible scores of 0 to 5, consisted of a series of five suggestions plus a score for the degree of presence (or absence) of amnesia. The suggestions—challenges not to be able to: (a) open the eyes, (b) raise the arm, (c) bend the arm, (d) separate the fingers, and (e) speak their name—are of less concern for my thesis than what preceded them:

> To obtain hypnotic suggestibility the subject was directed to lie on a couch with head slightly elevated and eyes focussed upon the head of a pin stuck in the opposite wall. The usual procedure for inducing *relaxation, drowsiness and sleep* (i.e., statements in a subdued, monotonous voice accompanied by pressure on the forehead and stroking) was employed for about five or six minutes before the specific suggestions to measure the degree of hypnosis were given. (Barry et al., 1931, p. 9, italics added)

Here along with the more modern, verbal form of induction, we see remnants of passes persisting into the third decade of this century. But more important, we see the subject placed in a position destined to promote relaxation and given "procedures" for doing so. This scale, like all of those of stages, depth, and susceptibility, perpetuates the common historical thread—relaxation and hypnosis. In fact, as we shall observe in Chapter 7, these authors found a significant positive correlation between their Hypnosis Index and suggestibility in the "relaxed state."

As with the foregoing, the Friedlander-Sarbin Scale (1938), on which Forms A and B of the Stanford Hypnotic Susceptibility Scales (SHSS; Weitzenhoffer and Hilgard, 1959) are based, begins with an eye-closure induction procedure (score 0−5 depending on when the eyes close), followed by five challenges (inability to open eyes, lift arm, bend arm, separate fingers, say name) and ends with a test of the degree of amnesia achieved—measured simply by the number of challenge items remembered (see Table 3.4). Again, the beginning of the scale marks it as both a depth (degree of) and a susceptibility scale, preserving the time honored relaxation-hypnosis relationship.

The verbal procedure accompanying the scale made this latter point all the more apparent. Period I of the eye-closure portion is mainly a rapport-gaining set of instructions, which includes: "you can easily fall into an hypnotic sleep." Period II begins: "Now relax and make yourself entirely comfortable"; but it is Periods III and IV that are particularly weighted with the relaxation-sleep relationship:

III. Relax completely. Relax every muscle in your body. Relax the muscles in your legs.

Table 3.4. Friedlander-Sarbin Scale of Hypnotic Depth

	Score Value
Final lid closure (Hull)	
1. Eyes close in Period I	5
2. Eyes close in Period II	4
3. Eyes close in Period III	3
4. Eyes close in Period IV	2
5. Eyes close in Period V	1
6. Eyes do not close	0
Negative suggestions test (Barry et al.)	
(Total the time required to resist "failed" items. Give one point for each multiple of ten seconds.)	
1. All five suggestions passed	5
2. Four suggestions passed	4
3. Three suggestions passed	3
4. Two suggestions passed	2
5. One suggestion passed	1
6. None passed	0
Test of Hallucination (Davis and Husband)	
1. Distinct hallucination, no prodding needed	5
2. Faint hallucination, prodding needed	3
3. No hallucination	0
Amnesia (Barry et al.)	
1. No items recalled	5
2. One item recalled	4
3. Two items recalled	3
4. Three items recalled	2
5. Four or five items recalled	1
6. More than five items recalled	0

(From Friedlander and Sarbin, 1938. Copyright 1938 by the American Psychological Association. Reprinted by permission.)

Relax the muscles in your arms. Make yourself perfectly comfortable. Let yourself be limp, limp, limp. Relax more and more, more and more. Relax completely. Relax completely.

IV. Your legs feel heavy and limp, heavy and limp. Your arms are heavy, heavy, heavy as lead. Your whole body feels heavy, heavier, and heavier. You feel tired and sleepy, tired and sleepy. You feel drowsy, drowsy and sleepy, heavy and drowsy, drowsy and sleepy. Your breathing is slow and regular, slow and regular.

Period V concentrates on the fatigue of the eyes and eyelids, before Period VI again reinforces the sleep-relaxation-hypnosis coupling:

VI. And then you will be completely relaxed, completely relaxed. Warm and comfortable, warm and comfortable. Tired and drowsy. Tired and sleepy. Sleepy. Sleepy. Sleepy. You are paying attention to nothing but the sound of my voice, listening to nothing but the sound of my voice. You hear nothing but the sound of my voice.

After returning to suggestions regarding the eyes in Period VII, Period VIII offers a counting deepening technique so that the subjects may feel themselves "going down, down, down, into a deep comfortable, a deep restful sleep" (Friedlander and Sarbin, 1938, p. 458).

In 1959 two forms of the Stanford Hypnotic Susceptibility Scales (Forms A and B) were published (Weitzenhoffer and Hilgard, 1959). Both of these forms contained eye-fixation and closure instructions as the second item in each scale. Since the Stanford scales were modeled on the Friedlander and Sarbin scale, it is not surprising that they very closely parallel the original's verbalizations. For example, compare the third step in the Stanford scales with Period III in Friedlander and Sarbin's:

> Relax completely. Relax every muscle of your body. Relax the muscles of your legs. . . . Relax the muscles of your feet. . . . Relax the muscles of your arms. . . . Relax the muscles of your hands. . . . of your fingers. . . . Relax the muscles of your neck, of your chest. . . . Relax all the muscles of your body. . . . Let yourself be limp, limp, limp. Relax more and more, more and more. Relax completely. Relax completely. Relax completely. (Weitzenhoffer and Hilgard, 1959, p. 14)

The rest of the instructions for this item reflect the same relaxation-hypnosis orientation, and end with a counting deepening procedure, as did Friedlander and Sarbin's instructions.

In 1962 a third form of the Stanford scales, Form C, appeared (Weitzenhoffer and Hilgard, 1962). As with Forms A and B, a series of gradated challenges are presented to the subject, with the exception that "the *induction* procedures . . . are optional, and *induction* is not scored (Hilgard, 1965, p. 82, italics added). The italicized words make it clear that the Stanford scales are *depth* scales of behavior *in* hypnosis, predictors of *future* behavior in hypnosis, rather than a purer susceptibility scale, *sans* induction, as is seen in the Barber Suggestibility Scale (see below).

To appreciate again the relaxation-hypnosis equation being made by the Stanford Scale, Form C, compare the third paragraph of the eye-closure induction with that in Forms A and B:

> Relax more and more. As you *think* of relaxing, your muscles will relax. Starting with your right foot, relax the muscles of your right leg. . . . Now the muscles of your left leg. . . . Just relax all over. Relax your right hand, your forearm, upper arm, and shoulder. . . . That's it. . . . Now your left hand . . . and forearm . . . and upper arm . . . and shoulder. . . . Relax your neck, and chest . . . more and more relaxed . . . completely relaxed . . . completely relaxed. (Weitzenhoffer and Hilgard, 1962, pp. 8−9)

The Harvard Group Scale of Hypnotic Susceptibility, Form A, also published in 1962 (Shor and Orne, 1962), was an adaptation of the Stanford Form A. As with its predecessor, an eye-closure, relaxation "induction" is included as the second of the scored items, preserving in group form what we have witnessed consistently throughout the scales of hypnotic "susceptibility." The final adult variation of the Stanford theme occurred in 1963 with the publication of the Stanford Profile Scales of Hypnotic Susceptibility, Forms I and II (Weitzenhoffer and Hilgard, 1963; Hilgard et al., 1963). These scales, intended primarily for research work in hypnosis with subjects who score well (above four) on the original Stanford scales, also contain induction procedures (through arm levitation and hand lowering) that reinforce the relaxation-hypnosis point made so often above.

Nor have the children been ignored. London (1962) has developed a two-part children's scale consisting of 12 challenge items in the first part and 10 in the second. Like the Stanford scales, an eye-closure, relaxation induction forms part of the first part, serving basically as an induction procedure for what follows. As in the Stanford scales, Form A and B, and the Harvard Scale, the Children's Hypnotic Susceptibility Scale (London, 1962) is a depth (degree of) scale and not strictly a "susceptibility" scale in the sense of predicting hypnotic from nonhypnotic behavior. The one exception is that postural-sway suggestions are used in all of these scales (head falling in the Harvard) prior to the eye-closure induction, thus constituting the only true susceptibility item as I have differentiated between depth and susceptibility scaling. However, with only one exception, all of the adult scales, individual and group, and the children's scale preserve and perpetuate the relaxation-hypnosis equation through their use of direct suggestions to this effect in the induction instructions.

The one exception is the Barber Suggestibility Scale (Barber and Calverley, 1963). Barber's scale does not involve an induction followed by tests for hypnotic depth, but rather presents eight challenges to the subjects after they have been directed to close their eyes. Thus based on the degree of nonhypnotic suggestibility displayed, Barber predicts the behavior that will follow any hypnotic induction procedure. Barber has included both adults and children and a method for scoring the subjective experiences of the subjects. While this scale does not reinforce the relaxation-hypnosis relationship, it is not intended to, because it does not involve hypnosis as it has been defined historically.

THE EVANS STUDIES

One of the major concerns of hypnosis investigators in recent decades has been the influence of subject variables on study outcomes. Ever since Orne's well-known "demand characteristics" paper of 1959, many researchers have been interested in the sociological aspects of hypnosis experiments, placing particular emphasis on the role played by the expectations (recognized or unrecognized) subjects bring to the experimental and clinical settings.

It was in the context of searching for a method to control the usual expectations and preconceptions that subjects have regarding hypnosis and hypnosis experiments that Evans (1967) conducted a series of studies pertinent to my hypnosis-relaxation thesis. His studies addressed the question: "Is it possible, in an experimental setting, to induce deep hypnosis without S's awareness or knowledge that the experimental procedure involves hypnosis?" (Evans, 1967, p. 73) The method of induction he chose was—relaxation.

Subjects were told that the experiment in which they were to participate was investigating "the effects of relaxation on behavior," and were further instructed that their "main task was to relax as completely as possible." The technique, partially modeled on Kubie and Margolin's (1944) work, included having the subject lie on a couch with a "blank mind" while listening to the experimenter talk and count in rhythm to the subject's breathing. Words such as "hypnosis" and "trance" were omitted. After 30 minutes of "induction," the subjects were tested with suggestions of the usual hypnotic phenomena: for example, arm rigidities, visual and auditory hallucinations, illusions, amnesias, anesthesias, age-regression, and the like.

Three samples of subjects were obtained over a five-year period for a total of 296. The depth of "hypnosis" was assessed in each of three different subject samples (obtained in 1958, 1960, and 1962−1963) by a four-point rating scale. The distributions, both with respect to central tendency and variability, were strikingly similar to those reported from subjects undergoing an ordinary hypnotic induction that is presented as such. For example, 13% of Evans's subjects were rated as achieving deep hypnosis; usual hypnosis studies yield 16% deep-trance subjects. In other words, subjects presented with a set of relaxation instructions in which any association with hypnosis has been carefully avoided distribute themselves in the same manner as subjects presented with a set of instructions explicitly offered as "hypnosis." Relaxation instructions elicit the same responses, in the same distribution format, as blatant hypnotic instructions.

In addition, Evans's last subsample of subjects (1962−1963) was rated on a seven-point scale assessing their perceptions and beliefs that the procedures were in fact a hypnosis induction. These 170 subjects were divided into 120 who received the relaxation instructions and a group of 50 who did not but were tested in the same manner as the relaxation induction group. The distributions were the same; 29% of the induction group recognized the procedure as similar to hypnosis, while 32% of the control group recognized the similarity. More important, "At least half of the Ss, even under some pressure, did not seem to recognize that an attempt had been made to induce hypnosis" (Evans, 1967, p. 79). Couple that result with the results of comparing the performance of the induction group and the control group on hypnotic task performance in this subsample and Evans's study becomes even more important. The clusters of hypnotic items used to assess the effectiveness of the relaxation, nonhypnotic induction in these 120 subjects appear in Table 3.5, and Evans's summary of the findings is as follows:

Table 3.5.   Clusters of Hypnotic Items Used in The Evans Studies

Item Cluster	Defining Variables
Perseverative dissociation	Posthypnotic compulsions, inhibitions, regressions, source amnesia
Amnesic dissociation	Posthypnotic amnesias, hyperamnesias, and recall interference
Challenge suggestions	Challenged or inhibited motor suggestions, rigidities
Motor suggestions	Non-challenge motor suggestibilities, arm movements
Relaxed reverie	Simple hallucinations, rated relaxation
Modified Stanford Scale	Items similar to Stanford Scales similar scoring criterion

(From Evans, 1967. Reprinted from the April, 1967 International Journal of Clinical and Experimental Hypnosis. Copyrighted by the Society for Clinical and Experimental Hypnosis, April, 1967.)

A comparison of the performance of the hypnotized Ss and the performance of the control Ss on the same tests demonstrates that the indirect induction technique did effectively induce hypnosis. There was a statistically significant difference in mean scores between the experimental group (i.e., following indirect induction of hypnosis) and the control group (no induction) for each item. (Evans, 1967, p. 80)

What Evans has shown is that when subjects are confronted with an explicitly nonhypnotic relaxation approach, all of the phenomena ordinarily associated with hypnosis occur, without the subject being aware that what may ordinarily be called hypnosis has taken place. The importance of the first part of this finding for my thesis that neutral hypnosis is relaxation, as depicted by induction techniques, is obvious. The latter part of the finding—that subjects may not be aware that hypnosis has occurred—raises some very interesting ethical and/or legal issues, which will be addressed in Chapter 9.

CONCLUSION

In conclusion, then, we continue to find that the relaxation-hypnosis equation pervades the history of hypnosis. We have seen it in early and modern theories. We have seen it in the induction procedures utilized throughout the centuries. We have seen it in the descriptions of the degrees of hypnosis and of hypnotic depth, and even in our present hypnotic susceptibility scales. While historical precedence does not a science make, it certainly arrests the attention of investigators. With this theme so prevalent in the historical antecedents of hypnosis, can we afford to ignore the relaxation-hypnosis equation on the basis of a few studies that suggest that "hypnosis is not sleep" and are themselves based on an oversimplified categorization of behavior into sleep and nonsleep, hypnosis and nonhypnosis? It is not clear that we should, particularly in light of the Evans's (1967) studies and the clinical and experimental evidence to follow.

CHAPTER 4

Relaxation as a Generalized Response

Having established the historical precedents of the relaxation-hypnosis equation in the theories, the observations on the degrees of hypnosis, the development of susceptibility scales, and, more particularly, the verbal and physical environmental emphasis on sleep and relaxation in induction procedures, it behooves us to look now at the equation in more detail. It is clear that we engender calm, quiet, lethargy, relaxation in our patients and subjects when inducing hypnosis. But what exactly is the nature of this relaxation we covet? How do we know when our subjects have achieved it? By what signs and by what processes do we attest to its presence?

In 1970 Wallace published a paper on the physiological changes occurring in the Transcendental Meditation® (TM) program. Using 15 college students as subjects, he showed that during the TM program oxygen consumption decreased by 20% (nine subjects only), heart rate decreased by 5 beats per minute, skin resistance increased fourfold, the electroencephalogram showed a predominance of slow alpha waves (8−9 Hz), and there was a steady respiration quotient as compared to a 20-minute premeditation period and a 15-minute postmeditation period. Unfortunately, Wallace did not enlighten us on his statistical procedures, although some of the average data were presented in tabular form (see Table 4.1). From his data and summary data elsewhere in the literature, the author concluded that the TM program differed physiologically from wakefulness, sleep, dreaming, and hypnosis.

Wallace's work was quickly followed by a paper with Benson and Wilson (Wallace et al., 1971) presenting essentially the same method on twice the number of subjects, and then by a more popularized version in the *Scientific American* (Wallace and Benson, 1972). A series of papers by Benson followed in which the phrase "the relaxation response" was coined. These early papers were quickly followed by a very popular book for laymen titled *The Relaxation Response* (Benson, 1975), in which little is presented not already in the original article by that title (Benson et al., 1974).*

The essential message of "the relaxation response" is that humans have,

---

*According to Wallace (personal communication) research has not established the degree to which Benson's methods reproduce the effects of the TM program.

Table 4.1   Physiological Measures Before, During, and After a Transcendental Meditation Session

Time	O_2 consumption (cm²/min)	Respiration Quotient	Minute Ventilation (1/min)	Skin Resistance (kohms)
	Premeditation			
10	246.8	.86	5.90	91.2
20	244.4	.87	7.56	101.2
	During Meditation			
35	208.1	.84	5.25	205.0
45	201.9	.85	5.28	188.8
55	200.8	.85	5.55	180.1
	Postmeditation			
70	233.1	.86	5.94	80.2

(From Wallace, 1970, Copyright 1970 by the American Association for the Advancement of Science)

inherent in their physical composition, the potential for a general behavioral and physiological response that is the antithesis of Cannon's famous fight-or-flight response. Whereas the latter is a readiness to respond with vigorous physical and emotional activity to a situation that is threatening or perceived as such, the relaxation response protects the organism from threat by withdrawing it from the situation into a slowed-down physiological and behavioral state. With respect to autonomic nervous system functioning, Cannon's emergency reaction may be thought of as a response governed by a predominance of the sympathetic system, while in the relaxation response, the parasympathetic system is regnant. Benson's popularized notion is that as individuals can utilize this latter state more often, they would suffer less from the disorders of civilization, for example, hypertension.

He proceeds then to show that TM technique, autogenic training, Zen and yoga, cotention, sentic cycles, Jacobson's progressive relaxation, and hypnosis all have in common the physiological parameters of the relaxation response. However, it is TM technique on which he dwells, indicating its efficacy for the treatment of hypertension, vascular headaches, drug abuse, and general tension states. This is certainly an impressive list of disorders to be treated by so popular an activity as meditation, and its choice as the treatment vehicle brought it quickly to the attention of the public. However, it is in the professional literature that the data of real interest to us appear.

THE TROPHOTROPIC RESPONSE

The early work and labeling of the behaviorally denoted central nervous system function that Benson popularized as "the relaxation response" was done by W.

R. Hess. The work, which began in 1925, was the tedious, detailed electrical exploration and mapping of the diencephalon. The experiments, carried out on 350 cats, consisted of the exploration of over 3500 areas eventually illuminating the interplay of function and morphology and culminating in *Das Zwischenhirn*, published in the same year Hess was awarded the Nobel Prize—1949.

The first part of the book covers the localization of various vegetative (autonomic) functions including pupillomotor, blood pressure, respiration, panting, sneezing, vomiting, sniffing, licking, chewing, micturition, defecation, moods, and sleep. By stimulating various areas in the diencephalon, Hess soon discovered that certain areas were consistently related to certain behaviors, and that these behaviors grouped themselves along a dynamic-adynamic, ergotropic-trophotropic, sympathetic-parasympathetic dimension. For example, stimulation of the "endophylactic-trophotropic" areas lowered blood pressure; decreased respiration rate; constricted the pupils; initiated micturition, defecation, and salivation; induced sleep; and produced *"hypo-* or *adynamia* of the skeletal musculature"* (Hess, 1957, p. 37). Although the trophotropic region is predominantly in the lateral and anterior hypothalamic area and lateral to the massa intermedia, the morphological separation of the dynamic and the adynamic areas is not absolute, and there is considerable overlap between them. Part of this apparent overlapping function, of course, may be due to *en passage* fibers in this very complex brain area.

Whereas Benson seems to have concentrated on the general behavioral response to stimulation of diencephalic areas, some of the details of Hess's work may be even more important. In the first place, Hess points out the physiological significance of the localized functions in the diencephalon: "the purely vegetative mechanisms, which occur isolated at lower levels, become associated with complex somatomotor functions to give a physiologically successful performance" (1957, p. 42). In other words, whereas the physiological functions of lower blood pressure or respiration, for example, can be elicited with stimulation of centers below the diencephalon, it is at the diencephalon that behavioral integration occurs. Here is where the connection between acts and their physiological concomitants occurs. This integration means that not only do changes in physiology have the capacity to cause behavioral changes, but vice versa. By creating the physical and skeleto-muscular atmosphere that usually *follows* these physiological changes, the physiological changes themselves can be elicited. By placing the individual in a comfortable position and instructing him to become "deeply" relaxed, we can create, through skeletomuscular manipulation and the diencephalon connections, the physiological concomitants of relaxation and hypnosis.

The second point worthy of note is contained in the following passage:

The trophotropic-endophylactic system of the diencephalon does not simply reproduce a mirror image of the functions of the dynamogenic zone, although perhaps there is some polarity between effects elicited from the two zones. One of the most prominent effects of the trophotropic-endophylactic system is adynamia, characterized by an over-all lowering of the organism's efficiency. The responsiveness of certain central nervous structures is reduced considerably—under some circumstances to zero. The respiratory and circulatory reflexes are also depressed. (Hess, 1957, pp. 39–40)

Thus the most striking aspect about the trophotropic response is the physical adynamia, the skeletomuscular lethargy of the animal. This response is a protective device, but like Victor Race's appearance and that of the patients of Braid, Liébeault, Bernheim, and Erickson, and that of Pavlov's dogs, it is the appearance of sleep and lethargy (adynamia) that is most striking. Hess continues:

Let us repeat at this point that we are actually dealing with a protective mechanism against overstress belonging to the trophotropic-endophylactic system and promoting restorative processes. We emphasize that these adynamic effects are opposed to ergotropic reactions which are oriented toward increased oxidative metabolism and utilization of energy. (p. 40)

This emphasis on the adynamic skeletomuscular lethargy accompanying stimulation of these trophotropic zones leads to the third point of Hess's work, which most directly pertains to my thesis. "The characteristic example of such accentuated antidynamogenic action is the *hypnogenic effect* . . ." (Hess, 1957, p. 40, italics added). The hypnogenic effect was noted when stimulation (at times of the lowest potentials) was applied to the areas lateral to the ventral half of the massa intermedia. Curiously, when undergoing this treatment, the cat does not suddenly collapse or pass out, but makes a number of postural adjustments, apparently seeking a comfortable position, often as in natural sleep. In addition, spontaneous movements diminish progressively, the eyes shut, and general activity is suppressed leading to an "artificially induced" sleep.

Two things that Hess noted about this hypnogenic effect are of particular interest. First is the role played by the exteroceptive sensory organs in arousing the animal from the induced sleep. Hess felt that these functions (vision, audition, olfaction) "play a decisive role in the activation of the ergotrophic system" (1957, p. 38). That is, they elicit the opposite of the trophotropic response, and thus can arouse the animal from a period of adynamia. This was most evident in the reversibility of the hypnogenic effect, which could be terminated by stimulating the cat with touch (eliciting the pinna reflex), odors (holding a piece of meat before its nose), or sound. The analogy to Braid's and Esdaile's methods of arousing their patients is clear. Braid blew on their eyes (tactile stimulation); Esdaile both blew and clapped his hands (auditory stimulation) to end the trance. Today we give verbal suggestions to end a trance, although some practitioners still use such devices as a snap of the fingers or a tap on a tabletop. The point is that the stimulation of the exteroceptive organs elicits a skeletomuscular and physiological behavior pattern that is the antithesis of hypnosis, *as well as* the antithesis of Hess's hypnogenic effect of the trophotropic response and Benson's relaxation response.

Finally, Hess notes that the hypnogenic effect varies between drowsiness and normal sleep and *varies according to the individual animal affected*. Some of the cats did not recline upon stimulation to the lateral massa intermedia, preoptic areas, and hypothalamus but rather sat down, drooped the head forward, and fell asleep in the sitting position. Others, who also did not make the customary postural adjustments, sank into an extraordinary, often awkward position as they entered the hypnogenic (adynamic) period. Hess notes:

We found repeatedly that a cat which slept while sitting was very difficult to awaken, while a reclining cat still reacted with relative ease to external stimuli. In the former case, it appears that what is especially reduced is the readiness to react to *sensory stimuli*, while in the latter case it is rather an involvement of the *motor system*. (1957, p. 27)

How reminiscent this observation is of the distinctions made in hypnosis (e.g., Braid) with respect to the various stages or depths of hypnosis. The early stages are usually denoted by challenges to the motor system (eye catalepsy, arm rigidity, muscular lethargy), while the latter, more profound stages are challenged by sensory suggestions (positive and negative hallucinations). As we observed in Chapter 3, scales of susceptibility follow the same pattern by considering those individuals capable of the "greatest depth" of hypnosis to be those who pass the sensory challenges in addition to the motor challenges. Hypnotized subjects then show the same sort of dichotomous behavior with respect to the involvement of the sensory and motor systems as did Hess's cats during the hypnogenic effect, with one distinguishing feature. In the human there is an apparent continuum of behavior that involves both the motor and the sensory systems; in the cat artificial stimulation yields either motor or sensory involvement. (This dichotomy is not pure, of course.) The human subject in hypnosis moves progressively through reduced motor activity to more and more sensory involvement. An individual in the early phases of hypnosis seems akin to the cat who, upon stimulation, makes postural adjustments before going to sleep; while the individual's behavior in the later stages (depths) of hypnosis—particularly somnambulism and the alert phases of de Puységur, Braid, and others—parallel the behavior of the cat who maintains posture (sitting) but appears to have lost much of its responsiveness to exteroceptive stimulation. In both cases, the analogy with sleep behavior and hypnosis is striking.

Hess continues with a statement that forms another analogy with the human hypnotic subject: "These different kinds of sleep are observed unequivocally in *different animals* . . ." (1957, p. 27, italics added). Unfortunately, he does not tell the numbers of cats yielding the hypnogenic effect in the sitting position and those yielding it while reclining. If he had, a percentage comparison could have been made between the relatively few human subjects who are considered "somnambules" and the number of cats displaying the sensory rather than motor involvement in the hypnogenic effect. As Hilgard suggested (1977), it may be that very few individuals are "truly" hypnotized in the sense that Braid (1855) used the term,* and that these few have a greater portion of the diencephalon involved (to draw upon Hess's findings) than those demonstrating only skeletomuscular involvement. But now I have become more speculative than present-day experimental techniques will allow us to verify. The point to be made is that Hess's work with cats made apparent a general, nonactivation pattern of behavior that serves to protect the organism in one way as the ergotropic response pattern does in another. That this trophotropic response pattern involves those physical and physiological responses that most resemble the relaxation half of our relaxation-hypnosis equation makes it all the more worthy of our attention. How closely the trophotropic response resembles the other half of our equation—hypnosis—will be the subject of the remainder of this chapter and those that follow.

THE RELAXATION RESPONSE

As indicated above, the phrase "the relaxation response" was introduced by Benson, Beary, and Carol (1974) and was based on the trophotropic response described by Hess (1957) and the physiological measurements of the TM technique published by Wallace (Wallace, 1970; Wallace et al., 1971). Two major aspects of the presentations of this protective response are of value to us in considering the relaxation-hypnosis hypothesis: (a) the description of the technique for eliciting the response, and (b) the physiological parameters of the vehicle for its production—the TM method.

Technique

Benson (Benson et al., 1974) outlines four basic elements in the production of the relaxation response: (a) a mental device, (b) a passive attitude, (c) decreased muscle tonus, and (d) a quiet environment. The similarities of these four principles to those generally pursued in hypnotic inductions is quite striking.

The *mental device*—Benson calls it "an object to dwell upon" in his popular book version—is some sort of a constant stimulus, something on which the subject concentrates to the relative exclusion of all else: "a sound, word, or phrase . . . or fixed gazing at an object" (Benson, 1975, p. 38). How like Braid's later monoideism is the concentration on a single compelling idea as a device through which to enter hypnosis. Or compare Braid's lancet case on which his patients concentrated their visual attention until fatigue and hypnosis overtook them. Consider also Chevreul's pendulum, or staring into the operator's eyes as devices for arresting the attention of the subject. Virtually all of the

_____

*"The term *hypnotism* ought to be restricted to the phenomena manifested in patients who actually pass into a state of sleep, who remember nothing on waking of what transpired during their sleep" (Tinterow, 1970, p. 370).

present-day induction techniques begin with some method for arresting the subject's attention—eye fixation; hand levitation, in which the hand and forearm are carefully watched and attended to by the subject, as, dumb-struck, he or she watches the limb rise in the air with no apparent effort; television, movie, or other visual imagery techniques; and even "the relaxation technique" in which the subject's attention is progressively drawn to various muscle groups to monitor their degree of tension or relaxation. Even the words of the operator can serve as a "mental device" to aid the subject in the task of excluding the external, the logical, the sensory input.

A *passive attitude* aids the concentration on the "mental device," just as hypnotic operators enjoin their subjects to "let the cares of the day fade into the background." Should the individual become distracted during the process, he or she is directed to bring the attention back to the technique (the mental device). In the Stanford scales we find: "Just relax. Don't be tense. Keep your eyes on the target. Look at it as steadily as you can. *Should your eyes wander away from it, that will be all right . . . just bring your eyes back to it*" (Weitzenhoffer and Hilgard, 1959, Form A, p. 14, italics added). The similarity is clear; in the passive attitude, concentration on the mental device is maximized.

The passive attitude has another feature that is very similar to hypnosis: The meditator is to be a participant, not an observer. He or she is not to be concerned with performance, is not to wonder how well the technique is working, but is merely to let the technique take effect. It is much like the individual trying to go to sleep. So long as the person *tries* he does not sleep, but once he becomes passive, not actively observing himself for signs of sleep, slumber ensues. In hypnosis it is the same. What do we tell our subjects?

Your curiosity will be satisfied [regarding what the experience will be like] before we are through, but you can best get the answers you want *by just letting yourself be a part of what goes on, and by not trying to watch the process in detail. . . .* Hypnosis is largely a question of your willingness to be receptive and responsive to ideas, and *to allow these ideas to act upon you without interference.* (Weitzenhoffer and Hilgard, 1959, Form A, p. 8, italics added)

Or further: ". . . your eyes will be so tired, will feel so heavy, that you will be unable to keep them open any longer and they will close, perhaps quite involuntarily. *When this happens, just let it take place*" (Weitzenhoffer and Hilgard, 1959, Form A, p. 14, italics added).

Like the foregoing, *decreased muscle tonus* is also encouraged during hypnosis. The subject is placed in a comfortable position, either seated or supine, often told to loosen tight clothing and remove contact lenses in preparation for the induction procedures. While there are some operators who claim to induce hypnotic trances while the subject is standing, such a procedure is the rare exception. Even while standing the subject inclines the head and droops the shoulders as the hypnosis takes effect. Remember, through the history of hypnotic induction a comfortable position was considered prerequisite. Even at Mesmer's *baquet* the patients sat, and Esdaile made constant use of the supine position, as did all of the investigators I have mentioned.

Esdaile (and others, of course) made a *quiet* (if not darkened) *environment* equally a part of the induction of hypnosis. Such an environment is used for TM training because, perforce, it reduces environmental distraction and what tendencies the subject may have to waver from the mental device. In addition, the eyes are often closed during the TM session. Again the similarities to the practice of hypnosis are striking. If the eyes are not closed at the outset (as they are in the usual relaxation induction technique), they soon close early in the process. In fact, as we have seen, the initial portion of the Friedlander and Sarbin susceptibility scale is based solely on the length of time that ensues before the eyes close. All of the Stanford scales and the Harvard Scale are concerned with when and how soon the eyes of the subjects close (see Chapter 3). And Hull (1933) made eyelid closure the foundation of his measure of the effectiveness of hypnotic induction and of many of his experimental studies.

Practitioners need only consider for a moment the nature of the environment they prefer and attempt to create for their patients during hypnosis to be convinced that a *quiet environment* is not a setting unique to TM practice and the elicitation of Benson's relaxation response.

The four elements used to elicit the relaxation response are basic to the induction of hypnosis. Practitioners of hypnosis have been using them for centuries, and at least these elements of the relaxation response and hypnosis appear very similar, if not identical.

Physiology of Relaxation

As indicated above, Wallace (1970) showed that the TM technique was associated with reduced oxygen consumption and heart rate, increased basal skin resistance and electroencephalogram alpha production, and a steady respiratory quotient. In 1971 Wallace, Benson, and Wilson expanded on Wallace's original work by using more subjects (36 total, although no more than 20 were used on any one measure and at times as few as 4 were used) and increasing the number of physiological parameters measured. In addition to replicating Wallace's findings, they also demonstrated significant decreases in carbon dioxide elimination, respiratory rate (breaths/minute), minute ventilation (1/minute), blood pH, base excess, and blood lactate (mg/100 ml). Rectal temperature, blood pressures, and arterial pressure of oxygen (P_{O_2}) and carbon dioxide (P_{CO_2}) did not change between the premeditation (10 to 30 minutes) and the meditation (20 to 30 minutes) periods.

Janda and Cash (1976) have also found similar changes during Jacobson relaxation training. Using five male and five female college students, measures of pulse rate, forehead electromyogram (EMG), and subjective experience were recorded before and after the relaxation exercises. The post-relaxation measure consisted of having the subject rate his or her "degree of relaxation" on a 1 to 100 point arbitrary scale (100 being extreme tension). All three measures showed a significant decrease after training: Pulse rate dropped from 75.10 to 67.40 beats/minute ($p < .01$); EMG, from 11.8 μv to 6.93 μv ($p < .05$); and scale ratings from 58.0 to 18.90 ($p < .001$). All in all these data were interpreted to indicate that during the relaxation response there is a general lowering of metabolism, which the authors labeled "a wakeful hypometabolic physiological state."

In the popularized version of Wallace, Benson, and Wilson's article (Wallace and Benson, 1972), extensive attention is paid to the decrease in blood lactate observed during the TM session. Since lactate production is an indication of anaerobic metabolism, its decrease signals a drop in this type of metabolism, accounted for either by an increase in oxidative metabolism or a reduction in norepinephrine-produced lactate. Figure 4.1 shows the rather precipitous decline

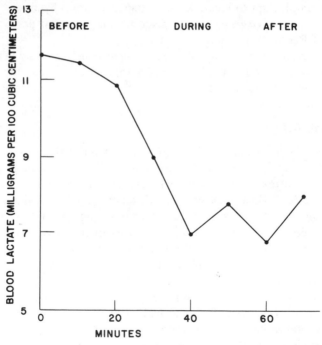

Figure 4.1.   Blood lactate concentrations before, during and after meditation. The rate of decline is three times faster than that of a subject at rest. (From "The Physiology of Meditation" by R. K. Wallace and H. Benson. Copyright © 1972 by Scientific American, Inc. All rights reserved.)

in lactate levels during TM practice. Unfortunately, the data are based on but eight subjects, as their own control, without the presentation of what these subjects' lactate levels would have been had they remained at rest for an equal time period (without meditation). However, the authors indicate that the rate of drop is more than three times the expected norm.

The same criticism can be offered with respect to the other significant changes in physiology—it would have been helpful to know what the changes and rate of changes would have been in these same subjects resting for equal time periods without meditation. Would, for example, a curve similar to Figure 4.2, which depicts changes in basal skin resistance, have been produced under these conditions? Be that as it may, by 1972 Wallace and Benson had established that the TM method did yield some physiological changes that pointed to a reduction in the meditator's metabolism.

In these early papers there was a clear attempt to divorce TM physiology from that appearing in other states of the organism—wakefulness, sleep, hypnosis. With respect to hypnosis, the claim was that any changes in physiology during it reflected the suggested state rather than hypnosis per se. In this appraisal there

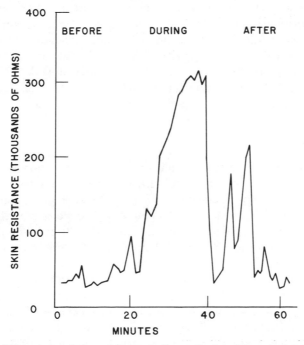

Figure 4.2. Skin resistance before, during and after meditation. The amount and rate of change exceeded that in sleep. (From "The Physiology of Meditation." by R. K. Walalce and H. Benson. Copyright © 1972 by Scientific American, Inc. All rights reserved.)

was a heavy reliance upon summary articles such as those by Barber (1961, 1971), Gorton (1949), and Crasilneck and Hall (1959); no attention was given to the Russian literature (e.g., Platonov, 1959).

By the time Benson had coined the phrase "the relaxation response," physiological similarities between TM training and hypnosis had been recognized. In the first article introducing the phrase (Benson et al., 1974), the authors review the many western and eastern techniques of eliciting the response (some dating back to the second century B.C.). Their aim (see also Benson, 1975; Benson et al., 1975) was to establish the fact that both ancient and modern techniques of relaxing took much the same form as Benson's four elements. The next section of the article (Benson et al., 1974) mentions briefly autogenic training, progressive relaxation, hypnosis, sentic cycles, yoga, Zen, cotention, and TM training first, to demonstrate the similarities of technique among the different practices and, second, to call attention to the physiological data of each. Unlike Wallace's original thesis that TM practice differed from hypnosis physiologically it now appeared that all of these "mental techniques" show a degree of physiological commonality, which Benson translates as the relaxation response.

This thesis was quickly followed up in another article (Beary and Benson, 1974) that, after reviewing the "essential components" again, reported data on 17 "healthy" subjects who were studied in each of three conditions: control (sitting quietly, reading nonemotional material), relaxation (meditation) and eyes closed (without further instructions). As with Wallace's original work (1970), oxygen consumption, carbon dioxide production, and respiratory rate all decreased significantly, while the respiratory quotient remained unchanged.

Side Effects

In addition to proposed clinical applications of the relaxation response (see Chapter 5), Benson, Beary, and Carol (1974) (echoed later almost verbatim by Benson, Greenwood, and Klemchuk [1975]) make passing mention of the potential side effects of TM practice. Claiming that there are no side effects when the relaxation response is limited to no more than two 20- to 30-minute periods per day, Benson reports that his personal observations indicate the potential for a severe withdrawal on the part of subjects, with "symptoms which range in severity from insomnia to psychotic manifestations, often with hallucinatory behavior . . . ." (Benson et al., 1974, p. 44) if the response is elicited more often. Unfortunately, no data are presented to substantiate either of these claims; the authors do point out that these observations are retrospective and thereby faulted by all of the attendant pitfalls of such recollections. It is most difficult to assess, post hoc, what symptomatology a given individual may have brought to the situation in the first place and to what degree the process enhanced, ameliorated, or released the presenting disposition of the subject or patient. Be that as it may, the development of side effects is a constant concern with any treatment modality, and has been even more so with hypnosis, given its historical misassocia-tion with the occult and the "powers of darkness" (see e.g., Braid, 1842).

The investigation of adverse sequelae to hypnosis has been clouded by two problems. First, most of the work is retrospective, and second, most of the reports are of negative effects occurring after hypnotherapy of some form rather than after hypnosis per se. It would seem that the investigation of the relaxation response side effects would not suffer as much from this later pitfall, except as the response is taught to patients with the suggestion, covert or overt, that its practice will have therapeutic benefit. In that case the two procedures share, once again, another aspect of their procedures and uses.

The Hilgards have been most prominent in attempting to bring some organized data to bear on the problem of assessing the "harmful effects" most laymen and a number of professionals attribute to hypnosis. According to Hilgard (1965), Schultz's 1922 retrospective questionnaire illuminated 100 cases reporting after-effects ranging from headaches to severe neurotic and psychotic symptomatology. However, the more recent literature indicates a scant 15 adverse "reactions" between 1949 and 1961 (J. R. Hilgard et al., 1961). Again the symptoms ranged from mild paranoid thoughts to severe psychotic "reactions" and suicide. The word *reactions* has been placed in quotes in accordance with my argument regarding what personality variables, dispositions, and symptoms the patient may bring to the hypnotherapeutic situation in the first place. It would be a disservice to our attempts to understand the nature of hypnosis to burden the field with "reactions" that may not be reactions to hypnosis at all but merely the manifesta-tions of the interpersonal context in which the hypnosis is performed. Even our interpretation of these relatively few cases of negative sequelae must be tempered with a broader perspective of the total environmental, personal, and interpersonal variables at work. As Hilgard opined: "Careful studies are needed in which entire samples of subjects or patients are studied *with the necessary controls* to determine and to understand the effects that are attributable to hypnosis itself" (1965, p. 54, italics added).

Hilgard, Hilgard, and Newman (1961) obtained better controlled data from a sample of 220 Stanford University students who had participated in a series of experiments in E. R. Hilgard's laboratories. Each of the subjects was interviewed extensively several days following the induction of hypnosis and was invited to report any aftereffects later on. This latter ploy makes evident the difficulty of obtaining totally uncontaminated data regarding sequelae. The mere act of invit-ing the subjects to report sequelae may be suggestive enough for some subjects to elicit the very responses the investigator is attempting not to suggest, but on which more rigorous data are needed. This dilemma is inescapable but should be attended to when assessing the percentage of reported sequelae. Some subjects may even perceive such a request as an indication that hypnosis, to be really effective, *should* involve some sort of aftereffect. Subjects with such a percep-tion will then be supersensitized to any change they may note in their physical and/or mental well-being, and report items that might well have gone totally unnoticed but for the investigators' query. The significance of these reports, therefore, is very difficult to assess.

At any rate, the percentage of subjects who reported any sequelae is small (7.7%), and those reporting persistent aftereffects even smaller (2.3%, or 5 subjects). None of the students had severe, psychotic or psychotic-like sequelae, the most severe apparently being a headache.*

More recently, Josephine Hilgard (1974) has presented continuing data along these same lines. This time 120 university students were interviewed following a group presentation of the Stanford Scale, Form A, and an individual presentation of Form C. The interviews explored not only longer aftereffects but the subjects' experiences during and immediately after hypnosis. Hilgard's results indicated that individuals reporting sequelae of short duration (5 to 60 minutes) comprised 16% of the population studied, while those reporting long-term aftereffects (longer than 1 hour) made up an additional 15%. The symptoms reported consisted of headache, dizziness and nausea, stiff arm or neck, drowsiness and sleep, cognitive distortion and confusion, anxiety, and night dreams. No symptoms of psychotic proportions were reported, although one subject, Bill, was "dazed" and "queasy" for about 24 hours, during which time he had a headache, hypnosis-related dreams, anxiety, and felt he "didn't come out of it."

As with the potential for aftereffects with the relaxation response, it appears that the sequelae to hypnosis should not cause the well-trained practitioner undue concern. To be sure, interpersonal concerns must be attended to, but the percentage of subject involvement in sequelae, the relatively mild nature of those sequelae, and the persistent difficulty of knowing to what variable their appearance should be attributed easily justify the continuation of hypnosis as an experimental and clinical technique. The studies by Hilgard, Hilgard, and Newman (1961) and J. Hilgard (1974), by being conducted in an experimental setting, give us a clearer hint of what sort of sequelae we can attribute to hypnosis per se in some subjects. In these studies there were no therapeutic manipulations, and the subjects did not participate with the conscious anticipation of therapeutic benefit. Hence we get a somewhat purer picture of hypnosis-related sequelae, although the unspoken perceptions and the personalities of the subjects could still have inflated the number and kind of aftereffects. With those precautions in mind, the sequelae to hypnosis can be considered generally mild and not of extensive duration.

CONCLUSION

In this chapter we have set forth the history, technique, and physiological data of "the relaxation response" and shown how similar its production is to hypnotic procedures. The extent of the similarity between the physiology of hypnosis and the relaxation response will be explored in depth in Chapter 6.

---

*In twenty years of experimental work the present author has only had one subject complain of a headache following hypnosis; it lasted less than eight hours.

ation response as a
raine and cluster
o fully appreciate
ectiveness of both
t chapter.

CHAPTER 5

Hypnosis and Relaxation: Clinical Studies

That hypnosis and relaxation as trophotropic responses are similar with respect to the techniques and procedures for their production is clear from the review in the last chapter. In this chapter we will review the similarities between hypnosis and the trophotropic response in clinical applications and therapeutic effectiveness.

CLINICAL APPLICATIONS

From the start, Benson's aim was to investigate the therapeutic efficacy of "the relaxation response" induced by Transcendental Meditation® (TM) sessions for a variety of disorders ranging from hypertension to addictions. Likewise, hypnosis has been put to a considerable number of uses, from surgical to medical to psychotherapeutic. A number of modern summaries of the general clinical applications of hypnosis are readily available (Kroger, 1977; Hartland, 1971; Haley, 1967; Wolberg, 1948); our concentration here will be on those areas of clinical application in which *both* hypnosis and relaxation have been applied.

Hypertension

Although hypertension (high blood pressure) affects over 20 million Americans and is estimated to cause the death of 200,000 a year (Deabler et al., 1973), few studies have been undertaken to assess the value of hypnosis in its treatment. A wide range of relaxation-related treatments—yoga, for example (Datey et al., 1969; Patel, 1973, 1975; Patel and North, 1975), autogenic training (Luthe, 1972) and Transcendental Meditation practice (Benson et al., 1974*a, b*)—have claimed some success at lowering either diastolic or systolic pressures, both, or an average of both.

Benson, Rosner, Marzetta, and Klemchuk (1974*a*), for example, were able to reduce both diastolic and systolic pressures significantly in 22 nonmedicated borderline hypertensive patients during a 25-week treatment period and in 14 medicated patients during a 20-week treatment period (Benson et al., 1974*b*). Meditation was practiced twice daily for 20 minutes at a time. Diastolic blood pressure (BP) dropped an average of 3.86 mm Hg between the premeditation and postmeditation periods, and systolic, an average of 6.98 for the nonmedicated patients and 4.85 mm Hg and 10.6 mm Hg, respectively, for medicated patients. Although significant in themselves, from the average premeditation BPs of 94.61/146.5 and 91.9/145.6, respectively, these figures do not approach the 20% reduction Blanchard and Young (1974) considered necessary for clinical significance.

In addition, Benson, Alexander, and Feldman (1975) reported being able to reduce premature ventricular contractions (PVCs) in 11 patients with demonstrated ischaemic heart disease. The patients were monitored for PVCs for two days prior to learning the relaxation response, which was then practiced by the patients twice a day for 20 minutes at a time. Four weeks later PVCs were again monitored and found to have decreased between 10.8% and 100% in 8 of the 11 patients. PVCs during sleep were significantly decreased over the entire group.

While a 20% reduction in BP as a clinical criterion for significant effect is considered by some to be rather "stringent," some of the data from the hypnosis studies approach that level. Deabler, Fidel, Dillenkoffer, and Elder (1973) evaluated diastolic and systolic pressure changes in 21 diagnosed hypertensive patients. Nine patients who continued their drug treatment during the study and six who were not taking antihypertensive medication received eight or nine treatment sessions that consisted of muscular relaxation à la Jacobson (1929) *followed* by a relaxation-hypnosis induction, in turn followed by deepening of the trance through continuing instructions to relax. The patients were also taught self-hypnosis, which they used in the last few sessions. Pressure readings were taken of basal levels, levels during relaxation, and levels during hypnosis. Patients not on medication showed a 15.5% reduction of diastolic pressure during relaxation and a 19.5% reduction during hypnosis. Systolic pressure drops for this same group were 8 to 12%, and 17%, respectively. Patients who continued medication during the relaxation-hypnosis treatment sessions reduced diastolic pressures 3 to 10% during relaxation and 14% during hypnosis. Systolic pressures in the medicated group dropped 9 to 15%, and 16%, respectively. The results for the medicated and nonmedicated groups are presented in Figures 5.1, 5.2, 5.3, and 5.4.

Figure 5.5 presents one final evaluation of the data for the nonmedicated patients. This graph is based on a formula that yields the percentage of decrease each patient achieved of the proportion that his or her systolic pressure was above clinically designated hypertension (140 mm Hg); that is, the patient's systolic pressure minus achieved reduction during treatment, divided by the patient's systolic pressure minus 140 mm Hg. In this presentation, relaxation reduced hypertension by 85%, and hypnosis reduced it by over 100%!

One point to attend to in the interpretation of Deabler et al.'s data is that the procedures used do not yield a direct comparison between a relaxation technique (progressive relaxation in this case) and hypnosis. Relaxation always preceded hypnosis in the treatment sessions; there was no counterbalancing of the two

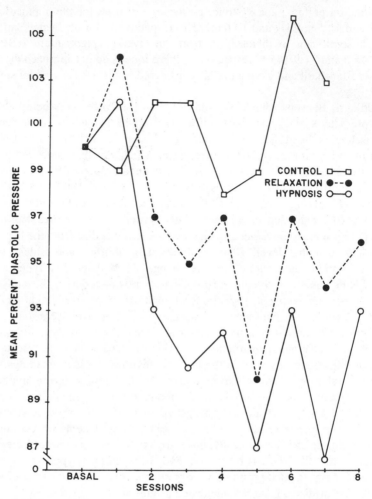

Figure 5.1.   Drug group. Mean percent diastolic pressure as a function of sessions. (From Deabler et al., 1973. Copyright © American Society of Clinical Hypnosis. Reprinted by permission.)

treatments. Thus the one significant difference between the two treatments in figure 5.1 merely reflect the further effectiveness of continuing relaxation instructions (hypnosis).

However, the major point made by the Deabler et al. (1973) data is the striking similarity of effectiveness between relaxation and hypnosis. The only place this similarity does not appear readily apparent is in figure 5-6, but this discrepancy can be accounted for by the methodological difficulty noted above. Since the

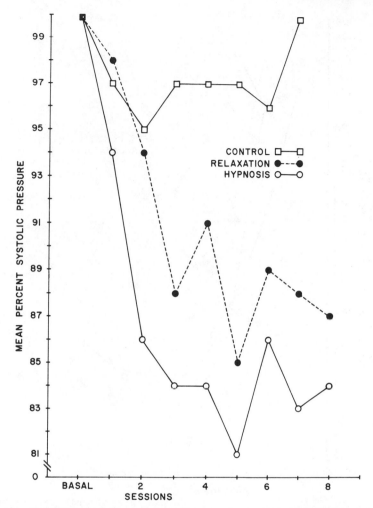

Figure 5.2. Drug group. Mean percent systolic pressure as a function of sessions. (From Deabler et al., 1973. Copyright © American Society of Clinical Hypnosis. Reprinted by permission.)

confounding of the two treatments yielded results in the expected direction—that is, the treatment that was presented second (hypnosis) yielded results that appear to be a continuation of those obtained with the first (progressive relaxation)—the study appears to suggest that hypnosis and relaxation are effective treatment vehicles for hypertension.

A more recent study offers a more clear-cut evaluation of the effectiveness of hypnosis as a treatment for hypertension and, in addition, demonstrates the

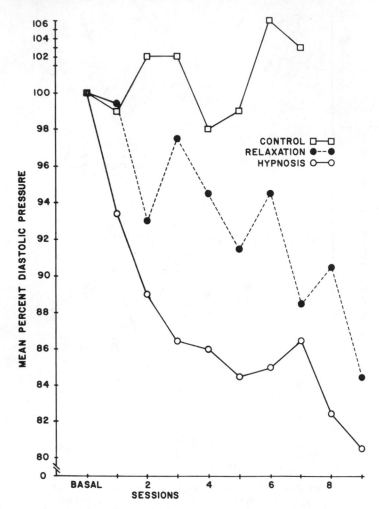

Figure 5.3. No drug group. Mean percent diastolic pressure as a function of sessions. (From Deabler et al., 1973. Copyright © American Society of Clinical Hypnosis. Reprinted by permission.)

longevity of its effect. Although it does not offer a comparison with relaxation techniques, it does, however, compare hypnosis with biofeedback techniques, which have gained attention since Miller and DiCara's application of operant conditioning techniques to visceral and autonomic responses (DiCara and Miller, 1968; Miller, 1969). In addition, we can consider the question of sustained treatment effectiveness. Friedman and Taub (1977, 1978) studied 48 hypertensive patients, all of whom were receiving medication throughout. Twenty-three highly hypnotizable patients (Stanford Hypnotic Susceptibility Scale [SHSS],

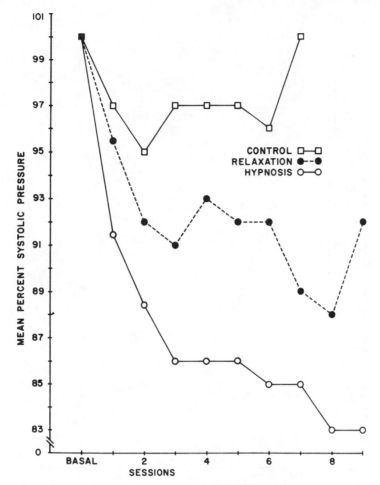

Figure 5.4. No drug group. Mean percent systolic pressure as a function of sessions. (From Deabler et al., 1973. Copyright © American Society of Clinical Hypnosis. Reprinted by permission.)

Form A, scores of seven or better) were treated either with hypnosis alone ($N = 13$) or hypnosis in combination with visual biofeedback ($N = 10$). Another 25 with low SHSS:A scores were assigned to a group receiving only biofeedback treatment ($N = 13$) or a no-treatment control group ($N = 12$).

Each patient received seven "treatment" sessions. Biofeedback was accomplished by having the patients observe a London Pressurometer, and hypnosis was initially induced through the eye-closure, relaxation instructions of the SHSS:A. Analysis of diastolic pressure changes at one week revealed that there was a significant reduction in pressure over time and a significant

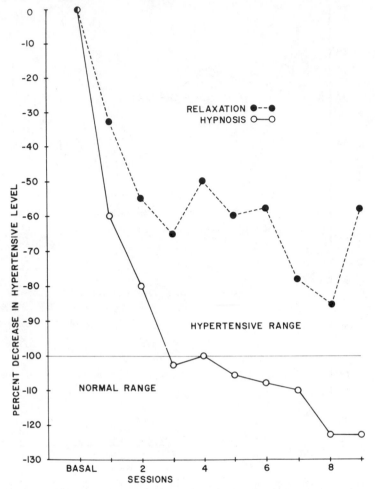

Figure 5.5. No drug group. Percent decrease in hypertensive level of systolic pressure as a function of sessions. (From Deabler et al., 1973. Copyright © American Society of Clinical Hypnosis. Reprinted by permission.)

difference among the treatment groups. Only the hypnosis group showed a significant reduction when compared to the controls and the other treatment groups. The same was true at the one month follow-up. Looking at the data from an intra- rather than an intergroup standpoint, the biofeedback group showed significant gains in diastolic pressure reduction, but not to the degree of the hypnosis group. The biofeedback group's systolic pressures, on the other hand, showed only a "trend" in the same direction at one week, but the same pattern of significances as for diastolic at one month.

Curiously, when hypnosis was used in combination with biofeedback no significant changes came to light. One might have thought that two treatments, which independently yield results in the same direction, would increase the direction and significance of those results when taken together. However, as we saw in our discussion of Barber's studies of the effectiveness of different induction variables (motivation and relaxation-sleep suggestions), hypnosis does not appear to interact in an additive manner with other treatments. Whether this is due to the invoking of different anticipatory response sets, as suggested by Benson et al. (1974a, b) and Friedman and Taub (1977), is not clear at present.

Six months after the original study, Friedman and Taub (1978) reported a follow-up on all but four of the patients originally studied. The follow-up data yielded essentially the same results as those reported at one month. In the hypnosis group diastolic pressures reduced as much as 12% (compared to 14% for Deabler et al.) and systolic as much as 11% (for Dealber et al., 16%). These results are shown in figures 5.6 and 5.7 respectively, and can be compared with figures 5.1 and 5.2 from Deabler et al., which also showed a clear advantage for hypnosis as a treatment for hypertension.

Hypertension is one of the disorders for which Benson feels the trophotropic-relaxation response to be a most appropriate treatment. Benson, Rosner, Mazetta, and Klemchuk (1974 a, b) report data on 22 nonmedicated hypertensive patients and 14 medicated hypertensive patients of a group of 86 who originally started a TM regimen eliciting "the relaxation response" twice a day for 20 to 25 weeks. Blood pressure was measured at random times during the day, but not during meditation. The authors report decreases in diastolic pressure of 4% in the nonmedicated patients and 5.3% in the medicated. Systolic pressure decreases were 4.8% and 7.2% for the nonmedicated and medicated patients, respectively. All of these decreases were statistically significant.

Table 5.1 summarizes the data from the Deabler et al. (1973), Friedman and Taub (1977, 1978), and Benson, et al. (1974 a, b) studies. The pretreatment

Table 5.1.   Comparative Data from Three Studies of the Treatment of Hypertension

Study	Treatment	Pretreatment Measure (mmHg)		% Decrease	
		Diastolic	Systolic	Diastolic	Systolic
Benson et al., 1974 a, b	Medicated	91.9	145.6	5.3*	7.2*
	Nonmedicated	94.6	146.5	4.0*	4.8*
Deabler et al., 1973	Medicated	95.0	158.0	14.0*	16.0*
	Nonmedicated	96.0	163.0	19.5*	17.0*
Friedman and Taub, 1977, 1978	Medicated	93.1	142.5	12.0*	11.0*

* Significant differences.

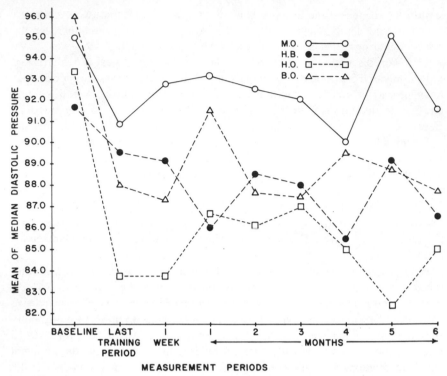

Figure 5.6. Means of mean diastolic pressure at each measurement period. Hypnosis alone = H.O.; Biofeedback alone = B.O.; Hypnosis and Biofeedback combined = H.B.; and Measurement only = M.O. (From Friedman and Taub, 1978. Copyright © American Society of Clinical Hypnosis. Reprinted by permission.)

measures indicate that all four studies were dealing with patients whose blood pressures were in the accepted range of hypertension (diastolic, >90 mmHg; systolic, > 140 mmHg). Although no statistical comparisons were made, the pressures across all four studies appear comparable. The percentage of decrease of the pressures under the different treatments are worth exploring in a little more detail. Although all of the percentages are significant in their respective studies, Deabler et al.'s patients appear to have obtained a greater percentage of decrease than those in the other studies. However, it should be kept in mind that although both Deabler et al. and Friedman and Taub used hypnosis as a treatment, Deabler et al.'s patients received relaxation induction instructions *after* having received progressive relaxation instructions. We might speculate that had Friedman and Taub offered the patients such a prolonged relaxation induction, they too might have achieved similar percentages of decrease.

Comparing Benson's TM relaxation with hypnosis, the percentages of change appear to be considerably different. Although we are not able to make direct

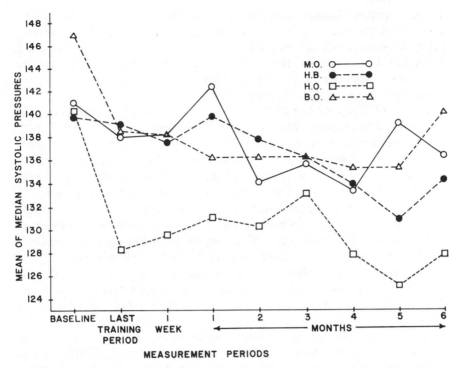

Figure 5.7. Means of median systolic pressure at each measurement period. Hypnosis alone = H.O.; Biofeedback alone = B.O.; Hypnosis and biofeedback combined = H.B.; and Measurement only = M.O. (From Friedman and Taub, 1978. Copyright © American Society of Clinical Hypnosis. Reprinted by permission.)

comparisons, the magnitude of the differences is suggestive. Does this mean that hypnosis and relaxation (the TM method, in this case) are dissimilar? Not necessarily. I suspect that the differences are of degree rather than kind. Remember, Deabler et al.'s data, because of the confounded presentation of the two treatments, made hypnosis appear to be more effective than relaxation. While hypnosis induced by relaxation-sleep instructions may be more effective than relaxation in the treatment of hypertension, the effectiveness of both indicates similarities of kind between them. At least in this clinical application the sparse data available suggest support of the relaxation-hypnosis equation.

Headache—Migraine

Another clinical application area where various forms of relaxation therapies have been applied is that of migraine and tension headaches. The former, a disorder that afflicts between 5% and 20% of the general population (Anderson et al., 1975), involves a disabling headache, often unilateral, accompanied by nausea, vomiting, diarrhea, and other symptoms (Wolff, 1963). The basis of the pain of migraine appears to be a redistribution of blood flow between central and peripheral areas, specifically vasodilatation of the vessels of the head region with a concomitant vasoconstriction of the distal vasculature. Considering the hypertensive literature, it is not surprising to find migraine treated with biofeedback, autogenic, and hypnotic techniques.

Basker (1970) reported on 28 cases of migraine treated with hypnosis from his private medical practice. The treatment varied considerably from patient to patient, who ranged in age from 15 to 77 years, but mainly included suggestions for reassurance, ego-strengthening, autohypnosis, and control of the "arteries in the head." Follow-up of the patients at from 11 to 38 months revealed complete remission in 16 and improvement in 7 others, in Basker's judgment. The percentage of complete remission, 57.1%, is quite comparable to those reported elsewhere in more rigorously evaluated populations. Cedercreutz, Lähteenmäki, and Tulikoura (1976) even report 50% complete relief from headache and 58% relief from vertigo in 155 patients who had suffered "skull injuries."

The most prevalent method of nondrug treatment of migraines has been some form of handwarming, whether by physically warming the hands to redistribute the blood flow away from the head region or by suggestions given in the context of autogenic training, relaxation, hypnosis, or biofeedback monitoring. Often suggestions for "cooling the forehead" are given concurrently with the hand-warming suggestions. Ansel (1977) has even reported success with a single patient who was refractory to hypnotic induction by having her rotate her arms in a rapid, circular motion to increase peripheral blood flow.

Attempting to find a more expedient form of treatment than the usual many hours spent in hypnotherapeutic endeavors, Daniels (1976) reported using tape-recorded treatment sessions with three patients. Each patient had six treatment sessions in which a 20-minute taped relaxation induction, including suggestions for hand warming and forehead cooling, was played. Through interviews before and after treatment the author assessed the frequency, duration, and intensity of the patients' headaches. All three of the patients reported reductions in frequency, duration, and intensity of their headaches over the period of treatment, one from a frequency of 1 per month and a maximum intensity of 9 (on a 10-point subjective scale) to complete freedom from migraine. In another, frequency dropped from 21 to 1 or 2 per week. Thus significant or complete relief was reported over the treatment period; Daniels did admit some recurrence on follow-up, but not to the extent of the original problem.

With another patient, Daniels (1977) combined the hypnosis, hand-warming, forehead-cooling tape with instruction in deep muscle relaxation (similar to Jacobson's progressive relaxation), a quick cue for achieving relaxation rapidly, and a procedure he has used with obsessive patients called "thought stopping." All of the procedures were used in combination by the patient at home for five weeks, at the end of which she was symptom-free. At 12-month follow-up she was still symptomless.

These case studies, as the studies to follow, point up a major confound in the clinical literature that makes the detailed assessment of treatment effectiveness difficult. Hypnosis is most often applied in combination with other therapeutic suggestions. This is true of virtually all of the clinical applications involving hypnosis, relaxation, and the other nonpharmaceutical treatments. With few exceptions no studies or clinical reports offer data relating to the effectiveness of hypnosis per se (or for that matter, relaxation per se). This is true in the present discussion of migraine, was true in the previous discussion of hypertension, and will be true in what follows. Consequently, to interpret the data presented as clearly indicating an equation in treatment effectiveness between relaxation and hypnosis is a bit of an extrapolation. However, I do not feel that the extrapolation is either unwarranted or excessive. What I am demonstrating herein is that treatment of disorders in the context of hypnosis is of the same order of effectiveness as treatment of those same disorders in the context of relaxation techniques, and thus, again by extrapolation, the two seem to share similar properties.

Returning to the sparce migraine-hypnosis literature, Stambaugh and House (1977) also reported a "shotgun-approach" to treatment, titled "multimodality treatment." However, their treatment techniques and the order of presentation are so confounded that reasonable interpretation, other than to say that massive doses (more than eight months' worth) of relaxation and suggestions and other instructions seem to reduce the severity and the frequency of migraine and the use of analgesics, is not in order.

Graham (1975), however, did give us a clearer picture of the effectiveness of hypnosis coupled with hand-warming suggestions in two patients. Graham's starting point was the work of Sargent, Green, and Walters (1973), who had earlier reported a 63% improvement in 19 migraine patients and a 33% improvement in 6 tension-headache patients through a temperature biofeedback technique. These authors used differential temperature feedback between the right index finger and the forehead in combination with self-administered suggestions to relax and increase the temperature of the hands, modeled on the autogenic training of Schultz and Luthe (1959). Since the temperature measures were relative, it is unclear whether index-finger temperature actually increased or forehead temperature actually decreased during treatment.

Graham hypnotized his two patients using Braid's eye-fixation technique and then administered suggestions to enhance the warming of their dominant hands. Five such treatment sessions, one week apart, were used; the patients practiced hand-warming on their own between treatment sessions. During a one-month pretreatment baseline period one patient reported 15 migraines with intensities of 9 (on a 10-point subjective scale) and with an average duration of 10 hours. The other patient's baseline measures were 10 migraines of 10 intensity with an average duration of 5 hours. At 9- and 12-month follow-ups, respectively, both patients were free of migraine headaches.

Considering the similarity between the procedures used by Sargent et al. (1975; biofeedback and relaxing, autogenic, hand-warming self-suggestions) and Graham (1975; relaxation-hypnosis and hand-warming suggestions), Graham raised the question of the necessity of including biofeedback information in the treatment of migraine. However, Graham's dissertation (1974) did offer some information relative to that question; he compared 30 migraine patients, equally divided among three treatment groups (hypnosis and biofeedback, biofeedback alone, and hypnosis alone), for frequency, duration, and intensity of symptoms. None of the groups showed any superiority over the others; treatments all led to significant decreases in the measures when compared to pretreatment levels.

Wickramasekera's (1972) preliminary report on tension headache had already spoken to that point. He presented data on five female headache sufferers who reported the intensity and frequency of their headaches while receiving either contingent frontalis or noncontingent frontalis electromyogram (EMG) feedback, 30 minutes each for five (contingent) or six (noncontingent) sessions spread over a three-week period. According to the author, the frequency and intensity of headaches were reduced during contingent feedback but not during noncontingent. Figure 5.8 shows the manner in which headache intensity follows frontalis activity, and figure 5.9 indicates the reduction of headache activity during contingent feedback. These data do not necessarily reflect the utility of biofeedback with migraine, but they do suggest that some form of feedback may be of benefit with certain forms of headache—in this case, tension headaches.

Along this same line, Zitz (1978) has also offered data indicating that EMG biofeedback alone is not reliable for reducing "physiological tension and psychological anxiety." The reason that her findings are so cogent here is that she discovered that *without the accompanying suggestions of relaxation,* EMG biofeedback is not effective, as measured. Zitz's 20 subjects, given six 50-minute training sessions, showed a very small drop in frontalis EMG (2.55uv), although a somewhat larger one for trapezius tension. This decrease is only a bit more than half of that reported by Wickramasekera (1972), and may serve to point up the very thesis of Zitz's dissertation. Thus relaxation instructions appear very crucial to the effectiveness of EMG biofeedback.

Let us now return to comparisons between relaxation and hypnosis in this same context. The question of the effectiveness of relaxation formed the basis of Andreychuk and Skriver's study (1975). These authors divided 33 respondents to a local news media ad equally into three treatment groups: (a) hypnosis, a self-administered, relaxation induction plus pain-reduction suggestions, (b) biofeedback for hand temperature coupled with autogenic relaxation instructions, and (c) biofeedback for electroencephalogram (EEG) alpha production also coupled with relaxation instructions. All instructions were tape administered.

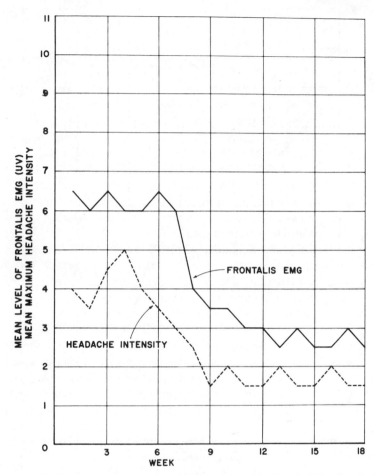

Figure 5.8. Headache intensity and frontalis EMG over time. (0−3 weeks is baseline; 3−6 weeks is noncontingent feedback; 6−18 weeks is contingent feedback) (From Wickramasekera, 1972. Copyright © American Society of Clinical Hypnosis. Reprinted by permission.)

Each subject had one treatment session per week for a period of 10 weeks. Comparisons of the effectiveness of the treatments were made between a six-week pretreatment period and the last five weeks of treatment. All three treatment groups showed significant improvement as measured by a headache index based on reports of frequency, duration, and intensity of the migraines, and none of the treatments was significantly more effective than the others. The hypnosis treatment yielded 36.1% improvement; the alpha feedback, 48.75%; and the temperature feedback, 74.45%. The authors noted "that each of the

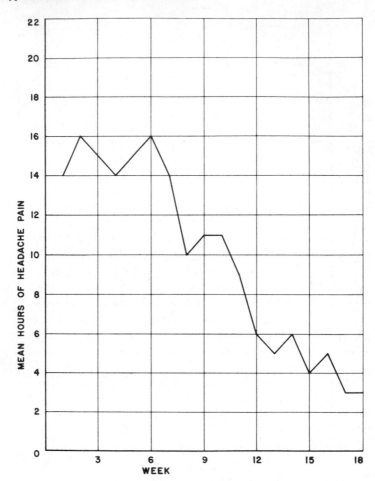

Figure 5.9. Headache activity over time. (0−3 weeks is baseline; 3−6 weeks is noncontingent feedback; 6−18 weeks is contingent feedback) (From Wickramasekera, 1972. Copyright © American Society of Clinical Hypnosis. Reprinted by permission.)

treatments also focused considerable emphasis on relaxation and that this may have been the crucial variable involved. There is no denying that relaxation can and does have a therapeutic benefit in many types of disorders'' (Andreychuk and Skriver, 1975, p. 180). But they interpreted the trend of their data as indicating the importance of suggestibility in the effectiveness of the treatments. This conclusion was based on the finding that significantly more (71.3%) of the highly suggestible subjects in all three groups (measured by the Hypnotic Induction Profile; Spiegel and Bridger, 1970; Spiegel, 1974) improved than the less suggestible subjects (41.4%). One of the problems with this interpretation is the susceptibility test used and its relationship to other standard scales. Hilgard (1978/79) has recently shown that there is little correlation between the newer induction score of the Hypnotic Induction Profile and the Stanford scales. Whether Andreychuk and Skriver's use of the older form ameliorates or exaggerates the meaning of this finding is not known, but further study of the scale itself may necessitate another look at their data. At any rate, what does seem to evolve from Andreychuk and Skriver's data, in addition to the possible suggestibility interpretation, is that treatment involving either hypnosis or relaxation, whether or not coupled with additional suggestions, is effective with migraine headaches.

Barabasz and McGeorge (1978) also raised the question of the necessity of biofeedback, not in the treatment of migraine, but in manipulating that which underlies the treatment—vasodilatation. Seventy-three New Zealand undergraduates were randomly assigned to four experimental treatment groups intended to aid them in increasing hand temperature. One group received typical biofeedback temperature information without "autogenic phrases"; another received false biofeedback information (a continuous tone); a third served as a relaxation-instruction control; and the fourth received passive-relaxation hypnosis induction instructions followed by suggestions for hand-warming. Although the analysis of the data is presented in a rather confusing manner, it appears that the hypnosis group alone yielded a significant increase in measured hand temperature (6.43° F).

While it would also appear that biofeedback information is not necessarily effective in raising hand temperatures, further study is clearly warranted. Although the relaxation instruction group did show an increase in hand temperature quantitatively higher than the biofeedback groups (1.3° F), hypnosis instructions seemed to hold the edge, except for one problem. The hypnosis group received additional suggestions for hand-warming that the relaxation group did not. This obvious confound makes clear interpretation difficult, though it could be suspected that with the same additional suggestions, the relaxation group might have faired as well. At least that is what could be assumed, based on all these studies taken in combination. Certainly, the studies indicate that hypnosis, particularly in combination with other post-induction suggestions, can be effective in combating the debilitation of migraine.

In fact, according to Anderson, Basker, and Dalton (1975), hypnosis is more effective than prochlorperazine (Stemetil®). Working through practitioners in England, they accumulated data on 47 diagnosed migraine patients. Twenty-three of the group were treated with Hartland's suggestive and ego-strengthening techniques (1971), which centered on controlling the dilation of the arteries of the head, decreasing tension and anxiety, and increasing relaxation. At least six hypnotic sessions were given every 10 to 14 days. The other 24 patients received 5 mg prochlorperazine four times per day for the first month and two times per day for the remaining 11 months of the assessment period. The practitioners reviewed each patient monthly and reported the frequency and severity of symptoms.

Table 5.2 presents the results, tabulated for symptom frequency and symptom severity, as measured by the frequency of "Grade 4 Blinding Attacks." The change from a frequency of 4.5 attacks per month to 0.5 for hypnotherapy was significant ($p < .0005$), while the change for the drug treatment was not. The same comparative balance held with respect to the severity measure. Hypnotherapy was accompanied by a significant reduction ($p < .005$) in the frequency of Grade 4 attacks, while prochloperazine was not. Finally, the 43.5% complete remission during the last three months of treatment by hypnosis is significantly greater than the 12.5% found for the drug treatment group ($p < .039$). The conclusion drawn by the authors was obvious: Hypnotherapy appears to be an effective treatment of migraine both in terms of reducing the number of attacks and the number of patients who suffer blinding attacks, and also in increasing the number who have a complete remission for three months (Anderson et al., 1975, p. 56).

In an attempt to assess the effectiveness of ego-strengthening suggestions in the treatment of migraine, Perkins (1975) treated 32 patients suffering from either classic, cluster, or common migraine. Using an arm-catalepsy induction, followed by progressive relaxation until muscle relaxation was apparent, Perkins coupled autohypnosis and ego-strengthening suggestions with: "The migraine attacks will become less severe; the migraine will not last long; the migraine will not come as often" (Perkins, 1975, p. 121) for six treatment sessions at one-week intervals. Specific reference to concentrating on the cranial blood vessels was not included. From records kept by the patients regarding frequency,

Table 5.2.   Treatment of Migraine by Hypnotherapy and Prochloperazine (Stemetil)

Outcome Criterion	Hypnotherapy $N = 23$	Stemetil $N = 24$
Median number of migraine attacks per month		
6 months prior to therapy	4.5	3.3
First 6 months of therapy	1.0	2.8
Second 6 months of therapy	0.5	2.9
Number of patients suffering Grade 4 attacks		
6 months prior to therapy	13	10
First 6 months of therapy	4	13
Second 6 months of therapy	5	14
Patients having complete remission during last 3 months of therapy	10 (43.5%)	3 (12.5%)

(From Anderson, Basker, and Dalton, 1975. Reprinted from the January, 1975 International Journal of Clinical and Experimental Hypnosis. Copyrighted by the Society for Clinical and Experimental Hypnosis, January, 1975.)

intensity, and duration of attack before, during, and 12 months after treatment, the following results were tabulated.

Although there were no significant changes in the severity of the attacks before, during, and after treatment, their duration showed a significant reduction (from 13.3 hours to 10.65 hours; $p < .025$), as did the number of attacks (from 1.19 per week to .37; $p < .0001$). Ego-strengthening suggestions added nothing to the treatment effectiveness. These results are reflected in figures 5.10 and 5.11. What is somewhat unique about these data is that the percentage of change (80% fewer attacks and 20% briefer) were accomplished *without* suggestions for

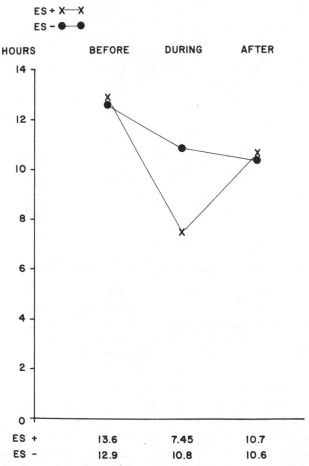

Figure 5.10. Duration of attack in hours in relation to the therapy. There is no significant difference between the two groups. There are significant differences for ES+ when values before treatment are compared with those during treatment ($t = 2.23; .050 > p > 0.025$). (From Perkins, 1975. Reprinted by permission.)

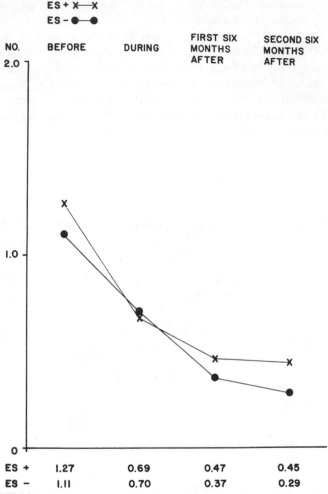

Figure 5.11. Frequency of attack in relationship to therapy. No significant difference between ES+ and ES− —but for each group there is a highly significant difference between initial and follow-up results ($p < 0.0001$, U-test). (From Perkins, 1975. Reprinted by permission.)

hand-warming, vasoconstriction or vasodilatation, or the like. Clearly here then is a study indicating that hypnosis—and primarily the element of muscle relaxation—can be effective as a treatment for migraine. While hand-warming suggestions may enhance the treatment effect, they are not required.

Benson's work with the TM method (his relaxation response) in the treatment of headaches has been scant and not very convincing. Only two reports have been forthcoming, and the first (Benson et al., 1973) merely indicated that 36 patients with severe cluster, migraine, and tension headaches were being treated with a TM technique, practiced twice daily for 15 to 20 minutes each. No results were reported.

The second report (Benson et al., 1974) involved 17 migraine sufferers and 4 patients with "incapacitating cluster headaches." Following a one-to three-months baseline period, during which each patient kept a personal record of headache severity, all of the patients were taught to relax through TM practice twice a day (15 to 20 minutes each, as above). Treatment was continued for 4 to 14 months and the results on a headache units index compared with the baseline period. Only three of the migraine patients had a statistically significant decrease in headache units with treatment. Clinically, six migraine patients were considered improved, while the same could be said of only one of the four cluster headache patients. Benson's conclusion is appropriately guarded: "regular elicitation of the relaxation response through the practice of TM has limited usefulness in the therapy of severe migraine and cluster headache" (Benson et al., 1974, p. 51).

His attempts to predict more success in the future based on the idea that the relaxation response reduces sympathetic nervous system activity, and therefore would reduce the "tension" that is clinically reported by many headache sufferers, was countered by Bakal (1975) in his review of the headache syndrome: "there is no research suggesting that high levels of sympathetic nervous system activity characterize headache sufferers" (p. 378). Certainly, from Benson's own data, it would be difficult to maintain any clear-cut advantage of the relaxation response in the treatment of migraine. What seems to be missing from his TM treatment is some sort of attempted manipulation of the vascular system, which the other studies reviewed (with the exception of Perkins, 1975) seem to indicate as critical if any sort of amelioration of symptoms is to be expected.

What can we then conclude from our brief comparison of the treatment of migraine in the context of hypnosis and relaxation? Basically, hypnosis per se, without further therapeutic suggestions, may not be very effective as a treatment. The same is apparent for relaxation. Alone neither provides adequate treatment. However, when combined with further suggestions directed at a redistribution of the blood flow—specifically increasing flow to the extremities and away from the head region—hypnosis *is* effective, and relaxation, not designated hypnosis, may be. Certainly hypnosis appears to be more effective than the usual biofeedback techniques, although even here the literature does not paint a totally clear image. Thus the generalized conclusion to be made is that there are similarities in clinical application between hypnosis and the trophotropic response when used as the context for additional treatment of migraine.

Addiction

Drugs

Transcendental Meditation. The concept of using the TM technique in the treatment of drug abuse was put forward rather forcefully in 1972 by Benson and Wallace, when they reported data from 1862 questionnaires filled out by individuals who had been attending meditation courses. Data on frequency of drug use, drug selling, and attitudes toward drug abuse were tabulated for five periods: 6 months before, and 0 to 3 months, 4 to 9 months, 10 to 21 months, and 22 months after starting meditation. The data on the first two periods, 6 months before and up to 3 months after starting meditation, were retrospective, while those for the other periods were obtained during the periods designated. The information was gathered with respect to marihuana, hallucinogens (LSD, mescaline, peyote), narcotics (heroin, opium, morphine, cocaine), amphetamines, barbiturates, alcohol (excluding beer and wine), and cigarettes separately, from subjects classified as heavy (> once a day), medium (one to six times per week), light (≤ three times per month) and nonusers. For LSD the definitions were once a week, one to three times per month, and less than once a month, respectively. Although most of the subjects were between 19 and 23 years of age, the range spread from 14 to 78 years, with a 58 to 42 percentage male/female split. All of the subjects practiced meditation as outlined by Marharishi Mahesh Yogi twice a day for 15 or 20 minutes each.

Benson and Wallace's data (1972) show a dramatic decrease in drug, alcohol, and cigarette usage during the period of eliciting the relaxation response through TM practice. However, the attrition rate over the 22 months may make their results seem better than they actually are. For example, table 5.3 is a reproduction of their table 6, presenting their data on narcotics. The percentage of usage decrease in each usage category is quite impressive across time, except that by 10

Table 5.3.   Use of Narcotics Before and After Starting the Practice of Transcendental Meditation

	Before (time in months)				After (time in months)					
	6−0		0−3		4−9		10−21		22−33	
Usage	N	%	N	%	N	%	N	%	N	%
Heavy	12	0.6	1	0.1	1	0.1	1	0.1	0	0.0
Medium	17	0.9	2	0.2	2	0.2	2	0.2	0	0.0
Light	286	15.4	47	2.5	39	2.1	30	2.1	10	1.2
Nonuser	1547	83.1	1812	97.2	1788	97.6	1384	97.6	842	98.8
Totals	1862	100.0	1862	100.0	1830	100.0	1417	100.0	852	100.0

(From Benson and Wallace, 1972. Copyright, 1972 by Lea & Febiger. Reprinted by permission.)

to 21 months there has been an attrition of 24% and by 22 months, 54%! Since the authors do not tell us the attrition figures per usage group, we do not know how much of the 0% use by the "heavy" users is due to an actual reduction of use or a loss in the number of respondents from that group. The other minor flaw (minor because the results are so apparent at an earlier point in the time sample) is that we do not know what the course of drug use would have been with other treatments; comparative data are lacking in this particular presentation. However, I will extract some comparisons from other studies, particularly using hypnosis as a treatment.

Since Benson and Wallace's drug-use data at the period of 4 to 9 months after beginning meditation do not show the high attrition rate of the 22-month data, they are presented in a composite table (table 5.4) comparing that post-period with the six-month premeditation period. (The alcohol and smoking data will be dealt with below.) The figures speak for themselves; over the 15-month period there is a consistent movement away from heavy usage toward nonusage in every drug category. In fact the increase of nonusers over this period ranged from 14.5% for narcotics to 41.4% for marihuana. Whether these figures should be

Table 5.4. Composite Table of Drug Use, Comparing Usage Before (6−0 months) with After (4−9 months) Beginning TM Practice.

| | Usage | | | | | | | |
| | Heavy | | Medium | | Light | | Nonuser | |
Drug	N	%	N	%	N	%	N	%
Marihuana								
6−0 months	417	22.4	618	33.2	422	22.7	405	21.7
4−9 months	39	2.1	137	7.5	500	27.3	1154	63.1
LSD								
6−0 months	132	7.1	301	16.1	467	25.1	962	51.7
4−9 months	13	0.7	36	1.9	151	8.3	1630	89.1
Hallucinogens								
6−0 months	5	0.3	56	3.0	665	35.7	1136	61.0
4−9 months	5	0.3	30	1.7	130	7.0	1665	91.0
Narcotics								
6−0 months	12	0.6	17	0.9	286	15.4	1547	83.1
4−9 months	1	0.1	2	0.2	39	2.1	1788	97.6
Amphetamines								
6−0 months	30	1.6	96	5.1	470	25.2	1266	68.0
4−9 months	3	0.2	9	0.5	79	4.3	1739	95.0
Barbiturates								
6−0 months	19	1.0	43	2.3	258	13.9	1542	82.8
4−9 months	3	0.2	3	0.2	37	2.0	1787	97.6

(After Benson and Wallace, 1972. Copyright, 1972 by Lea & Febiger. Reprinted by permission.)

interpreted to mean that TM programs are an effective treatment for drug abuse or that the individuals involved merely substituted a different, albeit less physically damaging, habit (Meditation) for the drug habit is not discernable from these data. At any rate, in the context of regularly eliciting the relaxation response through meditation a high percentage of individuals either reduced or eliminated their drug usage.

Hypnosis. The literature evaluating the use of hypnosis in the treatment of drug abuse is equally sparse. Baumann (1970) reports working with 177 adolescent drug abusers individually, while Ludwig, Lyle, and Miller (1964) worked with 22 patients in groups at the United States Public Health Service Hospital (Lexington, Kentucky).

Baumann reveals a serendipitously discovered technique for helping the adolescent drug user. While treating a 15-year-old, he asked her to "hallucinate" a pleasant experience in the past; it turned out to be a "high" at a "pot" party. So effective was this hypnotic hallucinated experience in stopping the actual behavior (smoking marihuana) that the author tried the technique on 80 patients. By making the "hallucinated" drug experience "more rewarding, more intense, more profitable than the original" (Baumann, 1970, p. 19), Baumann found that 50% of the patients who had used marihuana stopped using it. Since all of his patients were apparently using more than one drug, it is difficult to tease out the exact effectiveness of his treatment. He reports that 40 of the 80 patient total stopped using marihuana and that of the 42 who had been using LSD, 26 stopped and 4 reduced usage. Of the 17 patients who had been using amphetamines intravenously, all stopped, but 4 continued orally; of those using oral amphetamines (26), 6 stopped and the rest reduced their intake. Nine of 10 barbiturate abusers improved, but none stopped.

The tacit assumption that the normal course of drug usage is continuation makes a sound judgment of the effectiveness of Baumann's technique difficult, but as with Benson and Wallace's data reported above, hypnotic treatment is associated with some changes in drug usage patterns. While Baumann's and Benson and Wallace's treatments were not totally comparable because Baumann's was administered by a practitioner and involved suggestions in addition to the hypnosis, and Benson and Wallace's was self-administered relaxation without further therapeutic instructions, some data comparisons can be observed. Table 5.5 compares the two studies on percentage of change from abuse to nonuse.

As with the data on the treatment of migraine and hypertension, hypnosis appears to hold an edge in effectiveness over relaxation (TM technique), but in all cases the hypnotic induction is accompanied by additional therapeutic suggestions. These additions may well account for the percentage differences in the first three drugs listed in table 5.5. With respect to the barbiturates, Baumann re-

Table 5.5.   Comparison of Percentage Change from Drug Abuse to Drug Nonuse Between Benson and Wallace (1972) and Baumann (1970)

Drug	Benson and Wallace (1972) (9-month follow-up)	Baumann (1970) (12-month follow-up)
Marihuana	41.4	50.0
LSD	37.4	61.9
Amphetamines	27.0	42.2[a]
Barbiturates	14.8	0.0

[a] Includes both oral and intravenous users (Benson and Wallace do not indicate the mode of administration in their population.)

ported 9 of 10 patients improved, but none stopped using the drugs. For reasons not totally clear in his report, he interpreted the drug behavior of these patients as an attempt to "shock" parents and cry for help.

Ludwig, Lyle, and Miller's (1964) study was rather more limited. They divided their prisoner patients into three groups numbering 6, 6, and 10 each. The first group of 6 was given individual instruction in hypnosis; the second 6 were taught hypnosis in a group; the last 10, who were also collectively taught, differed from the first two groups by being nonvolunteers. Otherwise the groups were treated similarly in that the hypnosis, which involved a relaxation-sleep induction and deepening through various standard challenges, was part of a total drug-treatment regimen that involved nonhypnotic discussions and educational talks in addition to a variety of hypnotically suggested ploys: hypnodrama (in one group only), autohypnosis for sleep and relaxing, posthypnotic suggestions, amnesia training for certain "charged" words such as "hate" and "drugs," pleasant fantasies and uncomfortable images like a branding iron to "burn" an idea into their brains. Due to the particular population used, long-term follow-up was difficult and the results reported were admittedly "impressionistic." The authors judged the degree of conviction of the patients to give up drugs on the basis of individual interviews. Since the prisoner-patients had no access to drugs while hospitalized and came from very diverse geographic locations, the effectiveness of the patients' convictions could not be tested. Even at that, only 31.8% (7) of the total group were judged to have developed a "marked" conviction to give up drug abuse and an equal percentage (31.8%) avowed a moderate conviction. Even these admittedly subjective judgments made by the authors themselves fall within the percentage range of change from abusers to nonusers reported by Benson and Wallace (1972) for treatment by TM practice.

Alcohol

Benson and Wallace's (1972) data on alcohol and cigarette use indicate trends similar to those reported with respect to drugs. A comparison between their figures at six months premeditation and nine months after beginning meditation, chosen for the same reason cited above (attrition rate at 22 months), appears in Table 5.6. According to these figures, over the nine month period of eliciting the relaxation response through meditation, 23.4% more individuals ceased using alcohol and 19.1% more stopped smoking.

With respect to the treatment of alcohol abuse through hypnosis, the literature is scarce. This may be in part due to the generally reported difficulty in achieving hypnosis with alcoholics, in particular those severely affected, such as the Korsakoff patients (Pattie and Griffith, 1962). Field and Scott (1969) found that alcoholics' performance on a hypnosis inventory was significantly (p <.05) poorer than that of student volunteers, but not than that of student nonvolunteers. Lenox and Bonny (1976) also found that the susceptibility of alcoholics was lower than nonalcoholics, but matching samples for age reduced the probability of the differences obtained to p <.10 ($t = 1.65$, df, 70) and was interpreted as not significant. Whether the difficulties commonly encountered in hypnotizing alcoholics are due to personality differences (Field and Scott, 1969) or age differences (Lenox and Bonny, 1976) matters little to the practitioner, although Field and Scott's notation that they show a "superficial compliance to hypnosis *without the true lethargy*" (1969, p. 89, italics added) does imply that the alcoholic may be unable to attain the fundamental of hypnosis—relaxation. (Curiously, an essay on the hypnotic treatment of alcoholism from Sweden, where the rate of this addiction is probably the greatest in the world, claims: "It is scarcely possible to find an alcoholic who is not maximally accessible to hypnosis" [Bjorkhem, 1956, p. 26]. Unfortunately, the author offered no data to substantiate his claim.)

Most reports (e.g., Hartland, 1971; Kroger, 1977; Langen, 1967) are oriented to the practitioner, indicating methods, but little in the way of firm evaluation of the technique. Paley (1952) did report therapeutic success with individual patients, and Smith-Moorhouse (1969) reported data with groups.

Table 5.6.   Comparison of Alcohol and Cigarette Usage Six Months Prior to Beginning TM Practice and Nine Months After

	Heavy		Medium		Light		Nonuse		Total
	N	%	N	%	N	%	N	%	N
Alcohol									
6−0 months	50	2.7	295	15.8	770	41.4	747	40.1	1862
4−9 months	16	0.9	100	5.5	551	30.1	1161	63.5	1830
Cigarettes									
6−0 months	503	27.0	180	9.7	203	10.9	976	52.4	1862
4−9 months	222	12.2	136	7.4	163	8.9	1309	71.5	1830

(After Benson and Wallace, 1972, Tables 9 and 10. Copyright, 1972 by Lea & Febiger. Reprinted by permission.)

Paley (1952) did one-year follow-up interviews on three of an original group of five who received group hypnotherapy for alcoholism. Two of the original group did not complete treatment and one of the three who did, did not return for follow-up. The other two patients found hypnosis "very nearly the total curative experience" (1952, p. 19). However, the author himself was not absolutely convinced that hypnotherapy was any better than other group techniques.

Smith-Moorhouse (1969) reported group data from treatment within the context of a Pavlovian viewpoint. Of 182 alcoholic patients, 43 had had hypnotherapy as part of their treatment and 27 of those were available for follow-up study (six months to two years). Categorizing the effects as "unchanged," "some improvement" (still drink occasionally), and "good result" (absolute sobriety), the author found that 85% of those receiving hypnotherapy manifested either good or improved results (55%, good) as opposed to only 59% (32%, good) of those not receiving hypnosis. Even more pertinent to the notion of a hypnosis-relaxation equation are the data shown in table 5.7. Of the 27 patients receiving hypnosis as part of their treatment, 13 received only simple relaxation, while the other 14 received the relaxation plus other hypnotherapy (direct suggestions of aversion, tension reduction, reduced emotional disturbance, etc.). The distribution over improvement categories is identical. Despite probable intersubject differences in personality makeup, severity of disorder, and the like, the fundamental of hypnosis, relaxation, was as effective as neutral hypnosis coupled with additional suggestions and therapeutic maneuvers.

With the exception of a few reports like Smith-Moorhouse's (1969), hypnosis has seldom been used without additional therapeutic suggestions of one sort or another. Most often these additional suggestions are motivational in character, hoping to induce the patient to give up drinking as an indirect consequence of the suggestions. Some of these approaches involve an educational program under hypnosis, informing the patient of the harmful effects of continual heavy usage. Others have attempted to elicit the effects of emetics through suggestion, or at least to impart a distasteful reaction by hypnotically suggesting that the drink either imbibed or just smelled has a bitter taste or acrid odor.

Table 5.7. Comparison of Relaxation and Relaxation with Other Hypnotherapy in the Treatment of Alcoholism

	Relaxation Only ($N = 13$)	Relaxation and Other Hypnotherapy ($N = 14$)
No improvement	2	2
Some improvement	4	4
Good result	7	8

(From Smith-Moorhouse, 1969. Copyright, 1969 by Longman Group Ltd. Reprinted by permission.)

Byers (1975), for example, used hypnosis (administered by "hypnotist techni-cians") as a simple relaxation therapy in an alcohol treatment center. Using an eye-fixation progressive relaxation technique, patients were seen once a day for approximately one hour. After induction was accomplished, the patients were given suggestions of well-being and self-confidence. Although the author pre-sents no statistical data, the patients reported being less nervous and irritable, having fewer sleeping difficulties and headaches, and being more amenable to the standard treatment given all patients in the center—Antabuse®.

A number of the "aversive" treatment approaches have been reported to achieve quite credible results. Kroger (1977) states that "in selected subjects" as high as 60 or 70% total abstinence has been achieved. Without more detail about the nature of the patient population parameters and the treatment itself, it is very difficult to compare these data with those of Benson and Wallace (1972). Beahrs and Hill (1971), admitting the imprecision of their follow-up, estimated that "approximately half" of their unnamed number of hospitalized alcoholic pa-tients remained "sober and healthy" following group hypnotherapy, which in-cluded analytic, supportive, and self-hypnosis suggestions.

Friend (1957) did report a 36% improvement using group hypnotherapy with 39 hospitalized males, as compared to 53% with Antabuse® treatment. However, if only those patients on whom reliable follow-up data are available (28) are used, the percentage improved rises to 50%. The original figure (36%) is more in line with the expectations we have from previous comparisons between hypnosis and TM practice in the treatment of migraine and hypertension. That is, while both demonstrate some value as treatment modalities, hypnosis generally achieves a bit higher percentage of remission. This, as stated above, could easily be accounted for by the additional suggestions usually accompanying hypnotic treatment.

In another use of hypnosis to create an aversion to alcohol, Miller (1959) treated 24 patients who had been alcoholic for 3 to 34 years with between one and four "hypnoreflex-aversion treatment sessions." During the treatment the pa-tient relived one of his or her worst hangovers in a "deep trance," thus creating an "unconscious" aversion to alcohol. At a nine-month follow-up, Miller re-ported 83% still abstaining.

Smoking

Probably the most explored area of clinical application on habit phenomena has been that of smoking. In addition, it is probably one of the areas that accounts for the most practitioner-patient interaction time in all of hypnotherapy, particularly since the public awareness of the carcinogenic properties of some of the compo-nents of cigarettes. Nor has any other malaise received so much recent attention in the hypnosis literature as the treatment of cigarette addiction. Although there were a few earlier journal reports of treating numbers of patients (Hershman,

1956; Von Dedenroth, 1964 a, b), it was not until the 1970s that a number of more carefully controlled studies began to appear. In fact, the subject was considered so important that the *International Journal of Clinical and Experimental Hypnosis* devoted an entire issue to it in 1970.

Von Dedenroth's 1968 follow-up summary of his previous work with "1000 tobaccomaniacs" is noteworthy if only because of the extraordinary success rate reported—940 patients of 1000 stopped smoking (94%)! The method used involved a great deal of motivational suggestion offered both before and during hypnosis, plus specific instructions about not smoking at specific times of the day. The treatment took a total of three one-hour sessions spaced over 21 days. Von Dedenroth's follow-up period ranged up to six years and three months. No one else, before or since, has reported as high a treatment effectiveness rate as Von Dedenroth, as table 5.8 indicates.

Table 5.8 is a summary of some of the major studies done on hypnotic treatment of smoking in the last decade. As the table makes apparent, it is very difficult to find a single dimension on which to compare all of the studies. Most of the studies have been carried out within a clinical setting, so that there is a good deal of variation among techniques, wording, and complexity of suggestions offered the patients. Follow-up periods, also, are not uniform, and data are presented for periods from immediately following treatment to two years after treatment. Attrition rates vary as well, from a high of 56% in Spiegel's (1970) report to none in several studies. The percentages in parentheses during follow-up reflect the percentage of abstainers, after attrition has been subtracted from the total initial N.

The one trend that does seem to be constant across reports is that as time goes on the percentage of abstainers decreases. Even with this statistic there is not complete unanimity, because the two reports with the longest follow-up periods (Kline, 1970; Hall and Crasilneck, 1970) show the highest rates of treatment effectiveness (88% and 82[92]%, respectively). If the decrease in abstention rate decreases with time universally, then we can only assume that the rates in these studies at, say, six months must have been even higher. These are the only two studies, by the way, reporting percentages of abstention that approach that of Von Dedenroth's 1000 "tobaccomaniacs."

As with the literature on the hypnotic treatment of hypertension and migraine above, the percentage of effectiveness (20−88%) exceeds that for the relaxation response (19.1%, see Table 5.6 for gain in nonuse during the treatment period). Again it appears that methodological differences between the two approaches could account for the discrepancy. Recall that Benson and Wallace's (1972) 1862 subjects practiced meditation individually, while the studies summarized in table 5.8 involved both individual and group approaches. Even *within* one of these two modes great variation of technique occurred. The number of sessions alone varied from one in Spiegel's (1970) and Stanton's (1978) studies to as high as

Table 5.8. Summary of Recent Studies on the Treatment of Smoking During Hypnosis

	Individual or Group	Number of Sessions	Total Weeks	Total N	Attrition	Percent of Abstainers; Follow-up (months)						
						0	3	6	9	10	12	24
Spiegel, 1970	I	1	—	615	344			20 (45)				
Kline, 1970	G	1	—	60	0						88	
Hall and Crasilneck, 1970	I	4	4[b]	75	8							82 (92)
Nuland and Field, 1970												
(old)	I	—[a]	—	97	15			25 (30)				
(new)	I	—[a]	—	84	3			60 (62)				
Watkins, 1976	I	5	5	48	12	78		67 (89)				
Sanders, 1977	G	4	4	19	0	84				68		
Barkley et al., 1977	G	7	2	36	7		50 (62)[e]		25 (31)			
Stanton, 1978	I	1	—	75	0		49	45				
Pederson et al.,												
1975	G	1/6[c]	6	48	0		56.25			50		
1979	G	6/3	6/3[d]	65	0		53					

[a] No set number.
[b] Three sessions one day apart, then one session a month later.
[c] One hypnosis session, six counseling sessions.
[d] Six sessions one week apart, then three sessions one month apart.
[e] ( ) = Percentage of patients reporting.

five (Watkins, 1976) for the individual approach, and up to seven or more for group techniques.

None of the studies used the induction of hypnosis alone to treat cigarette addiction. All used some form of additional suggestion or counseling applied before, during, or after trance induction. Spiegel (1970), for example, verbally reinforced three points both in and out of trance: (a) smoking is poisonous to the body, (b) a person needs the body to live, and (c) a person owes the body respect and care. A number of studies used the patients' own stated reasons for desiring to quit as feedback during and before trance (Nuland and Field, 1970; Watkins, 1976; Stanton, 1978), while some concentrated on no longer having the "craving" for cigarettes (Hall and Crasilneck, 1970). Individual approaches even involved meditation in conjunction with relaxation-hypnosis and additional suggestions (Nuland and Field, 1970). Watkins called her technique a "concentration-relaxation technique." She told her patients that the procedure (hypnosis) was "only a state of relaxation" (Watkins, 1976, p. 382).

Despite the elaborate definitions we have developed for hypnosis, at least some clinicians recognize the hypnosis-relaxation equation. However, where the practitioner uses this equation not out of recognition of the state of things, but as a strategem to assure the patient staying in therapy—whether "for his own good" or not—we approach a very difficult ethical problem, as will be seen in chapter 9.

Stanton's (1978) article is one of the best examples of the extent to which a practitioner will go in elaborating his technique to help his patients. His method begins with a pretreatment (hypnosis) interview reinforcing the notions that treatment will be successful and that the patient's mind has great power over his or her body. After hypnosis is induced, no less than four additional techniques are applied, each with its own degree of shading and variation: (a) ego-enhancing suggestions, emphasizing feeling physically healthy and the ability of the patient to achieve his or her goals; (b) suggestions regarding smoking, continuing what was begun in (a) and further suggesting reasons to stop smoking; (c) Red Balloon Visualization, a visual technique in which a large red balloon lifts a container the patient has "filled" with cigarettes into the sky along with his or her feelings of need and desire; and (d) Success Visualization, in which various images are used to project a future in which the patient has successfully stopped smoking. Little wonder with such an array of additional treatment elements that it is not possible to compare the TM method directly with hypnosis per se in the treatment of smoking.

Studies using group techniques are no less confounded. Sanders (1977), for example, used brainstorming ideas about smoking, time progression and imagery, hypnotic dreams, imaginary rehearsals of self-control, and self-hypnosis in conjunction with an eye-fixation relaxation induction technique. Kline (1970) put his patients through a 12-hour marathon of on-again, off-again relaxation hyp-

nosis with a variety of suggestions, including enhancing the feelings of depriva-
tion the patients are going through — a kind of negative practice technique
designed to show the patients they can control even so strong a deterrent to
obtaining from smoking.

Only three of the studies in table 5.8 obtained comparative data on other
treatment techniques. Barkley, Hastings, and Jackson (1977) compared a hypnosis condition in which the subjects were hypnotized by relaxation and arm
levitation with a group that took a drag on a cigarette every 10 seconds for 30
minutes and a group that watched films on the dangers of smoking. Their findings are interesting in that, although they found that the hypnosis group yielded
the percentage of abstention indicated in table 5.8, the rapid-smoking group
faired considerably better at three-month (58.3%) and nine-month (41.7%)
follow-ups. Those readers interested in treatment might consider a combination
of these techniques with their patients.

Pederson, Scrimgeour, and Lefcoe (1975) compared hypnosis and counseling
with counseling alone and no-treatment in 48 patients, equally divided among
the treatment groups. Each patient in the first two groups received six weekly
counseling sessions; the hypnosis counseling groups had 90 minutes of hypnosis
in addition to the six counseling sessions. As Table 5.8 indicates, at three-month
follow-up 56.25% of those receiving both hypnosis and counseling had abstained
from smoking. This figure dropped to 50% by the ten-month following-up. The
group receiving counseling alone yielded abstinence percentages of 12.5 and 0,
respectively. However, another group of 50 patients who had received only the
one-shot hypnosis sessions were able to muster only an 8% abstention rate at
ten-month follow-up. The authors concluded that neither hypnosis nor counseling alone were effective in the treatment of smoking.

A more detailed study followed four years later. This time Pederson,
Scrimgeour, and Lefcoe (1979) compared additional different treatment techniques: (a) "live" hypnosis and counseling, (b) videotaped hypnosis and counseling, (c) relaxation-hypnosis and counseling, and (d) counseling alone. The
difference between groups (a) and (c) was that no suggestions regarding smoking
were given during hypnosis for group (c). In a sense then we get a picture of the
effects of just entering a trance, without further suggestion, on smoking behavior. The results are not encouraging. The percentage in the table (53%) is for the
"live" hypnosis and counseling group. The percentage of abstention for the
relaxation-hypnosis (no no-smoking suggestions) and counseling was in the
neighborhood of 18%. While this figure does not bode well for practitioners who
might wish to use an unelaborated hypnotic treatment, the figure is comparable to
Benson and Wallace's (1972) abstention rate of 19.1%.

In the main, treatment within the context of hypnosis yields better results
(larger percentages of abstention) than those reported by Benson and Wallace.

However, the best direct comparison between TM practice and hypnosis per se yields quite comparable results (19.1% and ~ 18%, respectively), and again points to a dramatic comparability in clinical application. The trophotropic (relaxation) response and hypnosis per se yield similar results in the treatment of cigarette addiction.

Insomnia

Yet another clinical syndrome has been treated by both relaxation techniques and hypnosis—insomnia. Relaxation techniques (mainly variants of systematic desensitization) have been effective in reducing sleeplessness when applied to either individuals (Geer and Katkin, 1966) or to groups (Kahn et al., 1968). In fact, when Nicassio and Bootzin (1974) compared progressive relaxation with autogenic training, both were reported effective. However, Montgomery, Perkin, and Wise's (1975) review of behavioral treatments concluded that a number of methodological issues need attention before reliable conclusions can be drawn about the effectiveness of anxiety-reducing behavioral techniques.

Two studies have compared a relaxation technique with a relaxation-hypnosis technique. The first, by Borkovec and Fowles (1973) treated 37 nondrug-using female college students for four weeks. Three different treatment groups were used: progressive relaxation, hypnosis induced by a relaxation technique, and self-relaxation, in which the subjects relaxed themselves by neutral image concentration. Each of nine subjects received three treatment sessions spaced one week apart and were told to practice the particular technique twice a day for ten minutes at a time. These treatments were also compared with a 10-subject no-treatment group on a daily self-administered questionnaire which gave indication of: (a) the length of time it took to fall asleep, (b) the number of awakenings during the night, (c) the number of awakenings in which there was difficulty going back to sleep, and (d) ratings of the difficulty going to sleep (five-point scale) and how restful the night's sleep had been (four-point scale). In addition, skin conductance, heart rate, muscle tension (EMG) from the forearm, and respiration were measured; but these measures did not correlate better than chance with any of the questionnaire data. All three treatments resulted in a significant decrease in the number of times the subjects awoke during the night and in how well rested they felt in the morning in comparison with the no-treatment group.

More pertinent for the present discussion are the results of the major measure usually used to determine the effectiveness of treatment for insomnia—the latency of the onset of sleep. Here progressive relaxation and hypnosis *both* effected a significant decrease. While the authors speculated that the common effective factor among the treatments leading to success may have been the refocusing of attention on "internal feelings," it is apparent that relaxation is significantly related to hypnosis. The two forms of treatment were indistinguishably effective in reducing latency of sleep onset. Clinically, an equation of hypnosis and relaxation emerges.

French and Tupin (1974) have reported a three-step relaxation technique for which they claim success in relieving sleep disturbances due to severe pain. Following muscular relaxation, the patient lets his or her "mind wander" to a pleasant memory on which he or she focuses. Five cases are reported in which patients were suffering from severe pain of varied origins. In each case the patients were able to use French and Tupin's method not only to gain sleep but to hold pain "out of consciousness" and to relieve depression and hopelessness.

Only one study has attempted to compare a relaxation technique with a relaxation-hypnosis technique. Graham, Wright, Toman, and Mark (1975) gave 22 college students who reported needing up to an hour or more to get to sleep at least once a week four modified autogenic training sessions defined either as systematic relaxation or self-hypnosis (11 subjects each). The instructions used to define the two treatments were the instructions for relaxation from the Stanford Hypnotic Susceptibility Scale, Form C, modified for the relaxation group by replacing references to "sleep" and "hypnosis" with "relax."

Subjects' ratings of the severity of insomnia (10-point scale) and reports of time to go to sleep and time of sleeping served as criteria. Both treatments yielded identical significant reductions in insomnia severity ratings, but only relaxation significantly reduced the sleep-time scores. Thus relaxation and hypnosis appear to produce comparable effects so far as the subjective reports of the subjects were concerned. That the less subjective (Graham et al. called them "objective") scores produced different results is, however, a moot point. The proportion of nights of insomnia reported after training was 12% for the hypnosis group and 13% for the relaxation group. *However,* the pretraining reports indicated that those individuals in the hypnosis group had 23% insomnia, while those in the relaxation treatment had 36%. Since no covariance techniques were applied, it is difficult to interpret these data with certainty; the authors chose *t*-test for each treatment separately from pre- to post-treatment. Granting the relaxation treatment significance, we still cannot assess the potential ceiling (floor, in this case) effect. It may be that 12% or so is about the best improvement obtainable with either treatment and if one group is more insomniac to begin with, it will show significant improvement and reach that optimal level of improvement, whereas another group whose members have a lesser degree of insomnia to begin with will not.

Hypnosis has been assessed as a treatment for insomnia with another patient population, and in comparison with another treatment technique—electrotherapy (Barabasz, 1976). Again subject ratings (on a one- to seven-point scale) showed hypnosis to be an effective therapy. In fact, although the author interpreted his data otherwise, hypnosis was, by group comparisons, the sole effective treatment technique among electrotherapy, electrotherapy placebo, electrotherapy and hypnosis, and electrotherapy placebo and hypnosis groups. As the reader might suspect, the hypnotic induction used was one of relaxation.

Anxiety

Further evidence for the hypnosis-relaxation equation comes from one of the few direct comparisons between hypnosis and the meditation-induced relaxation response. Benson, Frankel, Apfel, et al. (1978) have compared the two treatment approaches in the treatment of anxiety in 32 of 100 patients presenting anxiety symptoms (37 did not complete the treatment and 31 were not treated in this manner due to more severe pathology). Baseline anxiety was assessed by (a) psychiatric interview, (b) physiological measures (blood pressure, oxygen consumption, heart rate), and (c) a self-assessment scale.

The patients were divided into four unequal groups on the basis of hypnotic susceptibility (measured by the Harvard Group Scale of Hypnotic Susceptibility) and the particular treatment received (meditation-relaxation and hypnosis). Moderately to highly susceptible patients scored five or above on the Harvard scale and low susceptibles scored four or below. Twelve moderate-highs and four lows were taught Benson's acultic relaxation response, and nine moderate-highs and seven lows were taught self-induced hypnosis by a psychiatrist. The latter included relaxation and suggestions of various bodily sensations (e.g., floating, tingling, arm levitation). All subjects practiced their treatments twice a day for a period of eight weeks; other than the general suggestion of calm relaxation inherent in both techniques, no additional therapeutic admonitions were given. After the self-administered treatment period all patients were reassessed on the same measures: the Hamilton Scale for the Assessment of Anxiety States (psychiatric interview); the self-rating anxiety questionnaire, which delineated both general feelings of anxiety and very specific symptoms; and the physiological measures.

Benson, Frankel, Apfel et al.'s data make quite clear that *the therapeutic effectiveness of hypnosis and the relaxation response is very similar, if not identical,* at least with respect to the treatment of anxiety states. This is not a statement based on indirect evidence gleaned from comparing several studies using hypnosis as a treatment with several others using relaxation. Both treatment techniques have been *directly* compared in this one study and their identical effectiveness demonstrated. With respect to the psychiatric assessment, 5 of 16 (31%) engaging in meditation were rated as improved; 6 of 16 (38%) using hypnosis were rated improved. There was no significant difference in effectiveness of the two techniques. Neither treatment group (assessed without regard to high or low susceptibility of the patients) yielded changes in systolic blood pressure, oxygen consumption, or heart rate. The hypnosis group did have a significantly lower diastolic blood pressure ($p < .029$). Finally, self-rating comparisons also showed no differences between the two treatments. The one difference that appeared in the data was that the hypnotically moderate-high susceptible patients benefited significantly more from treatment, regardless of whether it was hypnosis or meditation.

In summary, then, what Benson, Frankel, Apfel et al. (1978) have shown quite conclusively is that hypnosis and TM-elicited relaxation, when directly compared on patients suffering from anxiety neuroses, yield the same therapeutic effectiveness.

Behavior Therapy and Hypnosis

It should be obvious to the reader at this point that many of the disorders that have been treated in the context of hypnosis or relaxation are those that have most often been attacked with the principles of learning—broadly labeled behavior therapy. It would not be appropriate here to attempt to present the vast literature of behavior therapy. However, it is worthwhile to note that much of what passes for the different forms of behavior therapy depends very heavily on the use of hypnosis (relaxation).

Initially it should be recognized that behavior therapy itself is not a singular, unified entity. While all behavior therapeutic techniques involve the application of the principles of learning in some sort of systematic manner in order to eliminate, reduce, or divert some maladaptive behavior patterns, the varieties of technique are as numerous as the practitioners who ply the trade. Although Wolpe (1969) noted three basic techniques—(a) counterconditioning (reciprocal inhibition), (b) positive reconditioning, and (c) experimental extinction—one has only to peruse the clinical literature in hypnosis to obtain some feel of the many subtechniques of application.

Since Wolpe's (1958) original approach to reciprocal inhibition depended heavily upon hypnotic techniques to vivify the imagining of the patient's hierarchy of anxiety-provoking situations, it is somewhat surprising that more of a rapproachement between the behavior therapists and the hypnotherapists has not occurred. If nothing else, hypnotic techniques hold historic precedence as a "behavior therapeutic" technique, as Weitzenhoffer's (1972) review and the clinical literature reviewed above ably point out. For example, many decades before behavior therapy was even formulated—much less became the current catch phrase—hypnotic techniques were used to create aversions to drugs, alcohol, and the like. Virtually all of the clinical literature mentioned above on migraine, alcohol, drugs, and smoking incorporate principles that have come to be known as behavior techniques.

The basic principle that pervades all of the varieties of behavior therapies is that of relaxation (for us, hypnosis). Wolpe himself noted that while hypnosis is more effective, even "those who cannot or will not be hypnotized but who can relax will make progress" (Wolpe, 1958, p. 141). Although this point of view is not without its detractors (e.g., Spanos, et al., 1973), traditional hypnosis and other relaxation techniques, most notably progressive relaxation, continue to be the dominant context in which learning principles are applied to behavior problems.

The communality between hypnotic and behavior techniques has been well described in the more recent hypnosis literature. Dengrove (1973), putting the historical cart before the horse, points out ways in which hypnosis can be an aid in behavior therapies, by facilitating treatment through: (a) relaxation, (b) visual imagery, and (c) easier patient management. Spanos, Demoor, and Barber (1973), still arguing the state-nonstate issue, pinpoint motivation, attitudes and expectancies, therapist verbalizations, and imaginative involvement as the variables hypnosis and behavior therapies have in common and that are critical to effecting behavior change. Weitzenhoffer (1972) had previously noted the importance of motivation and attitudes, but also discussed perceptual factors, (particularly in relation to stimulus discrimination or the patients' ability to discern appropriate and inappropriate stimuli) and the facilitation of the transfer of learning through hypnosis. The value of hypnotic techniques in facilitating stimulus generalization is of particular importance to the therapist whether he or she considers therapy to be hypnotic, behavior therapeutic, or psychoanalytic. One of the most vexing problems of any psychotherapy is the general difficulty in obtaining carryover from the therapy room to the patient's everyday environment. Here then is another area of communality between hypnotic and behavior techniques, in which the behavior therapists have claimed a better than usual batting average.

So central is the issue of relaxation, despite Spanos, Demoor, and Barber's (1973) claim that the literature does not support the notion that it is crucial for behavior change, that there is intramural discussion among various factions of behavior therapy as to which forms of relaxation are more efficient and effective. Greenwood and Benson (1977) contend that the usual Jacobsonian progressive relaxation used in reciprocal inhibition therapy does not serve to decrease automatic nervous system (ANS) function and produce a competing response to the patient's anxiety. While proposing Benson's relaxation response as an efficient and effective way of reducing ANS activity and facilitating behavior therapies, these authors drew attention to the dichotomy between cognitive and muscular relaxation as outlined by Rachman (1968).

Rachman contends that muscular relaxation is not a necessary element in effective desensitization therapy. Rather, he opts for mental relaxation, calmness, inner peace, presenting several supporting reasons and data. For example, he points out that therapeutic effects are achieved even with very brief relaxation training (this is reminiscent of the many one-session hypnotic treatments for smoking) rather than the 100 hours Jacobson originally proposed or the six training sessions developed by Wolpe. Rachman also points to the fact that desensitization therapy produces behavioral change when applied *in vivo,* where the patient is not relaxed in the usual muscular sense but is actively, physically participating. As we will see in chapter 8, Vingoe (1968) has used the reverse (cognitive alertness with muscular relaxation) in his group alert trance.

Unlike Spanos, DeMoor, and Barber (1973), Rachman did not abandon muscular relaxation altogether: "There is clear evidence to show that the use of this *preliminary training facilitates the desensitization process and contributes to the reduction of anxiety*" (Rachman, 1968, p. 164). What he did do was deal with relaxation as a dichotomy—muscular and cognitive—in which each can accompany the other or stand alone. In his view it is the cognitive "feeling of calmness," whether verbally or motorically induced, that is crucial for effective desensitization therapy.

While some may feel Rachman's point of view merely further confounds a confusing area of behavior therapy—hypnosis, relaxation, progressive relaxation, inner calm, reciprocal inhibition, and desensitization therapy—Greenwood and Benson (1977) apparently view it as the logical lead into the use of the TM relaxation response as a more efficient substitute for progressive relaxation. Thus in their view the effect of cognitive relaxation decreases autonomic functioning, allowing for a nonphobic, nonanxiety response to compete with its disturbing counterpart.

Despite Ollendick and Murphy's (1977) admonition to attend to such intersubject variables as locus of control when interpreting the effectiveness of either muscular or cognitive relaxation, Greenwood and Benson concluded: "Relaxation decreases arousal by providing a low level of afferent and proprioceptive input and thereby restricts attention to internal events" (1977, p. 341). The resemblance to a description of hypnosis is striking, so much so that the meaning of the foregoing sentence would not be at all changed by substituting "hypnosis" for "relaxation." Just as hypnosis focuses attention, so also does relaxation; just as hypnosis enhances patient motivation, so does relaxation; just as hypnosis is an effective treatment for a variety of disorders, so is relaxation; and just as hypnosis influences patients' perceptions, so does relaxation.

CLINICAL QUESTIONNAIRE STUDY

Not only do the clinical applications of hypnosis and relaxation (not presented as hypnosis) support the equation of the two procedures, but the perceptions of the hypnotic process by those most involved—the patients—lend credence to the thesis. Although it is quite clear that how one asks a question can quite often influence the nature of the response obtained (see Barber et al., 1968), this pitfall in experimentation with subjective experiences is surmountable. Since hypnotic subjects are particularly prone to both overt and covert influence (suggestion) by prestigious figures, even greater caution must be used in obtaining their subjective reports to avoid contamination by experimenter bias. One simple method is to provide the hypnotic subject with relatively open-ended queries and analyze the responses obtained by a classical content analysis; that is, one in which simple word counts are made prior to interpretation of the meaning of the data. While such analyses have been accused of offering only superficial information, the strength of the method lies in its objectivity. In fact, in the case described below the data obtained have a profound, rather than superficial, bearing on my thesis and are less open to the general criticism of experimenter bias than data otherwise obtained.

Another criticism that the experimental (as contrasted with the clinical) hypnosis investigator often confronts is the accusation that his or her data are obtained on too limited a population and in too limited and confining an experimental design to be of any clinical value to the practitioner. To avoid these possible confounds to investigation, the experimental investigator need only cooperate with the practitioner, so that both may benefit from each other's expertise. Thus the one can contribute more rigorous measurement, while the other brings a broader perspective and base of operation. The "storm" of controversy surrounding the "clinical versus experimental hypnosis" discussions is in reality little more than the inability of some investigators and some practitioners to recognize the worth of their fellow professionals' methods of observation and data gathering. (see e.g., Sutcliffe, 1960, 1961; August, 1967; Erickson, 1967; Edmonston, 1970.)

The study about to be described (see Edmonston, 1977) has attempted to respond to both of these difficulties in the process of obtaining data on the subjective perceptions of hypnosis by patients. With respect to experimental and clinical investigative cooperation, the study was carried out on patients of practitioners who use hypnosis in the context of their clinical practices. Thus questionnaires were sent to 191 fellows of the American Society of Clinical Hypnosis and the Society for Clinical and Experimental Hypnosis, requesting that they distribute them to their "three best hypnotic patients" for response. Such a procedure, of course, meant that a number of extraneous variables operated in the selection of the subject pool. No doubt a number of practitioners did not distribute the questionnaires. No doubt a number of patients who did receive the questionnaires did not return them, although their complete anonymity was assured by the system used to identify the questionnaires. Some may have even been lost in the mails. In fact, only 17% of the 573 questionnaires distributed were returned, a bit under the usual 20 to 25% return in survey studies.

The second caution to be considered in assessing the meaningfulness of subjective data, the grammatical structure of the statements eliciting the subjects' responses (Barber et al, 1968), was attended to by presenting the respondents with but four open-ended statements or questions and having the word-count content analyses done by two individuals unaware of the original experimenter's intent and by the experimenter himself. The interjudge reliabilities of the content analyses ranged between .93 and .99.

The four items on the questionnaires were as follows:

1. In your own words, describe what being in a hypnotic state (trance) is like for you. Please be as detailed as possible.

2. What, for you as a hypnotized individual, is unique about hypnosis?

3. How do you determine when you are hypnotized? For example, is there some feeling, some sensation, some change you perceive? Please describe in detail.

4. Please describe anything else about hypnosis which seems important to you.

Obviously any statement or question presented to an individual is going to direct the response obtained in one direction rather than another. That is, after all, the purpose of inquiry. What I tried to avoid with the above quesions was directing the subject's response toward the suspected relationship between hypnosis and relaxation. As the results showed, the second and third questions were leading to some extent; they elicited more responses in the different categories than the first request. Despite that, relaxation and words to that effect were used by most patient-subjects in response.

Table 5.9 presents the tabulations for question 1, as tables 5.10 and 5.11 present the data for questions 2 and 3, respectively. In response to the first question, 85% of the individuals responding mentioned "relaxation" in describing what hypnosis was like for them. When the second category (carefree, at peace, calm, loss of fear, well-being) was included, the percentage rose to 87%. Thus the notion of relaxation and/or calm peacefulness (one is reminded here of Rachman's [1968] distinction between muscular and cognitive relaxation) dominates the descriptive categories used by practitioners' patients when queried about their subjective experiences with hypnosis.

Table 5.10 presents a similar pattern of responsiveness, although it is somewhat attenuated by the nature of the query. As I suggested before, the shift in category emphasis to such things as "therapy aid, pain reduction" and "increased body control" may reflect a number of patients' concerns with application. In this sense the patients were reporting the unique importance of hypnosis for them—therapeutic application. Patients, unlike experimental investigators, are interested in the uses, rather than the fundamental nature, of hypnosis. Despite this self-centered emphasis (What is hypnosis doing for me that is unique?) the dominant word used to describe the uniqueness of hypnosis is "relaxation" (35%). Again, when the second category in the table is included the percentage increases to 38%.

Table 5.11 reflects a similar mixture of the fundamental (relaxation) with the

Table 5.9. Number of Individuals Responding to Item 1 with the Designated Content Categories

Content Category	Male (28)	Female (71)	Total (99)
Relaxation	20	64	84
Carefree, at peace, calm, loss of fear, well-being	19	45	64
Concentration, focused attention	10	22	32
Floating	5	10	15
Spinning sensation	1	0	1
Numbness	3	6	9
Heaviness	1	1	2
Breathing changes	1	0	1
Awareness of heart beat	0	1	1
Feeling of warmth	0	5	5
Individualized physiological or sensory phenomena	4	4	8
Reduced sensory perception	3	5	8
Increased sensory perception	0	0	0
Inability to move	0	1	1
Increased body control	2	0	2
Dissociation, transcendental experience	5	9	14
Increased anxiety	0	4	4
Time distortion	3	3	6
Automation	0	0	0
Therapy aid, pain reduction	0	0	0
Other	5	3	8
No response	0	2	2

(From Edmonston, 1977. Copyright © American Society of Clinical Hypnosis. Reprinted by permission.)

question-determined overtones (other categories). Question 3, by asking for feelings of sensations, leads the respondents into physical and/or physiological responses. Hence we see increases in such content as "numbness," "floating," "physiological or sensory phenomena," "reduced sensory perception" and "heaviness." But again, despite the obvious leading character of the inquiry, relaxation dominates the patients' choice of words used to respond (53%). As before, the percentage increased (63%) when calm peacefulness was included.

The unanimity of the data in response to these three questions is striking but not absolutely convincing. The major criticism of interpreting these data as final evidence of a hypnosis-relaxation equation is that the patients may "merely" be reporting back what they have been told by the prestigious clinician in the process of induction and treatment. Nowhere is this more suspect than in the category shifts in table 5.11. It is well known that such terms as "numbness," "heaviness," "floating" are used extensively in some inductions—not to mention, of course, "relaxation"—and both sensory-restrictive and physiologically enhancing suggestions are often used in treatment phrases. Does the possibility that the patients are reporting the words used in their induction abrogate the

Table 5.10.   Number of Individuals Responding to Item 2 with the Designated Content Categories

Content Category	Male (28)	Female (71)	Total (99)
Relaxation	12	23	35
Carefree, at peace, calm, loss of fear, well-being	2	10	12
Concentration, focused attention	4	6	10
Floating	0	1	1
Spinning sensation	0	0	0
Numbness	1	0	1
Heaviness	0	0	0
Breathing changes	0	0	0
Awareness of heart beat	0	0	0
Feeling of warmth	0	0	0
Individualized physiological or sensory phenomena	2	2	4
Reduced sensory perception	4	0	4
Increased sensory perception	0	7	7
Inability to move	0	0	0
Increased body control	4	10	14
Dissociation, transcendental experience	5	0	5
Increased anxiety	0	0	0
Time distortion	0	2	2
Automation	0	0	0
Therapy aid, pain reduction	3	17	20
Other	2	9	11
No response	0	7	7

(From Edmonston, 1977. Copyright © American Society of Clinical Hypnosis. Reprinted by permission.)

interpretation that to patients in the therapeutic process hypnosis is predominantly relaxation? I think not, for several reasons.

First, as has been developed in the preceding chapters, relaxation is historically inseparable from hypnotic techniques. Thus there is nothing fortuitous about the use of the word "relax" in induction procedures; it is not an accident of history. In fact, the accident of history was de Puységur's observation of sleeplike relaxation in Victor Race. Through the years practitioners have found the use of "relaxation" efficacious in the treatment of patients, as has been amply exemplified earlier in this chapter.

Second, Aaronson (1973) presented data that showed "physical relaxation" as the dominant descriptive category offered by subjects instructed only to experience themselves in a trance. Aaronson recognized the fact that "any hypnotic induction may weight the experiences of persons responding to it according to the variables manipulated in the particular induction" (1973, p. 113). Since he regarded any inductions as variations on telling the subject to "have a trance," he decided to compare the effects of his Altered States of Consciousness Induction Device (ASCID) with a usual hypnotic trance by instructing his hypnosis sub-

Table 5.11. Number of Individuals Responding to Item 3 with the Designated Content Categories

Content Category	Male (28)	Female (71)	Total (99)
Relaxation	12	40	52
Carefree, at peace, calm, loss of fear, well-being	0	14	14
Concentration, focused attention	2	4	6
Floating	3	12	15
Spinning sensation	3	4	7
Numbness	4	16	20
Heaviness	3	9	12
Breathing changes	0	8	8
Awareness of heart beat	0	4	4
Feeling of warmth	0	4	4
Individualized physiological or sensory phenomena	8	6	14
Reduced sensory perception	9	5	14
Increased sensory perception	1	4	5
Inability to move	3	6	9
Increased body control	0	0	0
Dissociation, transcendental experience	3	0	3
Increased anxiety	0	0	0
Time distortion	1	0	1
Automation	3	0	3
Therapy aid, pain reduction	1	0	1
Other	4	6	10
No response	1	6	7

(From Edmonston, 1977. Copyright © American Society of Clinical Hypnosis. Reprinted by permission.)

jects: "Experience yourself as being in a trance. Don't say to yourself, 'I'm going into a trance.' Don't say to yourself, 'Go into a trance.' Just experience yourself as being in a trance" (1973, p. 113).

Aaronsen asked 100 ASCID and 20 hypnosis-trance subjects to write a chronological, detailed description of what they had experienced. These descriptions were scored by independent judges (93.3% agreement). Of the 50 descriptive items, physical relaxation was used by 70% of the "trance" group and 55% of the ASCID group. Mental relaxation was reported by 52.5% of the "trance" group and 30% of the ASCID group. These data, with particular attention to the "trance" group, developed *without* the use of a customary induction procedure and its attendant confound of providing the responder with the words to be fed back to the investigator in the desciption of the experience. Coupled with the historical perspective on the use of "relaxation" in hypnotic induction procedures, these data seem to reduce the impact of the criticism noted above.

In addition, an example of the exact verbal descriptions offered by one of the subjects in my 1977 study may allay the fears of critics that the subjectively reported descriptions are unduly tainted by the words of prestigious hypnotic operators. While the practitioner may have originally suggested "relaxation" in the induction, it is quite clear that, once having experienced hypnosis, patients find that it entails much more than a simple compliance with the suggestion to relax. The relaxation becomes their own, with the individualized nuances and vagaries.

The individual chosen to illustrate this point is a 29-year old female patient of a psychiatrist. She is verbally quite skilled and expresses a depth of involvement that goes well beyond simple compliance. While the prestige of and the trust in the operator ease the patient's path to hypnosis, the hypnotic state is relaxation. In answer to question 1:

Being in a hypnotic trance is being as totally relaxed as is possible while still in a "conscious" state. It is a state of well-being, of not caring about otherwise troubling situations. It is a rest from "reality" which causes that reality to become important. A feeling of "everything will be all right" and "My God! how could that have seemed as important to me" (although I at least don't reach exclamation point stages while in hypnosis). It is a stable, comfortable, good, warm, unanxious state to be in—nothing pulls at one's decision-making centers, no demands are made, nothing has to be done. If questioning by the doctor is going on, cooperation is, of course, expected but the effort (and it is an effort to disturb this comfortable state) is minimized, I would suppose, by the confidence in the person asking the questions. In my experience, too, hypnosis has been a state of feeling "someone will help me now, he will make things right again, etc.—." It's an "I could stay here and this way all day" feeling—retrospectively, time does, indeed, pass more quickly than expected in hypnosis.

In her response to question 2, this patient describes the uniqueness of hypnosis by comparison to other forms of relaxation.

Unique as compared to other means of relaxation? Alcohol gets me high then sick then headachy—even in small quantitites. Tranquilizers never seemed to really effectively take care of anxiety because my conscious mind could fight them off. Hypnosis, while not introducing any foreign agents into the body, results in ultimate relaxation and has none of the unpleasant side effects. Of course, I am sure that unless the subject had trust and confidence in the operator, it would be very difficult to give in to the abandonment of relaxation.

Again we see the strong influence of the relationship with the operator, not as a definition of hypnosis but as a prerequisite for "giving in to the abandonment of relaxation" (hypnosis).

The response to question 3 illustrates the difficulty patients have in putting their feelings into words. I suspect that this difficulty is not a part of whatever general problem led this patient to seek treatment, because she makes a concerted effort and is even able to interject some humor into her response. She shows us two things: that hypnosis is not an easy condition to describe adequately, even for those who have experienced it; and that the feelings and sensations determining hypnosis are those generally associated with relaxation.

It is difficult to describe in words something that must be felt. A try: At first a heaviness when the limbs become flaccid and muscles are consciously loosened. Then something happens in the head; a distance swimming through, taking away the daily visions which have habitually caused the teeth to clench and the brow to crease. It might be called "tingly" but it is not so sharp. It might be called dizziness but it's not a loss of control as such. A *stillness* is also there. And a special emptiness. Physically, there is an unwilling-ness to move—in this way I feel rather like a statue—it is almost *absurd* to make an effort to move—I suppose, more concretely (pardon the pun), the limbs and muscles are some-how heavy (but not really!) and immobilized. In an apparent contradiction, I am also going to say that there is a certain floating feeling which however does *not* cause a lack of control nor does it cause fear.—there, I knew I couldn't describe it!

This particular description also illustrates the relationship between physical and cognitive relaxation (Rachman, 1968), which some may interpret as a dis-sociation (Hilgard, 1977). The problem may be whether we are discussing the cart or the horse; I think that the horse (relaxation, hypnosis) precedes the cart (hypnotic phenomena, including dissociation).

Finally, this patient's response to question 4 is reproduced here because it is fairly typical in content (although certainly not in presentation style) of the sort of responses this directive elicited. A number of patients mentioned the power over their own destiny that hypnosis afforded, as well as expressions of enjoyment and admonitions to try it.

The greatest importance, it seems, of hypnosis is that it enables the individual, that is, it has enabled me, to realize that I have within myself the ability, power to control my own behavior, attitudes and actions to a certain extent. The idea of me talking to myself is amazingly right! I know better than anyone how I feel—therefore *I* have to be the most sympathetic person for me to receive advice and suggestions from. Self-hypnosis, particu-larly, insures the utmost in private counseling. I love hypnosis! It's great! Everyone should try it!

CONCLUSION

In this chapter I have attempted to show that in the realm of clinical application at least one type of therapeutic relaxation (the trophotropic response produced during TM sessions) and hypnosis yield similar results. One area omitted in this comparison is surgery. While reports of the uses of hypnosis as analgesics or anesthetics date from at least the time of Esdaile and occupy considerable space in the medical and dental clinical literature, attempts to use meditation in this manner have not appeared. In addition to the clinical comparisons, data have been presented that indicate that the perceptions of patients being treated with hypnosis reflect a heavy emphasis on equating (descriptively) hypnosis with relaxation.

These data are suggestive rather than definitive. Direct comparisons between hypnosis and nonhypnotic relaxation are needed to confirm the suspicion of an equation between hypnosis and relaxation. These data will be presented in the following chapter.

CHAPTER 6

Hypnosis and Relaxation: Physiological Comparisons

In the preceding chapters I have traced the history of the association of hypnosis with the concepts and appearances of relaxation, and the similarities between the clinical results reported from the applications of hypnosis and relaxation elicited by Transcendental Meditation (TM) practice. As noted, all of these data suggest a striking similarity between hypnosis and relaxation, but do not present a conclusive demonstration of the equation.

In this chapter I will provide the reader with more evidence of the relationship between the two by reviewing those studies in the hypnosis literature that relate to certain physiological changes occurring during hypnosis that have been shown to occur in TM relaxation (see Chapter 4). This review of the physiological literature will merely be an extension of the foregoing arguments by analogy, and thus will present additional indirect evidence of the equation of hypnosis and relaxation.

The direct proof-of-the-pudding, that is, studies that have used a nonhypnotic relaxation group or condition as a control comparison to hypnosis, will be presented in Chapter 7. The reason for handling the literature in this manner is to finish the argument by analogy before giving emphasis to the studies that have directly compared hypnosis and relaxation on the same parameters. Although some studies that compare the two conditions directly cover some of the same responses as those taken up in this chapter, their impact and meaning for interpreting the nature of hypnosis is far greater than the indirect comparisons being made here and deserve a separate presentation.

THE PHYSIOLOGY OF HYPNOSIS AND RELAXATION

In Chapter 4 I briefly outlined the physiological changes that Benson reported accompanied the relaxation response. Wallace had originally concluded that

TM-produced relaxation was physiologically different from hypnosis (Wallace, 1970; Wallace et al., 1971; Wallace and Benson, 1972), basing his work in large part on summary articles of the physiological concomitants of hypnosis. However, physiological similarities between hypnosis and TM relaxation became apparent as Benson developed the notion of the relaxation response (Benson et al., 1974). During this trophotropic response Wallace (1970), Wallace, Benson, and Wilson (1971) and Beary and Benson (1974) measured respiration (decreased oxygen consumption, carbon dioxide consumption, respiratory rate, minute ventilation, and an unchanged respiratory quotient), blood chemistry (decreased pH with concomitant increased base excess and decreased blood lactate), cardiovascular function (decreased heart rate and no change in systolic or diastolic pressures, or pressures for oxygen or carbon dioxide, separately), electroencelphalogram (EEG) functioning (increased alpha production), body temperature (no change in rectal temperature), and skin resistance (increased basal resistance). All of the reported changes were significant and were derived from a comparison between pre- and post-meditation periods with a 20- to 30-minute meditation period. As I indicated in Chapter 4, these physiological changes were interpreted as a decrease in the general metabolic activity of the subjects. For comparison's sake, Wallace, Benson, and Wilson's table (1971) is reproduced here (Table 6.1).

While authors of general surveys of the physiology of hypnosis conclude that there is no stable physiological concomitant of the hypnotic state (see, e.g., Gorton, 1949; Crasilneck and Hall, 1959; Barber, 1961, 1970), isolated and more recent studies indicate that the physiology accompanying hypnosis is not different from that described by Wallace and Benson (1972) for the trophotropic response. Since the physiological changes associated with TM-induced relaxation are associated with the relaxation elicited, rather than being the results of some combination of relaxation and further suggestions of change, the hypnosis literature surveyed here will, by and large, deal only with those studies that measured physiological changes in the context of neutral hypnosis; that is, hypnotic induction without the addition of therapeutic or other direct suggestions regarding the physiological or emotional states. This approach necessarily limits the survey presented, but allows a more accurate comparison with the relaxation response and keeps us from the mire of confounding neurral hypnosis and suggestions in hypnosis. Besides, the effects of direct and indirect suggestions for changes in the physiology have been reviewed in depth elsewhere (see Gorton, 1949; Crasilneck and Hall, 1959; Barber, 1961, 1970). Occasionally, where the literature does not offer the study of certain physiological responses in the context of neutral hypnosis alone, reports including confounding additional suggestions will be mentioned as suggestive evidence for the thesis of an equation between hypnosis and relaxation.

Table 6.1. Physiologic Changes Before, During, and After Meditation

Measurement	Number of Subjects	Precontrol Period, mean ± SD	Meditation Period, mean ± SD	Postcontrol Period, mean ± SD
Oxygen consumption, ml/min	20	251.2 ±48.6	211.4 ±43.2*	242.1 ±45.4
CO_2 elimination, ml/min	15	218.7 ±41.5	186.8 ±35.7*	217.9 ±36.1
Respiratory quotient	15	0.85 ±0.03	0.87 ±0.04	0.86 ±0.05
Respiratory rate, breaths/min	5	13 ±3	11 ±3**	11 ±3
Minute ventilation, 1/min	4	6.08 ±1.11	5.14 ±1.05**	5.94 ±1.50
Blood pressure, mm HG				
Systolic	6	106 ±12	108 ±12	111 ±10
Diastolic	6	57 ±6	59 ±5	60 ±5
Mean	9	75 ±7	75 ±7	78 ±7
pH	10	7.421 ±0.022	7.413 ±0.024**	7.429 ±0.025
P_{CO_2}, mm Hg	10	35.7 ±3.7	35.3 ±3.7	34.0 ±2.9
P_{O_2}, mm Hg	10	103.9 ±6.4	102.8 ±6.2	105.3 ±6.3
Base excess	10	−0.5 ±1.5	−1.3 ±1.5*	−1.0 ±1.8
Blood lactate, mg/100 ml	8	11.4 ±4.1	8.0 ±2.6*	7.3 ±2.0
Heart rate, beats/min	13	70 +8	67 ±7	70 ±7
Rectal temperature, °C	5	37.5 ±0.4	37.4 ±0.3	37.3 ±0.2
Skin resistance, kilohms	15	90.9 ±46.1	234.6 ±58.5*	120.5 ±92.0

P is the probability of the mean value of the precontrol period being identical to the mean value of the meditation period.

*$P < 0.005$; **$P < 0.05$.

(From Wallace, Benson, and Wilson, 1971. Copyright by The American Physiological Society. Reprinted by permission.)

Respiration and Metabolism

Respiration

Whether respiration rate decreases, increases, or remains unchanged following the induction of hypnosis has not been fully resolved and, judging from the number of recent studies making this measurement, will not be for some time to come. The earliest study of this response (Walden, 1900−01) indicated a slower respiratory rate in hypnosis than during wakefulness. Using a single male subject on whom repeated measures were made during hypnotic sessions that lasted approximately five hours, Walden measured peripheral blood flow, blood pressure, pulse rate, rectal temperature, skin temperature, and respiration. He found a drop in respiration rate from 18/minute to 15 or 16/minute with the onset of hypnosis. This lower rate continued through the hypnotic period and rose sharply (to 20/minute) upon termination of the trance five hours later.

Talbert, Ready, and Kuhlman (1924) indicated from their study of a single subject that "one can expect changes in respiration [with suggestion]" (1924, p. 113), but they failed to tell us in which direction. Goldwyn (1930) did find a significant reduction in respiratory rate from wakefulness to hypnosis in 18 subjects ($t = 3.15, p < .01$).

Jenness and Wible (1937), although noting that Walden (1900−01), Kirschberg (1925), Goldwyn (1930), Zynkin (1930*b*), and Bier (1930) all report lower respiration rates in hypnosis, offered data that they interpreted as indicating no difference in respiration between hypnosis and wakefulness. Like a number of Hull's students of that era, Jenness was concerned with differentiating hypnosis from "sleep," a point we have taken note of in Chapter 2. It was his and Wible's intention to test whether or not respiratory and heart rates were lowered in hypnosis, as they are in sleep. Using eight subjects (four of each sex), Jenness and Wible measured respiration and heart rate during ordinary sleep, resting hypnosis, hypnosis with other stimulations (pain) and/or suggestions (analgesia, heart rate acceleration), and waking control periods prior to and after hypnosis. The authors used initial waking control periods as a reference against which to compare the rates during various periods of hypnosis and ordinary sleep. It is the performance during the "resting" hypnosis period with which we are concerned.

When hypnosis is compared with waking, 6 measurements yielded an increased rate, 5 remained the same, and 15 decreased in rate; for sleep with waking, the figures were 1, 3, and 11, respectively. The average difference between the waking and hypnosis rates was 0.7/minute. The probability that such a difference could have occurred by chance was .12, not significant, but certainly a trend in the direction of a decreased respiration rate in hypnosis. In ordinary sleep the rate decreased by an average of 2.3/minute, a significant difference from the waking measures at the .001 level of confidence.

Since the probability of significance between wakefulness and hypnosis only reached the 0.12 level, the authors concluded that the respiration rate in hypnosis was similar to that in wakefulness and that hypnosis is not sleep. However, it appears to me that these data are open to another interpretation. The trend toward a difference between hypnosis and wakefulness ($p < .12$), coupled with the significant difference between sleep and wakefulness ($p < .001$), may place hypnosis somewhere on a continuum between wakefulness and sleep with respect to this measure (see Chapter 2). Commenting on their own comparison of hypnosis and wakefulness, and, incidentally, indirectly acknowledging the presence of a trend, Jenness and Wible state: "Even if this represents a 'true' decrease, however, it is no greater than the decrease which would ordinarily result from ten minutes of relaxed rest on a bed" (1937, pp. 213–214). This is precisely the point; the physiological concomitants of hypnosis yield data that demonstrate a striking resemblance to relaxation.

In addition, these authors did not compare hypnosis and sleep measures directly, but used only the waking data for comparison with each. The confounding element in such a procedure lies in the fact that different waking periods were used for the comparisons. In other words, the waking period just preceding hypnosis was the comparison period for hypnosis, and the waking period just prior to sleep was the comparison period for sleep. These two waking periods were not the same; in fact, the average respiration rate for the prehypnosis waking control period was 15.4 respirations per minute, while that for the presleep period was 17.2/minute! Thus the potential for a small change during sleep being significant and a large change during hypnosis not being significant was fostered by the initial difference between the two comparison periods. Covariance techniques would have helped resolve this data dilemma, but a simple comparison between the sleep rates and the hypnosis rates helps to clarify the meaning of the data.

When such a comparison is made, we find that no difference exists between the respiration rates in hypnosis and those in ordinary sleep ($t = .15$, n.s.). The average rate in hypnosis was 14.7/minute, while that for sleep was 14.9! Not only is the trend noted in the original data meaningful, but it seems that the hypnosis respiration rates lie closer to sleep than to wakefulness. Thus the data of Jenness and Wible are much more in accord with the findings in the older literature than the authors themselves noted, and these early studies do seem to indicate a communality between hypnosis and relaxation in respiration rates.

Jenness and Wible (1937) also measured respiration amplitude. The same faults reported in the respiration rate data obtain in these data, although the two waking comparison periods appear to have more similar amplitudes than they had rates: 7.6 mm for prehypnosis and 8.0 mm for presleep. Of the 27 amplitude measurement comparisons made during hypnosis, there were increases in 10 instances, no change in 2, and decreases in 15. During sleep the figures were 3, 2, and 10, respectively, in a total of 15 measures. Neither averages were different from waking, although the authors indicated a trend for amplitude under sleep conditions to decrease. When the average differences between hypnosis and sleep are compared directly, again we find no difference between hypnosis and sleep ($t = .48$, n.s.).

Sears and Beatty (1956) make mention of Sears's unpublished research report at the University of Minnesota in 1953 in which significant ($p < .0125$) decreases in respiration rates were found between waking and hypnotic measures. The Russian literature, as reported by Platonov (1959), also indicates a decrease in respiration rate and amplitude as the general rule. Tsinkin (1930 c), for example, reported decreases of three to six respirations per minute during hypnosis (24 subjects).

Dudley, Holmes, Martin, and Ripley (1963) studied 11 male students for changes in certain respiratory functions associated with hypnotically induced emotion, pain, and exercise. These authors found no change in respiratory rate upon induction, although, as with Jana (1967) below, expected changes should have been minimal since the subjects rested for upwards of 30 minutes before induction, meaning that some initial phases of relaxation had already been accomplished prior to hypnotic induction. Despite the lack of change in respiratory rate, there was a decrease in oxygen consumption with the initiation of hypnosis, indicating an increasing hypofunction during hypnosis, as in nonhypnotic relaxation.

A more recent research report appears to contradict these findings, however. Jana (1967) measured oral temperature, pulse rate, blood pressures, and respiration rates in 15 to 41 students during hypnosis. These measurements were compared with the same measurements taken following 30 minutes of bed rest. All measures were taken in both the morning and afternoon. Respiration rates were calculated from either observations of the rise and fall of the chest or from spirograms, and were found not to differ between hypnosis and nonhypnotic control periods. As we will see in the following section on metabolism, the use of a fully relaxed "waking" control in such studies does not necessarily produce results that are at variance with the theme of this book. In Jana's (1967) study, for example, the half hour's bed rest prior to the control measurements would appear to assure that the subjects were in a fully relaxed but "nonhypnotic" condition. The virtues of this sort of a control group to assure investigators of obtaining true basal physiological measurements has been extolled by Gorton (1949) and Barber (1970). When, however, no difference is found between such a control group and hypnosis, it does not, methodologically, mean that hypnosis is physiologically identical with waking, as Jana claims. The waking condition is generally considered to be more alert and interactive with the environment than relaxation in a subject who has had 30 minutes of bed rest or extensive training in relaxation before measurement. What these sort of control groups do is to ascertain that hypnosis does indeed differ on certain measures from the alert wakefulness state and is not indeed dissimilar from a relaxed state that lies somewhere between being fully alert and being asleep. Jana's (1967) data then are not as contradictory as they are confirmatory of the idea that hypnosis and relaxation are physiologically similar.

Regarding pulmonary ventilation, some of the Russian investigators (e.g., Nemtzova and Schattenstein, 1936) have reported ventilation rates of 4.35 liters/minute, a rate below that which Wallace, Benson, and Wilson (1971) found in TM-elicited relaxation (see Table 6.1). Jana (1967), however, reported no change in pulmonary ventilation, but, as indicated, his control measures were taken after 30 minutes of bed rest; a no-change result tends to support the thesis of no difference on this measure between hypnosis and relaxation.

Reid and Curtsinger (1968) have also measured respiration rates in a study involving the assessment of respiration, pulse rate, systolic and diastolic blood pressures, and oral temperature. Although the study is better known for its findings with regard to temperature changes during hypnosis, the other findings are pertinent to our comparisons. Reid and Curtsinger used a total of 20 subjects, only 4 of whom had had much experience with hypnosis. Physiological measurements were taken before, during, and after hypnosis. The induction procedure used was heavily laden with references and direct suggestions to relax, beginning with "we are only going to relax you," followed by specific instructions to relax different muscle groups from the neck down, and ending with brief arm-levitation suggestions. In all, the word relax or other verb forms of "relax" appeared over 50 times in an induction that took a total of 8 to 20 minutes.

Unfortunately, the authors analyzed only the data on oral temperature, although they did present data representing the number of subject measurements (37 inductions over 20 subjects) showing increases, decreases, or no change in the other physiological parameters. These data, minus those for oral temperature (see the section on body temperature below) are presented in Table 6.2. With respect to respiration, 73% of the measures indicated a decrease in respiration rate, the average being 4.5 breaths/minute, following trance induction. After trance, 62% of the measures indicated an average increase of 4/minute. Without statistical analysis of the raw data it is difficult to interpret these findings, but such percentage changes certainly suggest that there was indeed a substantial decrease in respiration rate during hypnosis induced by instructions heavily weighted with relaxation instructions. Furthermore, this change is in the same direction as that predicted for the relaxation response.

The general finding with respect to respiration rate is that hypnosis and relaxation share a common ground; both elicit a reduction in breathing rate. Crasilneck and Hall's (1959) comment seems justified: "There are suggestive reports that respiration is slowed by neutral hypnosis" (p. 23).

Table 6.2.   Effect of Hypnosis on Vital Signs of 20 Ss

	Increase	Decrease	No change	Average change
Measurement during Trance compared to before Induction				
Pulse	12	15	10	−2.5 per minute
Respiration	4	28	5	−4.5 per minute
Systolic	6	25	6	−6 mm Hg
Diastolic	12	16	9	−3 mm Hg
Oral temperature	36	0	1	+0.6°F
Measurement after Trance compared to during Trance				
Pulse	7	19	11	−5 per minute
Respiration	23	7	7	+4 per minute
Systolic	19	12	6	+2 mm Hg
Diastolic	11	13	13	−1 mm Hg
Oral temperature	2	34	1	−0.5°F

Note: The 20 Ss received a total of 37 inductions of hypnosis.
(From Reid and Curtsinger, 1968. Reprinted from the April, 1968 International Journal of Clinical and Experimental Hypnosis. Copyrighted by the Society for Clinical and Experimental Hypnosis, April, 1968.

Metabolism

Because of the close association between respiratory function and the measurement of metabolic rate, it is appropriate to explore the sparse literature on basal metabolic rate (BMR) and neutral hypnosis at this juncture. The main controversy in comparing BMRs in hypnosis with those in nonhypnotic states is one of the degree that precautions were taken to obtain an absolutely *basal* BMR to which to compare the hypnotic BMR. Goldwyn (1930) compared the BMR of 18 subjects in waking and hypnotic conditions, finding that when he assured maximum relaxation during hypnosis, the BMR decreased in each case, the average being close to 4% ($t = 7.20$, $p < .001$).

In 1932 Whitehorn, Lundholm, Fox, and Benedict studied two subjects on six different days in a newly developed breathing helmet. The female subject yielded an average decrease of 0.8 cc/minute oxygen consumption during hypnosis when compared with wakefulness, and the male an average decrease of 3.0 cc/minute ($< 2\%$). (The female did show as high a decrease as 3% on a single day and the male, 2%.) Although the authors noted that the consistency of the man's decreased oxygen consumption "appears significant," they concluded that "the metabolic rate was not reduced by hypnosis, in either subject, below the normal basal level" (1932, p. 778). Their attempts to obtain BMR measures during sleep were thwarted by the fact that each time the male subject fell asleep, he began to snore. His snoring was amplified by the metal helmet and awoke him.

Whitehorn et al. (1932) considered their results more reliable and more accurate than those of Goldwyn because they had taken great pains to ensure that their nonhypnotic measurements were taken only after several days of training their subjects in relaxation. They considered such a procedure necessary to obtain a "true" basal reading. More recent reviewers have hailed this methodological feature (Gorton, 1949; Barber, 1961, 1970) and use this one study alone to justify the conclusion that the BMR in hypnosis is not different from that in wakefulness, abrogating both Goldwyn's older study and von Eiff's more recent work (1950) in which he found an average decrease of 7% in 16 subjects.

However, it is Whitehorn et al.'s (1932) methodological expertise that makes it clear that the BMRs in hypnosis are similar to those obtained in relaxation. Reviewers argue that neither Goldwyn nor von Eiff paid enough attention to obtaining a truly "basal" BMR by producing maximum relaxation in their subjects prior to taking nonhypnotic, awake, control measurements. Thus they concluded that BMR decreases in hypnosis, because they were comparing their hypnotic measurements against measurements taken in a less than fully relaxed (basal) condition. The subjects were more alert than they should have been during control measures. However, when the subjects *are* fully relaxed for the control measures (Whitehorn et al., 1932), no difference in BMR is noted. Of course this is the case, because both states (the relaxed, basal measurement state and hypnosis) are relaxation. As we have seen, and will continue to see, when hypnosis is compared with nonhypnotic relaxation, no differences appear. Thus the conclusions from all three of the above studies are: BMR decreases in hypnosis when compared to a waking, more or less alert state, but shows no difference when compared to a relaxed waking state.

Jana (1965), on the other hand, concluded the opposite in his study of 14 males, reporting that "a hypnotic trance does not alter the metabolic rate in a basal condition" (p. 308). Since in a later study Jana (1967) used a 30-minute reclining rest period prior to obtaining measures and in his 1965 study he indicated that the subjects were hypnotized after "constant BMR values were obtained," my first suspicion is that the same difficulty that plagued the previously reviewed articles also influenced the data in this one. That aside, a reanalysis of Jana's (1965) data calls into serious question his original conclusion.

Jana reports three sets of data, one for "waking" BMR, one for hypnosis, and one comparing presleep with natural sleep. When he compared the "waking" BMR with that obtained in hypnosis, there was indeed no difference ($\bar{X}s$ = 35.63 and 35.59 kcal/hr/m², respectively). However, the mean prenatural sleep reported for nine subjects was 41.48 kcal/hr/m²! This latter figure appears much more similar to a waking BMR than that reported in the "waking BMR" table. In fact, the mean BMR for the nine sleeping subjects was 36.79 kcal/hr/m²—higher than either the "waking" or the hypnotic BMRs! If one compares the BMR reported in hypnosis with that reported for presleep and that reported during sleep, one finds that the BMR in hypnosis does not differ from that in sleep (t = .745, n.s.), but does differ significantly from that occurring prior to sleep (t = 7.096, p < .001). In fact, the mean "waking" BMR of Jana's (1965) data does not differ from that obtained during sleep, according to his own figures. I cannot help but feel that the author's original conclusion needs revision.

Blood Chemistry

With the exception of articles by Goldwyn (1930), Lovett Doust (1953), and Jana and Patel (1965), little is known about the condition of the blood chemistry in neutral hypnosis. Goldwyn (1930) reported no changes in nonprotein nitrogen, urea, uric acid, sugar, creatinine, hemoglobin percent, red blood cells, white blood cells, polymorphonuclears percent, lymphocytes, eosinophils, transitionals, and basophils in 18 subjects. A year earlier Wittkower (1929) reported no changes in leukocyte count. According to Lovett Doust (1953), however, arterial oxygen saturation was reduced upon the induction of hypnosis (see Chapter 2).

Jana and Patel (1965) attempted to assess the "mental alertness and hypersuggestibility" that they feel is characteristic of hypnosis by measuring blood glucose, calcium, and inorganic phosphorus levels in 18 individuals. Although they reported no change in these measures between a blood sample taken in the "waking state" and one taken following hypnotic induction, the "waking state" sample was taken following 30 minutes of bed rest. As with the data on BMR, when the comparison condition is essentially one of nonhypnotic relaxation (lengthy bed rest), it is not surprising that no changes were noted. The authors did not actually make the comparison they intended; the comparison they made was not between hypnosis and a "waking state," but between hypnosis and a nonhypnotic resting relaxation. The lack of differences in the comparisons the authors actually made indicates, once again, the relationship between hypnosis and relaxation.

Since Benson placed major emphasis on reduced blood lactate levels during TM-elicited relaxation (Wallace and Benson, 1972), future studies on hypnosis and relaxation should concentrate on this measure. Indeed, blood chemistry changes in hypnosis is an area of study that has received too little attention.

Cardiovascular Functioning

Two areas of cardiovascular functioning in neutral hypnosis will be considered here. First I will review studies of blood pressure changes and then those dealing with heart rate. A number of the studies reviewed here have been presented earlier, so their methodology will not be discussed in detail unless it is pertinent to data interpretation.

Blood Pressure

Walden's 1899 (1900–01) studies constitute one of the earliest works on physiological measures and hypnosis. As indicated above, he measured a number of parameters in the course of trances lasting up to five hours. In his subject he found a drop in arterial pressure upon induction, averaging 7 mm Hg, followed by a gradual rise in pressure, but never reaching prehypnotic levels. However, the variability of the pressures during the prolonged hypnosis make clear conclusions difficult.

According to Jenness and Wible's review (1937), Berillion (1900) and Zynkin (1930 a) reported decreased systolic pressure during hypnosis, and Platonov (1959) indicated that Tsinkin alone and in cooperation with him found lower arterial pressures during "suggested sleep." These decreases ranged from 8 to 25 mm Hg in different subjects. Sears (1953) also reported a decrease at the .001 level of confidence, although Laudenheimer (1925) reported no change, as did Goldwyn (1930) and Nygard (1939).

Nygard's (1939) work, however, was primarily intended to test some general theories of sleep through measurement of cerebral circulation. Three of his four subjects had had severe head trauma in automobile or toboggan accidents and the fourth was an epileptic boy. Each had a section of skull removed, which allowed Nygard to measure cerebral blood flow and pressures. While these subjects were of advantage for Nygard's measurement purposes, they can hardly be considered typical. His 20 hypnosis measurements were made on but two of the four subjects and were summarized merely as follows: "The arterial pulse cannot be distinguished from that in a corresponding wake period in amplitude, or form of pulse wave [or volume]" (Nygard, 1939, p. 12). No data were offered and there is nothing in the report to indicate the manner in which hypnosis was induced. Consequently, because of the unusual subject sample and the sparsity of information regarding data and methodology, it is difficult to fully assess the importance of Nygard's work in relation to the thesis of this book.

On the basis of the state of evidence from these older studies, it is difficult to draw parallels between hypnosis and relaxation with regard to blood pressure changes. Reid and Curtsinger's (1968) data, however, do offer a strong hint that at least systolic blood pressure does consistently fall with hypnotic induction and rise again after trance termination. In Table 6.2 it can be noted that 67% of their measurements of systolic pressure fall an average of 6 mm Hg upon trance induction and 51% rise an average of 2 mm Hg upon trance termination. The data on diastolic pressure are not as clear, because while 43% of their measurements fell an average of 3 mm Hg upon induction, a similar percentage (35%) continue to fall an average of 1 mm Hg after termination of the trance. These data are similarly inconsistent with their data on pulse rate (see below) and may well be interrelated.

Recently, Benson, Frankel, Apfel et al. (1978) have provided evidence of a parallel between hypnosis and relaxation. In the context of comparing hypnosis and meditation-induced relaxation as treatments for anxiety neurosis (see Chapter 5), blood pressures were measured before and after eight weeks of the patients' practicing either technique. Although patients highly susceptible to hypnosis did have a significant drop in systolic pressure (from 126.1 to 122.5 mm Hg; $p <$ .048), a comparison between the two treatment techniques yielded no significant systolic blood pressure changes. Hypnosis did reduce diastolic pressure; meditation did not. Unfortunately, the authors did not present a direct comparison on the latter measure, but they did make clear that systolic pressures were comparable for the two treatment techniques.

It seems reasonable then to accept the generality of Crasilneck and Hall's conclusion: "the hypnotic state itself has not been shown to cause alteration [in blood pressure]" (1959, p. 21), although some room for interpretation clearly remains at this point.

Heart Rate

Probably the earliest study of the modern literature on heart rate (HR) during hypnosis was that by Hoover and Sollmann (1897), who reported a decreased HR of over 30 beats/minute during hypnosis. Nothing in the modern literature compares to these results; most studies show a decrease of 2 to 6 or 7 beats/minute.

Once again it is Walden's (1900–01) study that takes the chronological lead in this century. Measuring pulse rate over the extended trances of his subject, he found a reduction in rate of 1 or 2 beats/minute. This reduction was particularly noticeable at the onset of hypnosis, gradually adapting back to near normal levels later in the five-hour trance.

In the case of HR, Goldwyn (1930) and Whitehorn et al. (1932) agree; both found lowered rates upon the induction of hypnosis. For Goldwyn this meant an insignificant average decrease of 1.89 beats/minute from an awake control period, which Whitehorn et al. considered insufficiently relaxed to obtain a true basal measurement (see the section on metabolism above). For Whitehorn et al. (1932) the decrease was from an already lowered rate due to the extensive relaxation training given their subjects in the first place. These authors found an average drop in HR of 4.4 and 2.3 beats/minute in their female and male subjects, respectively. A detailed analysis of their data revealed that since the control period HRs did not change over four test periods, the drop during the hypnosis test periods was even more clearly due to the hypnosis. Thus in this case it would appear that hypnosis is somewhat more effective in lowering heart rate than is nonhypnotic relaxation.

The Russian literature also provides evidence of a decreased HR during hypnosis. Tsinkin (1930 c) conducted 67 studies on 24 subjects and found not only a consistent reduction of pulse rate, but one that was related in magnitude to the depth of hypnosis achieved. While the overall reduction varied from 3 to 6 beats/minute, deep hypnosis yielded reduction of from 6 to 12 beats/minute and medium trances from 3 to 7. Platonov (1959) reports decreases of 8 to 10 beats/minute from his 1930 studies.

Jenness and Wible's (1937) review also cites Kirschberg (1925) and Zynkin (1930*b*) as reporting reduced HR during hypnosis, while acknowledging Deutsch and Kauf's (1923) finding of accelerated HR and Bier's (1930) finding of no change. Bier, however, did find that suggested emotions of happiness and excitation increased HR, while suggestions of "rest" decreased it. In their own work, Jenness and Wible (1937) compared resting hypnosis with the pre-awake control period and found no difference. Even when hypnosis was compared with a second awake control period that followed the first and all of the various hypnotic procedures, the HR in resting hypnosis was higher than that in the control period. As with their data on respiration, Jenness and Wible (1937) compared a sleep condition with a different waking control than that used for hypnosis and discovered a significant difference—sleep averaging 68.4 beats/minute and waking, 79.3 beats/minute. The hypnosis condition yielded a rate of 84.4 beats/minute. Unlike my reanalysis of their data with regard to respiration, comparisons between their hypnosis and sleep periods reconfirm their original conclusion that, unlike ordinary sleep, hypnosis does not decrease heart rate.

However, a closer look at their procedures reveals some clue to the discrepancy between their results and those of most other investigators except Deutch and Kauf (1923) and Bier (1930). Data for the waking control period for comparison with hypnosis was taken during a two-minute rest period, following a ten-minute rest period. This latter period was followed by pain stimulation and then by hypnotic induction. *Before* the "at rest" hypnotic measurement period began, the subjects were asked to hallucinate four different visual images (a word on a door, a light on a metronome, a change in color in a saline solution, and a black cat) in a four-minute period. *Following* these hallucinations, three minutes of "resting" hypnosis measurements were made. Since mental imagery and emotions attached therefore are known to affect cardiovascular functioning (see Gorton, 1949; Crasilneck and Hall, 1959), it is unlikely that the heart rate of the subjects would have changed appreciably in a brief three-minute "resting" hypnotic period, in the midst of mental activity and previous pain stimulation.

The other methodological variable that might have influenced HR in hypnosis was that a metronome was constantly beating during that period. The metronome beat was an attempt to keep the hypnosis and sleep conditions comparable. Jenness and Wible (1937) had argued that studies prior to theirs had not measured precisely when their subjects had fallen asleep. Consequently, during the sleep measurement period their subjects had to "follow" the beat of a metronome by squeezing a small rubber bulb. Fifteen minutes after they stopped squeezing, the subjects were considered asleep. Although the authors did not require their subjects to squeeze the bulb during hypnosis, the metronome remained part of the experimental situation. We do not know the rate of the metronome, but the authors themselves note: "Another possible criticism of this procedure is that our constant stimulation of the subject may have kept his cardiac rate from decreasing'' (Jenness and Wible, 1937, p. 205). Not only is this a reasonable possibility, but the activating activities of the subjects prior to the hypnosis measure may also have obviated any downward change that may have occurred.

At any rate, these considerations do leave the results of this study open to an interpretation other than that given by Jenness and Wible. This is particularly true when we return to their data (rather than their methodology) and find that HR decreased in 15 of the 30 observations, remained the same in 2, and increased in 13. Considering also that two of the subjects yielded three observations of HR of over 100, and in two instances over 120, the data are not as easily interpreted as they may have first appeared. This becomes somewhat more apparent when we look at Wible and Jenness's article (1936) in which they analyzed the details of the electrocardiogram waveform. In these data they found that the P-Q interval was longer in hypnosis than waking by 0.003 sec ($p < .07$), and that the Q-T interval exceeded the waking measure by 0.002 sec. Comparable figures for their sleep-waking comparison were 0.001 and 0.009 sec. Since the lengths of these intervals are negatively correlated with HR, one would expect to find decreased HR in hypnosis, considering the increases noted in the P-T and Q-T intervals. Why the authors did not report such changes may hinge on the fact that the two waking periods used for comparison with hypnosis and sleep were themselves not comparable. As a brief example: The average P-Q and Q-T intervals for prehypnosis waking period were 0.160 and 0.350 sec, respectively, while those for the presleep period were 0.165 and 0.363 sec. Had some sort of covariance techniques been used the data interpretations may have been different.

Certainly this is not to say that Jenness and Wible's interpretations of their data were incorrect, but it does demonstrate that the results of this one major study, which were at variance with most others in the field, do not necessarily obviate all other results. If nothing else, the variable of HR measures across subjects makes clear interpretation difficult, regardless of the apparent direction of reported results.

More recently Sears (1953) reported a decreased HR significant at the .0025 level of confidence, while Jana (1967) showed no change in HR during hypnosis when compared to a half hour's bed rest control period, again demonstrating that when the control group or control period used for comparison involves nonhypnotic relaxation, the strong tendency is to find no differences in the measures taken.

In the course of an abortive attempt to assess the influence of hypnotic induction on a conditioned HR response in my laboratories, we did obtain some rate data pertinent to the present discussion (Conti, 1968; Edmonston, 1972b, 1979). The main purpose of the studies was to compare the effects of hypnosis with those of instructions to relax but not be hypnotized on conditioned HRs. (The use of groups of subjects instructed to relax but not enter hypnosis has only recently been recognized as a valuable comparison for understanding the fundamentals of hypnosis. This point and data obtained by such comparisons will be discussed in detail in Chapter 7.) The subjects received 20 trials of conditioning (pairing the onset of a 10-watt light, to which the subjects had previously been habituated, with the sounding of an automobile horn) prior to either a relaxation-type hypnotic induction or instructions to relax but not to enter hypnosis. Following these instructions 10 extinction trials were presented, after which the instructional sets were terminated (arousal from hypnosis or instructions to become alert). Since it was not clear that a conditioned HR had been established in the groups as a whole (10 subjects in each), only the data for two of each group, in which the conditioned HR was established, were scrutinized.

Following hypnotic induction instructions (Stanford Hypnotic Susceptibility Study, Form B, eye-closure instructions), there was an average reduction in HR of 8 beats/minute. Following the termination of hypnosis, the HR rose an average of 5 beats/minute. In the relaxation subjects, the HR declined an average of 5 beats/minute following relaxation instructions and rose an average of 2 beats/minute after the instructions to become alert. The pattern of HR is the same in both groups; both showed a decrease following instructions and an increase after the instructions were terminated. In both cases the changes in the hypnosis were greater than those in the nonhypnotic relaxation condition, although neither group returned to its preinstructional rate immediately upon termination of either hypnosis or relaxation.

As noted in Table 6.2., Reid and Curtsinger (1968) also presented data suggesting a decrease in pulse rate during hypnosis (see section on respiration for an outline of their study) when comparing hypnosis with a preinduction baseline measure. However, an unexplained continued decrease followed trance termination. Forty-one percent of their measures in the first instance yielded an average decreased pulse rate of 2.5 beats/minute. However, an even bigger percentage (51%) continued the downward trend after hypnosis had been terminated (an average drop of 5 beats/minute). The first datum appears to be consistent with the other studies showing that hypnosis is associated with a decreased heart rate, as is relaxation, but the latter is at odds with the former.

Tebēcis and Provin's (1976) data make it clear that although HR decreases during awake relaxation, it decreases to a significantly greater extent in hypnosis. These authors compared HR, skin temperature, and skin resistance in 14 highly hypnotizable subjects with the same measures in 14 randomly selected subjects who had never been hypnotized. Counterbalanced measures were taken for the first group during waking and hypnotic relaxation. In both instances the HR dropped, but the decrease was greater in the hypnosis period ($p < .02$), echoing some previous data that both relaxation and hypnosis promote differences that are similar in kind but not always in degree.

Collison (1970) also reported a significant difference in HR in two subjects between an awake resting period and a neutral hypnosis period. The average difference was 15 beats/minute, 80 beats/minute during wakeful rest and 65 beats /minute during hypnosis.

It seems reasonable to conclude that there is sufficient evidence for inferring that there is a similarity between hypnosis and relaxation with respect to cardiac functioning. Those studies that have yielded data not fully in accord with this conclusion have by and large been orientated toward demonstrating a difference between hypnosis and natural sleep. With this orientation, different aspects of the data become important, to the detriment of others. Hopefully, my refocusing on the relaxation-hypnosis aspects of older data will make the thesis of this book more readily apparent.

Peripheral Blood Flow

Closely related to other cardiovascular functions is that of peripheral blood flow. Although not part of the early major statements by Benson and his coworkers, the reported success of TM-elicited relaxation with migraine headaches (see Chapter 5) certainly implied a shift in peripheral blood flow, in particular an increase. In 1972 Levander, Benson, Wheeler, and Wallace reported a study indicating, in fact, an increased forearm blood flow during relaxation (waking hypometabolic state). Flow was measured 180 times in five male subjects by a water plethysmograph and compared on measures before and during either a TM session or sitting quietly. A consistent average increase of 0.45 ml/100 ml tissue volume/ min was found during TM relaxation. No change was found during the control period, indicating an increased blood flow with TM-induced relaxation.

The hypnosis literature generally yields the same finding, although Gorton (1949) offered the opposite conclusion in his review. Tamburini and Seppelli (1882) reported finding vasodilatation during what they termed "lethargic" hypnosis and constriction during "cataleptic" hypnosis. The distinction here, however, seems to be between hypnosis per se (relaxation-induced hypnosis) and suggestions (i.e., catalepsy) during hypnosis, with the former being more akin to what I mean when I speak of neutral hypnosis.

Walden's (1900−01) early study indicated a decrease (vasoconstriction) in the peripheral blood flow for the first 10 minutes of hypnosis, followed by slowly rising flow back to near normal and beyond levels until near the end of the five-hour trance, at which time the peripheral flow again fell. This finding was replicated by Talbert, Ready, and Kuhlman (1924), who found essentially the same blood flow changes in a single subject; they noted a constriction at induction, followed directly by dilatation of the vessels as hypnosis progressed. Initial responses such as this vasoconstriction could be attributed to initial anxiety on the part of the subject, as discussed with respect to body temperature changes below and in Cogger and Edmonston (1971). After all, the Russians (Tsinkin, 1930b; Povorinskii, 1949) have consistently reported peripheral vasodilatation during "suggested sleep" (hypnosis) that often closely mimics that found in natural sleep.

Except for the works in the first two decades of this century, only three recent studies have explored peripheral blood flow. Following an initial apprehension-induced peripheral constriction (see above), Bigelow, Cameron, and Koroljow (1956) noted that pulse and blood volume variability increased in the fingers of their two deeply hypnotized subjects. Although no analysis of their data is presented, a representative figure from their recordings appears to indicate greater peripheral blood volume during hypnosis.

In my own laboratories plethysmographic measures to two types of situational anxiety were taken in 12 undergraduate subjects (May and Edmonston, 1966). Photoelectric finger plethysmography was used to assess peripheral blood flow during: (a) either a hypnotic induction (Stanford Hypnotic Susceptibility Scale, Form A) or listening to tape-recorded short stories, (b) an automobile horn stimulus, and (c) verbally induced anxiety. Here we will look only at the nature of peripheral blood flow during the hypnotic induction-short story control period, since our major interest is in the effect of neutral hypnosis on the physiology. Figure 6.1 depicts the relative blood volume changes in the two groups during the 18 minutes of induction or control listening. Relative volume was computed by tabulating the amplitude of the plethysmographic pulse-wave deflection from an arbitrary baseline to the apex. A comparison of the relative volume between the two groups' average change yielded a significant difference ($t = 5.26; p < .01$).

However, this finding did not exactly support the notion that during hypnosis there is an increase in peripheral blood flow, as in relaxation. The *average* blood volume for the hypnotized group did not differ from a two-minute preinstruction measure. On the other hand, the *average* blood flow for the control group dropped significantly from their premeasure level. *On the average* then the significant difference between the groups during the instruction period was due to a decrease in peripheral blood flow in the control group, not a change in the hypnotized group.

In the original interpretation of these data May and I attributed this finding to the ability of the hypnotic induction to hold the attention of the subjects better than short stories, thus maintaining their arousal level. However, a look at the first four minutes seems to indicate that only after an initial increase in peripheral blood flow during the induction does the attention revert to its preinduction level. During this early period there is a significant rise in relative blood volume from the preinstruction baseline.

In a 1973 study Peters and Stern also found that vasodilatation marks hypnosis induced by the relaxation induction used by Reid and Curtsinger (1968) ($F = 3.192$, $df = 1/15$, $.05 > p < .10$). The crucial thing about Peters and Stern's work is that they used a relaxation control group that showed *the same vasodilatation*. These findings will be discussed in depth in Chapter 7. At any rate, it is clear that while the hypnosis data do not show complete unanimity of the direction of peripheral blood flow, there is sufficient evidence to suspect that as more studies consider this question, we will see increasing support for blood flow

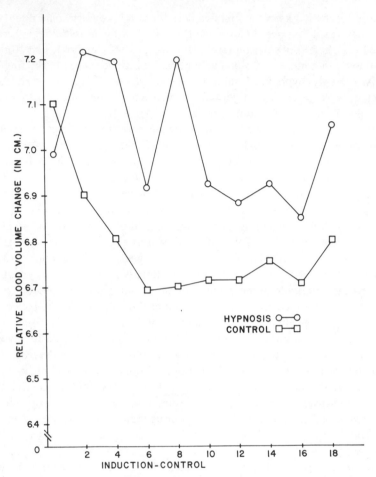

Figure 6.1. Relative blood volume changes during base-rate induction-control periods for experimental (hypnosis) and control (non-hypnosis) groups. (From May and Edmonston, 1966. Copyright © American Society of Clinical Hypnosis. Reprinted by permission.)

pattern distributions in hypnosis being similar to those reported for TM-elicited relaxation.

EEG Functioning

As Evans (1972, 1979) cogently points out, the variability of both hypnosis and electroencephalogram functioning makes it exceeding difficult to assess adequately the relationship between the two. At least since the advent of Pavlov's writings on hypnosis, investigators have concerned themselves with distinguishing hypnosis from ordinary sleep. To this point a number of reviews already exist

(Gorton, 1949; Weitzenhoffer, 1953; Sarbin, 1956; Crasilneck and Hall, 1959; Barber, 1961, 1970; Evans, 1972, 1979), and although the general weight of evidence is against a similarity between the two, Evans's conclusion that "without independent criteria of both . . . any hypothesized similarity is difficult to evaluate conclusively" (1979, p. 149) is probably considered the most reasonable at this time.

However, the fact remains that a few studies have suggested a relationship between EEG sleep stages and various stages of hypnosis. Barker and Burgwin (1948, 1949), for example, reported that when suggestions reduced sensory stimulation and enhanced muscular relaxation, EEG patterns became sleeplike. In addition, they found that the word sleep as part of the suggestions given produced the beginnings of EEG sleep patterns. Two brief reports by Darrow et al. (1950) indicated similar patterns between drowsiness, light sleep, and hypnosis. Otherwise most western studies have ruled out a consistent relationship between EEG patterns in hypnosis and those in sleep.

Russian investigators, on the other hand, report that "the electric activity of the cerebral cortex coincides both in suggested (hypnosis) and natural sleep" (Platonov, 1959, p. 61). Marenina (1959) reported that EEG changes in three stages of hypnosis (light, medium, and deep) demonstrated the progressive overall "quieting" that appear in similar stages of natural sleep. To emphasize this, she showed that EEG reactivity to a light stimulus became progressively diminished as the subject moved through the three hypnosis stages, as it did with progressively deepening sleep. Earlier she had reported a decrease in alpha density and amplitude during hypnosis, a finding at variance with Benson's notation of an increase in alpha production during TM-elicited relaxation.

Alpha Production

Using sophisticated computerized analyses, the lack of which hampers adequate interpretation of hypnosis studies of EEG activity (Evans, 1979), Wallace, Benson, and Wilson (1971) found an increase in intensity of the slower alpha rhythms (8−9 Hz.) during TM relaxation. In addition, some of the subjects yielded occasional trains of slower theta waves (5−7 Hz.), with a concomitant decrease of the more active waveforms (e.g., 12−14 Hz.). The hypnosis literature on this point does not show as clear a relationship with the relaxation response as did the previous physiological responses reviewed.

Concern with alpha production and hypnosis stems from the confluence of two research interests, that of Miller (1969) and his concern with the possibilities of conditioning autonomic responses through operant techniques and that of Kamiya (1962, 1969) and his concern with transcendent states, particularly alpha states, and their enhancement with biofeedback techniques. Kamiya was convinced that optimal alpha production occurred under the subjective states of "relaxed awakening" or "uncritical relaxation." Miller, on the other hand, sought a method to reduce the interference of skeleto-muscular mediation on autonomic conditioning. Rather than continue using curare with human subjects (Lapides et al., 1957; Birk et al., 1966), Miller proposed "hypnotic suggestion to achieve similar results . . . by producing relaxation distraction by irrelevant cues" (1969, p. 444).

Instead of directly measuring alpha production during hypnosis, however, most investigators have been more interested in assessing the relationship between individual subjects' susceptibility to hypnosis and their general alpha productivity. In part this approach to EEG functioning and hypnosis is the consequence of the very great emphasis placed in recent years on understanding the nature of individuals who are more or less susceptible to hypnotic inductions. By and large this impetus has come from the work of the Hilgards in their Stanford laboratories, which has dominated the last two decades of hypnosis research and turned much of the research in the field to the assessment of individual differences of subjects involved in the process, in contrast to understanding the process per se. This is not to say that the two lines of investigation are separable but to take note of a particular emphasis. Assessing hypnosis indirectly by assessing the personal attributes (physiological or otherwise) of individuals who respond to hypnotic suggestion is but one way of understanding the basic processes involved. Another is a more direct assessment of changes, if any, that take place during hypnosis, rather than either measuring the influence of suggestion during hypnosis or comparing a one-step-removed measure of hypnosis (e.g., susceptibility) with subject attributes. As pointed out in Chapter 3, most of the susceptibility measures (except the BSS) are a potpourri of susceptibility, depth scales in hypnosis, and induction procedures.

The studies on alpha production and hypnotic susceptibility present a confusing array of findings, as Evans (1979) has indicated in his detailed analysis. For example, London, Hart, and Leibovitz (1968) showed a positive correlation between the two measures and that highly susceptible subjects produced more alpha in a nonhypnotic period than those less susceptible. Engstrom, London, and Hart (1970) replicated these findings and showed that alpha enhancement training increased susceptibility scores. On the other hand, others have not replicated these relationships (Galbraith et al., 1970; Travis et al., 1973; Evans, 1972, 1979). Similar results were obtained from two studies in my laboratories, one of which is presented in detail below (Edmonston and Grotevant, 1975). In the first, baseline alpha densities were compared with BSS scores for subjects ranging in age from 21 to 40. The correlations were small and insignificant for both an eyes-closed ($\rho = .22$) and an eyes-open ($\rho = .32$) condition. In the second, baseline eyes-closed and open alpha densities were compared with Harvard Group Scale of Hypnotic Susceptibility scores, as used by London et al. (1968), Galbraith et al. (1970) and Engstrom et al. (1970), in subjects aged 18 to 21. Here too correlations were small and not significant (eyes closed, $r_b = .17$; eyes open, $r_b = .23$).

Paskewitz and Orne (1973) have suggested that the differences are due to situational variables, a point echoed by Evans in his conclusion "that waking alpha frequency, density, and amplitude are probably not correlated with susceptibility to hypnosis" (1979, p. 155). The place of this finding in comparing EEG functioning in hypnosis and relaxation is undetermined, mainly because the data to which Wallace and Benson (1972) refer when discussing the relaxation response are changes occurring during the elicited response, not measures of their subjects prior to TM practice. A more cogent comparison, therefore, must involve measures of individuals taken during hypnosis to see if this condition, like relaxation, increases alpha density.

The literature of direct measurement is sparse. As noted above, Marenina (1959), in the context of demonstrating that EEG functioning during natural sleep and hypnosis was similar, found a decrease in alpha density and amplitude. Brady and Rosner (1966), on the other hand, reported that some of their deeply hypnotized subjects produced greater alpha densities than when they were not hypnotized and not asleep.

As of 1979, Evans felt that no definitive study had been carried out, arguing that comparisons of alpha densities during hypnosis and no-hypnosis should be made with insusceptible subjects. His preliminary data using such a comparison looks comparable to that of Marenina (1959), in that both his hypnosis and simulator subjects produced less alpha (density) when hypnotized (or simulating hypnosis) than when in the awake condition. In the hypnosis group there was a 10% decrease and in the simulators, a 7% decrease ($p < .01$). It should be noted also that the simulator group was significantly different from the hypnosis group in baseline alpha density (hypnosis = 27%; simulator = 52%; $p < .001$), a finding also in contrast to earlier reports of a correlation between susceptibility and alpha production. What is important here is that the hypnotized group did not yield an increased density upon entering hypnosis.

Two studies from my own laboratories, mentioned above, measured alpha densities under baseline and hypnotic conditions and during attempted alpha control through biofeedback techniques (Edmonston and Grotevant, 1975). The purpose of the first study was to assess the influence of hypnotic induction on the ability to increase alpha densities through biofeedback.* Measurements of alpha density during 10 two-minute alternating eyes-closed and eyes-open periods formed the baseline, which was followed by a nonhypnotic period of attempted alpha control for two four-minute eyes-closed and two four-minute eyes-open periods. Next a standard hypnotic induction (based on the Stanford Hypnotic Susceptibility Scale, Form A) was presented, followed by the hypnotized subjects' attempting to keep the alpha indicator (a change in a tone stimulus) on

---

*The second study (also Edmonston and Grotevant, 1975) will be presented in Chapter 7, since it involved a direct comparison between hypnosis and relaxation.

or off for four alternating two-minute periods. Each operation (baseline, alpha control, hypnotic induction, and alpha control in hypnosis) was conducted in separate experimental sessions and appropriately counterbalanced across subjects. The results appear in Figure 6.2. The dashed lines indicate the average baseline alpha densities for the eyes-closed (35.20%) and eyes-open (21.9%).

Since much of the purpose of this study was to assess the efficacy of using hypnosis as a control of skeleto-muscular mediation in autonomic conditioning (as measured by alpha feedback control), most of the analysis concentrated on comparisons of alpha control in the baseline-control and control-under-hypnosis conditions. Briefly, these results may be summarized as follows: (a) hypnosis did not enhance the subjects' ability to control alpha production; (b) subjects were able to manipulate their alpha densities, but not beyond the limitations set by the baseline measures; and (c) higher alpha densities were produced with the eyes closed then with the eyes open.

Two comparisons in this investigation are relevant to alpha production in hypnosis as a basis for comparing that condition to relaxation. When we com-

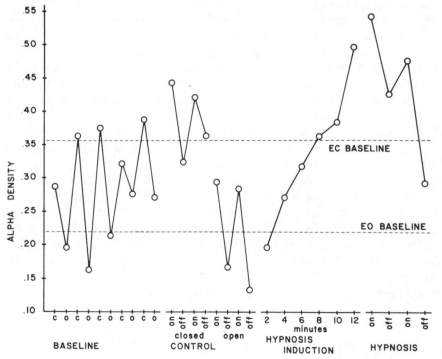

Figure 6.2. Alpha densities in percent alpha for baseline, baseline control, hypnotic induction and control under hypnosis. (From Edmonston and Grotevant, 1975. Copyright © American Society of Clinical Hypnosis. Reprinted by permission.)

pared the alpha densities during the alpha control period under hypnosis with those during the baseline period, the data indicated a trend toward higher alpha densities during hypnosis ($t = 2.22$, $p < .07$). This was not true when we compared the nonhypnotic control period to the baseline ($t = .61$, n.s.). In addition, during the hypnotic induction per se, alpha production began within the baseline range (19.71%) and gradually increased as the induction progressed. The dramatic increase in alpha density between 10 and 12 minutes of induction corresponded approximately to the average time it took for the subjects' eyes to close (9.73 minutes). Our partial interpretation at the time of the study was that this merely served to support the general finding that it was more the condition of the eyes (closed or open) that determined alpha densities than the subjects' attempts at alpha manipulation, whether in or out of hypnosis. A reanalysis of this hypnotic induction portion of the data shows that the alpha density does in fact increase significantly over time as hypnosis is induced ($F = 16.48$, df, 3/24, $p < .001$). This result was obtained whether or not the last dramatic increase in alpha density upon eye closure was included. Thus in two portions of this study there is some hint that alpha densities may increase during hypnosis, as reported with the relaxation response but in contrast to Marenina's (1959) and Evans's (1979) findings.

One of the clearest demonstrations of an increased alpha production during hypnosis comes from Melzack and Perry's (1975) study of the pain-reducing properties of alpha feedback training and hypnosis. Using 25 out-patients suffering from various pain syndromes (back pain, peripheral nerve injury, cancer, arthritis, phantom limb, etc.), alpha density was measured under baseline, training, and practice conditions. One group received training in both alpha feedback and hypnosis, one in hypnosis alone, and one in alpha training alone. Although the authors' major concern was subjectively evaluated pain reduction (58% of the patients achieved a 33% or greater decrease in subjective pain), their data comparing alpha density under the three group conditions are pertinent to the present discussion. The mere act of engaging in relaxation-induced hypnosis (without alpha feedback training) raised alpha density an average of 11 to 14% in 60 to 80% of the subjects in this group. Those receiving both hypnosis and alpha training increased their densities by 13 to 23% (82 to 88% of the subjects), and those receiving only alpha training by 13% (33 to 50% of the subjects). Melzack and Perry's conclusion that the subjects who did not receive alpha training (their hypnosis-alone group) "increased their EEG alpha output to levels that compare favorably with subjects that actually received alpha training" (1975, p. 465) is instructive.

The best conclusion we can draw from all of these indirect comparisons of EEG functioning in relaxation and hypnosis is that alpha density changes in hypnosis parallel those reported by Wallace, Benson, and Wilson (1971) in TM-elicited relaxation.

Theta Production

One more recent study reports on theta activity during hypnosis, further supporting the thesis of the similarity of hypnosis to relaxation. Tebēcis, Provins, Farnbach, and Pentony (1975) analyzed the analogue power frequency spectrum of the EEG during hypnosis, relaxation, and an imagination-control control period. The results were consistent across all measures (BSS; a self-report depth scale of one to five; EEG in delta, theta, alpha, slow beta, and fast beta ranges). Differences were found between the imagination-control and the other two groups, which the authors designated hypnosis and "awake" control, in that the latter two had significantly higher BSS scores and self-rated depth estimates. With regard to EEG functioning, the only consistent differences obtained were in the theta range; both the hypnotized and "awake" controls produced significantly more theta than the imagination controls but *did not differ from one another*. "The experimental group displayed more theta activity in the EEG, both during hypnosis *and* the awake conditions, than a random sample of subjects (who had never been hypnotized) in the awake state" (Tebēcis et al., 1975, p. 14).

A critical point to be made here is that what the authors' designated as the "awake condition" was, in reality, a relaxation control condition! The fact that they have used the word awake to denote the condition can easily lead the careless reader to an erroneous conclusion. The condition designated "awake" received the following instructions: "Close your eyes and *relax,* but don't go into hypnosis and don't fall asleep (awake, eyes closed)" (Tebēcis et al., 1975, p. 5, italics added). These instructions are virtually the same as used to instruct a nonhypnotic relaxation control condition in other studies (see Chapter 7) and do not deserve the label "awake." In fact, by this semantic quirk, the authors reached the conclusion that there were no differences in theta production between an "awake" condition and hypnosis, when what their data showed was that hypnosis and relaxation were equated with respect to theta production.

This major interpretative difference leads to a further interpretation that may also need revision. Because the subjects who participated in the "awake" (relaxation) and hypnosis conditions had had previous experience with hypnosis (mostly self-hypnosis), the authors attributed the increased theta production to either a hypnotic susceptibility factor or to brain changes occurring with repeated hypnosis. While this conclusion may have considerable merit, the more parsimonious explanation of the change in theta production lies in the relaxation that is common to both the hypnosis condition and the "awake" (relaxed) control period. Such a shift in interpretation would not obviate the authors' other conclusion, which is wholly consistent with my thesis: "We suggest that descending stage I sleep is one type of hypnotic state . . ." (Tebēcis et al., 1975, p. 15).

The important point to be understood from this study is that theta production, which is generally associated with early sleep patterns in the EEG literature, increases during hypnosis. Further, it increases significantly beyond that found in a reasonably defined awake condition, and does not differ from a nonhypnotic relaxation condition (the condition Tebēcis et al. labeled "awake").

Body Temperature

The data available on body temperature and the trophotropic (relaxation) response is particularly scanty, and essentially consists of Wallace, Benson, and Wilson's (1971) data of the rectal temperatures in but five subjects (see Table 6.1). Since the temperatures of these five subjects showed basically no change during TM-elicited relaxation, it has been assumed that body temperature remains stable during relaxation, although temperature can be influenced both by respiratory and vasomotor changes. Respiratory changes probably affect oral temperatures, while vasomotor changes may influence peripheral skin temperature measures.

The hypnosis literature is certainly more plentiful, if not as unanimous. As early as 1939, Doupe, Miller, and Keller (1939), testing the same subjects in a series of experiments (all with identical hypnotic induction procedures), reported no change in either skin or rectal temperature during hypnosis. More recently, three studies have reported unsuggested oral (Reid and Curtsinger, 1968; Timney and Barber, 1969; Jackson et al., 1976) and skin (Reid and Curtsinger, 1968) temperature increases upon the induction of hypnosis.

The Reid and Curtsinger (1968) study found a significant average, unsuggested rise in oral temperature of 0.6° F in 20 subjects following a relaxation hypnosis induction procedure. A follow-up study of four subjects measured body temperatures from the forehead, the palm of the hand, the chest, and the volar surface of the foot, as well as orally. According to the authors, the increases from all these locales except for the foot were even more dramatic than in the original study (average changes: forehead = 2.9° F; hand = 2.6° F; chest = 1.3° F; foot = 0° F; oral = 0.9° F.)

For a control group Reid and Curtsinger tested nine subjects under the same condition, except that they were "instructed to relax" instead of receiving the extended relaxation induction of the other 20 subjects. After ten minutes of "relaxation" no change was found in oral temperature. Two difficulties arise with this control group: (a) the verbatim instructions are omitted from the report, and (b) the participants were allowed 10 minutes of relaxation, while the other group was given 8 to 20 minutes of induction. Regarding the first difficulty, we do not know if the subjects received constant repetitive instructions to relax during the 10 minutes or whether they were simply told to "relax" and left alone for the 10 minutes. Thus both the degree of exhortation to relax and the time allowed for the relaxation to take place differed between the two groups, and an adequate, comparative interpretation of the two sets of data is not possible. In addition, as Sarbin and Slagle (1972, 1979) have suggested, the rise in oral temperature could be linked to respiratory changes and the skin temperature changes to peripheral blood shifts (see the section on peripheral blood flow above). One other problem with the interpretation of these data will be discussed below, as it pertains to the study by Timney and Barber (1969) as well.

Timney and Barber's (1969) work was essentially a replication of Reid and Curtsinger's (1968) study with refinements and better control conditions. Nineteen subjects had their oral temperature measured five times in each of the experimental and control sessions. Timney and Barber used Reid and Curtsinger's induction procedure *verbatim* during the experimental session and administered parts of the Wechsler-Bellevue Intelligence Scale, Form II, during the control session.

Statistically, Timney and Barber replicated Reid and Curtsinger's data. Oral temperature rose significantly ($t = 3.2, p < .01$), an average of 0.21° F (far less than Reid and Curtsinger's), after the relaxation hypnotic induction. However, these findings were due to only 53% of the subjects who yielded a temperature increase (six showed no change and three had a decrease), whereas Reid and Curtsinger found that 36 of their 37 measures showed an increase (the other remained the same). Timney and Barber's control group actually showed a significant drop in oral temperature during the administration of the Weschler subtests. As with almost all of the studies of hypnosis, there are individual differences influencing the consistency (or inconsistency) of the results across groups of subjects.

But it is not so much individual differences that direct us to interpret these data with caution as a factor that Timney and Barber directly measured, one that Reid and Curtsinger did not seem to consider—the subjects' apprehensions, anxiety, or fear of the hypnotic situation. As indicated above, the majority of Reid and Curtsinger's subjects were totally or partially naive with respect to hypnosis upon entering the study (ten had never experienced hypnosis and six had experienced it only once or twice before). Timney and Barber found that there was a significant *negative* correlation between the oral temperature change and the number of times the subjects had been hypnotized ($r = -.38, p = .11$). "The implication of this *negative* correlation is that Ss with the *least* previous hypnotic experience had a greater tendency to manifest a rise in oral temperature" (Timney and Barber, 1969, p. 129). They interpreted this finding to mean that it may have been initial apprehension and anxiety about hypnosis that accounted for the initial rise in oral temperature rather than the induction of hypnosis itself. In fact, as a further test of this interpretation, they recalled the ten subjects who had accounted for the significant findings in the first place and reran the eight who returned through the hypnosis session a second time. This time six of the eight (75%) had a *smaller* temperature increase than during the first experiment.

Thus, just as I have suggested that initial apprehension about the hypnotic situation could have accounted for the peripheral vasomotor constriction reported by Walden (1900−01) and Talbert, Ready, and Kuhlman (1924) at the beginning stages of hypnosis, so too could subject anxiety account for what many investigators had fervently hoped was, at least, a physiological sign of the hypnotic condition. At the very least, caution is required in the interpretation of these oral temperature data.

The same sort of criticism, of the possibility of initial subject anxiety, is a consideration with the data of Jackson, Barkley, and Pashko (1976). These authors used 33 subjects recruited from a psychology class, equally divided them among three conditions ("neutral hypnosis," high motivation, and no treatment), and measured their oral temperature before and after the three instructional sets. The reason for placing quotation marks around the words "neutral hypnosis" in this case is that the instructions used involved relaxation, finger twitching, hand-palm warming, and hand levitation. While the first and last elements may be similar to those used by Reid and Curtsinger (1968), no detail is offered, and it would seem that a suggestion of hand warming in a study of body temperature hardly qualifies the induction for the title of "neutral."

As with the two previously outlined studies, a significantly increased oral temperature was reported, the average change being 0.13° F (even less than that reported by Timney and Barber, 1969). Increases were found in 9 of the 11 experimental subjects and 2 and 3 of the subjects in the other groups, respectively. As implied, subject anxiety may have been a factor in the findings, as might have another element that appears in all three of these works—subject movement during the latter stages of the induction. All three studies ended their induction procedures with a hand levitation procedure, which demanded physical activity of the subjects. Physical movement was not required of the various control groups (Timney and Barber's control group was mentally active). Physical activity itself may result in body temperature changes, and could have played a part in the results reported by Reid and Curtsinger (1968), Timney and Barber (1969), and Jackson et al. (1976).

That body temperature increases with hypnosis (unlike the lack of a change reported with TM-elicited relaxation) is not a consistent recent finding is apparent in two other studies. Although reporting 8 of 15 subjects (53%) showing an increase in oral temperature averaging 0.2° F (greater than that reported by Jackson et al., 1976), Jana (1967) was unable to find a significant change between a nonhypnotic rest period and hypnosis. (See the section on respiratory changes above.) No change was also reported by Cogger and Edmonston (1971) in the context of group hypnosis. Since this latter study involved a direct comparison with nonhypnotic relaxation, it will be discussed more fully in the next chapter. It is sufficient to note here that the procedures used were a combination of the Reid and Curtsinger induction and the Timney and Barber measurement sequence.

Most of the work on changes in *skin* temperature, with the exception of those reported by Reid and Curtsinger (1968), have measured responsivity to suggestions of heat and/or cold rather than just to hypnotic induction. Since my concern is with the comparability of relaxation and hypnosis without further confounding suggestions, these studies will not be reviewed here except to note that some report no skin temperature changes to suggestions of warmth and cold during hypnosis (Tebēcis and Provins, 1976; Peters et al., 1973) while others (Maslach et al., 1972) report significant changes in the direction suggested.

One study of skin temperature should be noted here, although it will be discussed thoroughly in Chapter 7. Peters and Stern (1973) found that while skin temperature does increase during hypnosis, it does so *no more than that during a nonhypnotic relaxation control* period. With all skin temperature studies, however, the reader must note where the measurement was taken, for, as noted above in the studies on peripheral blood flow, differential blood flow will affect a variety of measures. Skin temperature measurements taken on the hands may be particularly affected by blood flow patterns occurring naturally during hypnosis. What happens to body temperature during hypnosis and during relaxation is not clearly resolved, although it appears, when all factors are considered, that body temperature may rise during both (see Chapter 7).

Electrodermal Measures

Electrodermal changes have been one of the favorite physiological measures of psychologists for decades. Studies have investigated (a) basal skin resistance (or its reciprocal, conductance), which generally demonstrates the relative arousal level of the subjects in that increased arousal or alertness is associated with decreased skin resistance (or increased skin conductance) to the passage of an imperceptible current, (b) electrodermal orienting responses (EDORs) of changes (usually decreases) in ongoing measures of skin resistance to internal or external stimuli, and (c) electrodermal spontaneous fluctuations (EDSFs) of changes in skin resistance or conductance measures due to unknown stimuli. The relationship between alertness and electrodermal measures has attracted the attention of investigators interested in correlates of hypnosis.

However, as in the case of the physiological responses reviewed above, the hope of establishing a stable index of hypnosis in electrodermal measures has not been fully realized.

Basal Resistance and EDORs

The early studies of basal skin resistance were equivocal. Levine (1930) found no evidence of a change in skin resistance during hypnosis, while Brown (1935) and Estabrooks (1930) observed a decrease in resistance with hypnosis, the latter finding that this response eventually generalized to the operator alone. Davis and

Kantor (1933) found both a decrease and an increase depending upon whether the subjects were in "active" or "passive" hypnosis, respectively.

The last two decades have not produced exactly unanimous agreement on the vagaries of basal resistance during hypnosis, but at least the studies offered are better controlled than their predecessors. In his unpublished study Sears (1953) reported a significant decrease in "galvanic skin response" (change in basal resistance associated with stimuli) at the .0025 level of confidence. In a second study (Sears and Beatty, 1956) no difference between hypnosis and waking was found. However, in this study galvanic skin responses (GSRs) were recorded during a series of questions regarding the recall of a group of objects that had previously been viewed. In addition, direct comparisons between the two conditions could not be made due to the slowness with which the subjects responded when hypnotized. Unfortunately, neither of Sears's studies reported information on basal resistance directly.

Using six "good" hypnotic subjects, Barber and Coules (1959) measured skin conductance before, during, and after hypnotic induction and during various hypnotic tests (analgesia, hallucinations, age regression) and found essentially no change in the group during hypnosis. During suggestion, however, they noted that "active" suggestions elicited increases in skin conductance, while "passive" suggestions yielded decreases in skin conductance. Since the hypnotic induction used in the investigation was one of relaxation, one would have expected the conductance to decrease in accord with the concomitance shown between the subjects' level of arousal and conductance in the rest of the study. Since it did not, Barber and Coules interpreted this finding as demonstrating that "good" hypnotic subjects do not need a hypnotic induction to be prepared to respond to further hypnotic suggestions. Such an interpretation appears to imply that the skin conductance of "good" subjects is at the level one would expect after an induction in naive or "bad" subjects. Such a comparison was not made, but the rest of the data imply that the skin conductance of the subjects reflects their rate of general activation whether or not a hypnotic induction has been presented. If this is the case, then skin conductance should reflect the degree of compliance with relaxation hypnosis instructions and show a downward trend with unselected subjects. One indication that a more detailed look at skin conductance is warranted was the fact that at the termination of hypnosis, all of the subjects showed a rise in skin conductance (drop in resistance), four of the six of which were quite dramatic (from 6 to 14 microhms).

The same sort of dramatic change in apparent skin resistance upon termination of hypnosis was reported by Stern, Edmonston, Ulett, and Levitsky (1963) in a study of hypnotically induced amnesia. Adaptation curves for the EDOR were generated by seven subjects under sequential conditions of hypnosis, hypnotic amnesia, hypnosis after terminating amnesia, posthypnotic amnesia, and post-posthypnotic amnesia. Seven equally hypnotizable control subjects were also tested under the same conditions except that instead of being hypnotized, they were instructed to be comfortable but to remain fully awake and alert. Resting resistance levels were measured 21 times during the experiment and appear in Figure 6.3. While there was no remarkable change in resistance as a function of becoming hypnotized, there was a trend toward a consistent increase in resistance as the hypnotic session progressed. This trend is not seen in the progressive skin resistance of the control group, who became progressively more alert during the hypnosis control period and returned to their pretesting level before the end of the test period.

What was most striking about these data (and similar to that seen in Barber and Coules's article) is the dramatic drop in basal skin resistance upon termination of hypnosis, followed quickly by a rise again to the level noted during hypnosis. Barber and Coules (1959) attribute such a change to the opening of the eyes and the light stimulation to which the subject is thereby exposed. Had this been the case, the resistances should have stayed at their initial posthypnosis

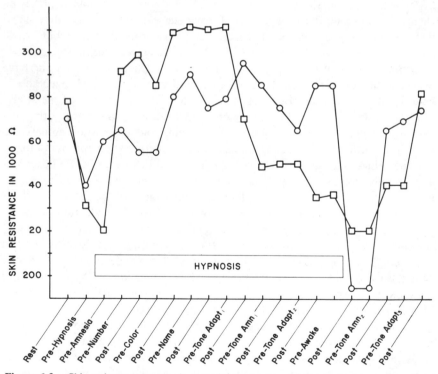

Figure 6.3.   Skin resistance measures in control and experimental groups at various points during the experiment. (Circles indicate hypnotic subjects; squares indicate control subjects.) (From Stern et al., 1963. Copyright 1963 by the American Psychological Association. Reprinted by permission.)

low levels because the subjects' eyes were open from the termination of hypnosis through the remaining test periods. Instead they quickly increased again, showing that if the visual stimulation created the dramatic drop in resistance, it had only a momentary effect.

On the other hand, some readers may be tempted to interpret the rapid decrease and then increase in skin resistance in the Stern et al. (1963) study as indicating that the subjects reenter hypnosis for the posthypnosis test period. However, the resistance of the control subjects seem to negate such an interpretation. Regardless of the explanation offered, it does appear that there are changes occurring in the basal skin resistance (conductance) that relate, in some way, to the state of the subject, including the presence or absence of a hypnotic condition.

The work of Tart (1963) further exemplifies this interpretation and again replicates the finding of a dramatic decrease in skin resistance upon the termination of hypnosis. Tart tested the concordance between basal skin resistance and hypnotic depth in 10 subjects carefully selected for hypnotic ability. Following two training sessions, each subject participated in one session of hypnotic dreams and one of sleep dreams. To ascertain the hypnotic depth of the subjects in relation to their self-reports, Tart tested for both hypnotic dreaming during the experimental sessions and posthypnotic amnesia for the experimental sessions. The average basal skin resistance of the subjects during the dream sessions is shown in Figure 6.4. Several points are noteworthy. First, there is a progressive increase in skin resistance during hypnotic induction (as during sleep onset), which consisted of a quick induction signal taught in a previous training session. Second, just as Barber and Coules (1959) would have predicted, the resistance drops during the hypnosis, as the subjects are required to participate actively in the process with an arm-rotation suggestion. Such a change is paralleled by the sleep session, further indicating that skin resistances or conductances reflect the arousal level of the subject in or out of hypnosis. Third, as indicated above, there is the repeat of the dramatic drop in resistance at hypnotic (or sleep) termination mentioned by Barber and Coules and presented by Stern et al. (1963). Finally, upon rehypnotization, the skin resistance of the subjects again displays a progressive increase.

Tart's main consideration was to explore the concomitant variation of basal skin resistance with subjectively evaluated hypnotic depth, which his data demonstrated. In addition, he showed that the sequence of skin resistance changes in hypnosis closely parallels those in sleep ($\rho = .96$), and, more important, "that BSR shows a general tendency to rise during hypnosis" (Tart, 1963, p. 91).

This same result, a tendency of the basal skin resistance to rise during hypnosis, was also demonstrated by Edmonston and Pessin (1966) in the context of an elaborate study on the influence of hypnosis on various forms of learning.

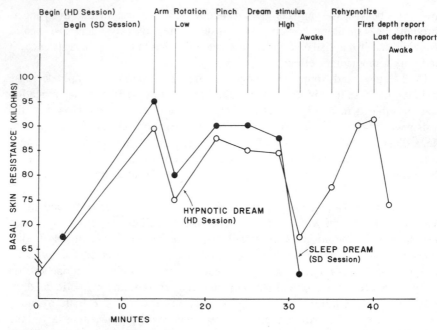

Figure 6.4.   Average basal skin resistance for all 10 subjects. (From Tart, 1963. Reprinted from the April, 1963 International Journal of Clinical and Experimental Hypnosis. Copyrighted by the Society for Clinical and Experimental Hypnosis, April, 1963.

Twenty-one subjects participated in three sessions in which measures were made on five learning tasks (meaningful material, random shapes, syllogisms, memory for digits, and coding), arm levitation, eye-closure time, and electrodermal activity. Basal skin resistances of a group who experienced a standard eye-closure induction procedure and a group instructed to sit quietly for a time period equal to the hypnotic induction were compared. The basal resistance for both groups showed a significant increase when compared to a nonhypnotic control period $(F = 20.21, p < .001)$, and a progressive increase over time for the hypnosis periods $(F = 12.74, p < .001)$. *However,* the hypnosis group did not differ in this measure from the nonhypnotized control group. Whether this particular study is at variance with those just reviewed is not certain, for if skin resistance does reflect the state of the organism, regardless of the presence or absence of hypnosis, then the data could be interpreted to mean that the control group had become as relaxed as the hypnosis group, and had they been instructed to be "alert" differences would, in fact, have been found. Regardless, the introduction of a relaxation eye-closure induction was accompanied by increasing basal skin resistance. As will be seen in the next chapter, that is what is expected, provided the control group used can reasonably be said to have been relaxed. In this case, however, the uniqueness of such a change for hypnosis is in doubt. It is this point, not the direction of basal skin resistance during hypnosis, that is moot in my and Pessin's (1966) report.

Pessin, Plapp, and Stern (1968) also measured basal skin resistance (as well as orienting responses and spontaneous fluctuations) while studying the attentional qualities of hypnosis. They opined that hypnosis is partially a state of concentrated attention, that should, like other such states, be denoted by a lessening of skin fluctuations (SFs) and EDORs, but not necessarily an increase in basal skin resistance, as one finds in sleep and relaxation. Their findings met their expectations, except that their data on basal resistance, coupled with the nature of their control conditions, leaves some room for interpretation. Splitting 40 subjects among four groups, the authors gave a relaxation, eye-closure hypnotic induction (Stanford Hypnotic Susceptibility Scale, Form A) to two groups and instructions to become relaxed, in a comfortable position (with eyes open), to the other two. One of each of these pairs of groups (hypnosis and nonhypnotic) received further instructions to concentrate their attention on either a visual (a picture) or an auditory (a series of tones) stimulus. The series of tones was presented to all groups and the electrodermal adaptation to the tone was recorded. In this manner the effects of hypnotic instructions and attentional sets on EDOR adaptation to a novel stimulus could be assessed. Prior to these measurements, basal resistance and SFs were measured during a *15-minute rest period* that followed both the hypnosis and the instructions to relax.

With respect to the basal skin resistance, the authors report no significant differences between hypnosis and nonhypnotic groups during the rest period, as measured by point-by-point comparisons (U-tests) of the two every three minutes. This result is not surprising, considering the fact that both groups were measured during a *rest* period, following instructions to become relaxed (one hypnotic and the other nonhypnotic). Thus, while they report no difference between the two groups, these findings are not inconsistent with the proposition that basal skin resistance during hypnosis is similar to that found in nonhypnotic relaxation. In fact, their graph of these data (see Figure 6.5) appears to reveal a progressive increase in resistance during the rest period. Statistical analysis for such a trend was not reported. The real puzzle in Pessin, Plapp, and Stern's data is not the similarity between the two groups, but that the hypnosis groups appear to have a lower basal resistance overall than the control groups. The authors make mention of this observation, but since they do not comment on any significance regarding this aspect of the data, intersubject variability on the measure must have kept the apparent difference from being a true difference.

The most recent study measuring basal resistance of a hypnosis and a nonhypnotized control group is that by Tebēcis and Provins (1976), outlined above in the section on heart rate. These authors also took their measures during either a relaxation-hypnosis or an awake-relaxed period, counterbalanced with the subjects as their own controls in two 40-minute experimental sessions (20

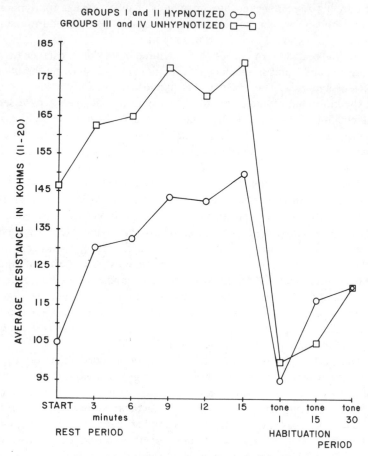

Figure 6.5. Basal resistance for hypnotized and non-hypnotized groups during the rest and habituation periods. (From Pessin, Plapp, and Stern, 1968. Copyright © American Society of Clinical Hypnosis. Reprinted by permission.)

minutes each for hypnosis-relaxed and awake-relaxed conditions). The data showed that "mean skin resistance increased progressively throughout the two consecutive 20-min. recording periods" (Tebēcis and Provins, 1976, p. 255), and that for both the hypnosis and the awake-relaxed periods the mean resistance at the end of the test period was significantly greater ($p < .05$) than at the start.

Both Pessin et al.'s and Tebēcis and Provine's studies touch on a major point to be elaborated in chapter 7:—With the appropriate control group comparisons—that is, with a relaxed but not hypnotized control group—the differences in various measures between hypnosis and "controls" wash out. No differences, in these instances, are exactly what should be predicted, if hypnosis is basically and fundamentally similar to relaxation.

The sparse data from the nonhypnotic (TM-induced) relaxation literature also indicate an increase in basal skin resistance as relaxation takes place. This is seen in Table 6.1 from Wallace, Benson, and Wilson (1971), and in works such as that by Mathews and Gelder (1969), who, in the second of two studies of relaxation treatment on phobic patients, found a significant decrease in skin conductance during relaxation as compared to a control group not instructed in relaxation. Just as with the hypnosis literature, such findings are not totally consistent, for Mathews and Gelder (1969) did not find a similar result in a previous study of 10 phobic patients.

Spontaneous Fluctuations

Although there is some controversy with respect to the origins of EDSFs (see Pessin et al., 1968), the general view is that there are changes in the basal skin resistance in response to unidentifiable stimuli, internal or external. A reduction in the number of EDSFs is taken as indication that the individual is less responsive to extraneous stimuli in the environment, as is the case in sleep.

However, Johnson and Lubin (1966) showed that spontaneous electrodermal activity is not uniform across all stages of sleep. They found that it is least frequent in Stage 1, but in Stages 3 and 4 it increases significantly over both Stage 1 sleep and wakefulness. These data appear to support the interpretation that the quantity of EDSFs indicates a focus of attention rather than a general, and progressive, response to ensuing relaxation. Amadeo and Shagass (1963) similarly felt hypnosis to be a focusing of attention when they found a reduction of rapid eye movements (REMs) during hypnosis. However, both of these sets of data (few EDSFs and reduced REMs) may indicate the resemblance of hypnosis to Stage 1 sleep, as suggested by Tebēcis et al.'s (1975) data on EEG theta activity. Whether the reduction in EDSFs is due to a focusing of attention on particular stimuli to the exclusion of others or a more general response system change accompanying relaxation and eventual sleep is still in debate, although it should be recognized that these two alternatives are not necessarily mutually exclusive.

Benson and his colleagues have not measured EDSFs with respect to the TM-induced relaxation response, although others in the field of relaxation and desensitization training have. One example is the two studies of phobic patients by Mathews and Gelder (1969) mentioned above. In the first they found a trend toward a greater reduction of EDSFs in the group that had received relaxation training (á la Jacobson), compared to another group who engaged in time-equated discussion sessions with the therapist. In the second study, patients taught relaxation yielded significantly fewer ($F = 8.1, p < .025$) EDSFs during and immediately after the instruction period than a control group instructed to "rest but not attempt to relax in the way that had been taught" (Mathews and Gelder, 1969, p. 5).

Unlike the literature on basal skin resistance (conductance), the findings on

EDSFs during hypnosis are much more uniform. By and large hypnotized groups show a reduction of EDSFs that is significantly different from the EDSFs of usual control groups (awake, uninstructed time-control, listening to nonemotional material, and the like) and remarkably similar to the appropriate control group of nonhypnotic relaxation.

One of the earliest notations of measuring electrodermal variability during hypnosis was in the study by Stern, Edmonston, Ulett, and Levitsky (1963) of the effects of hypnotic amnesia on EDR habituation. As noted before, the basal resistance results showed some peculiarities, which implied an effect of the hypnotic instructions. Variability of EDSFs was also evaluated, with the following conclusion: "During hypnosis, our experimental subjects demonstrated less EDR variability than did our control subjects during a similar, but nonhypnotic, period $(F = 6.45, p < .005)$" (Stern et al., 1963, p. 401). Thus the level of skin resistance made hypnosis appear to be more of an active process, while the variability of this measure indicated "a passive process." A similar discrepancy between these two electrodermal measures reported by Pessin, Plapp, and Stern (1968) is discussed below.

The one study that did not find a difference in EDSFs between a group receiving an eye-closure hypnotic induction and what was thought to be a usual control group (uninstructed time-control) was by Edmonston and Pessin (1966). We measured EDSFs during an arm-levitation (nonhypnotic) period before and after instructions and during the instruction period. No group differences were found, although there was a significant reduction in EDSFs following the instruction period *for both groups* $(t = 2.49; p < .01)$. A strict interpretation of this finding is that the two groups did not differ despite the fact that one had received hypnotic instructions and the other had not, and that hypnosis is not similar to relaxation on this measure. On the other hand, it might be said that the control group relaxed as much as the hypnotized group and therefore no differences were found. The latter view, however, is simply *post hoc* speculation (the control subjects were not queried concerning their degree of relaxation), and for the moment the finding must be taken as the only data not compatible with the rest of the findings regarding EDSFs and hypnosis.

In the context of investigating electrodermal correlates of hypnotic depth, O'Connell and Orne (1968) also reported a reduction in spontaneous activity during hypnosis. Figure 6.6 depicts an example of the change in EDSFs during hypnosis in "a highly electrodermally responsive subject." The virtual total lack of EDSFs during hypnosis in the record may be attributed either to the fact that their 51 subjects were all experienced in hypnosis and may not have had to contend with the apprehension about hypnosis that some subjects experiencing it for the first time do (see discussion of body temperature above) or the negative correlation between EDSFs and hypnotic susceptibility as reported by Plapp (1967). O'Connell and Orne (1962) had reported similar findings in an earlier study of the origins of bioelectric changes during hypnosis.

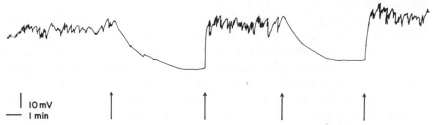

Figure 6.6.   Endosomatic electrodermal activity during two periods of passive hypnotic induction. Note spontaneous activity during intervening waking periods. (From O'Connell and Orne, 1968. Reprinted with permission from the Journal of Psychiatric Research, vol. 8. Copyright 1968, Pergamon Press, Ltd.

Pessin, Plapp, and Stern (1968) also reported not only a significant difference in the mean number of EDSFs between their hypnotized and their nonhypnotized subjects ($p < .025$) but a progressive reduction in EDSFs over time. These authors interpret this finding, coupled with their findings of no difference between the groups on basal skin resistance, to mean that hypnosis is more of a redirection of attention than "heightened relaxation." Their view is that if relaxation were paramount, then *both* measures would have shown a difference between the groups; a difference in one without the other led them to conclude redirected attention rather than relaxation. However, my reinterpretation of the basal resistance data raises the relaxation issue even in the context of their data.

The nonsignificance of the basal skin resistance data can be associated with the nature of the period in which both groups were measured—a rest period. This might indicate that when subjects are resting their basal resistance is not dissimilar from when it has been suggested to them that they are in a deep state of relaxation (hypnosis). However, as I have pointed out in the review of some of the clinical literature, hypnotic instruction may be more effective, but this effectiveness is not reflected in the basal resistance measure but in another electrodermal measure—EDSFs. Thus two groups, one hypnotically relaxed and the other resting quietly, may yield similar basal measures but different EDSFs measures. Even the attentional factor to which Pessin, Plapp, and Stern attribute their results may be accounted for by the state of their subjects—relaxed.

Thus the interpretation of the hypnotized subject as being more vigilant and less responsive to extraneous internal and external stimuli (Fehr and Stern, 1967) may not be a complete description of what transpires. The basic factor that allows the subject to exclude the influence of other stimuli is the degree of relaxation achieved through traditional hypnotic procedures.

While studying the effects of hypnosis on conditioned EDRs, I have collected data on the fate of EDSFs during hypnosis. These studies have been described in detail previously (Edmonston, 1968, 1972b, 1979) and will be reiterated in Chapter 7 when we look at all of these responses in direct comparison between hypnosis and relaxation.

For the time being, I will present only the data comparisons between groups who had been hypnotized and a control group who sat in the experimental room for a time period equivalent to the hypnotic induction. The induction used was the eyelid-closure portion of the Stanford Hypnotic Susceptibility Scale, Form B, modified by substituting the word relaxation for "sleep." Prior to the presentation of the instructions all 45 subjects (15 control, 15 nonhypnotic relaxation, and 15 hypnosis) had received 20 trials habituating their EDORs to a tone and 20 trials conditioning their habituated EDORs by a tone-shock pairing. The hypnosis group was naive of the purpose of the study. Figure 6.7 shows the EDSFs produced by the three groups during the instruction period, a 10-trial extinction period (tone without shock), and a second set of extinction trials following the termination of hypnosis and a "become fully alert and aroused" instruction for the control group.

The data clearly show that during the instruction period, the hypnosis group yielded a progressively decreasing number of EDSFs over time, which is significantly greater than the slight reduction noted in the control group. Looking at the last four minutes of the instruction period, the hypnotized subjects produced significantly fewer EDSFs than the control group ($t = 2.38, p < .03$). The same relationship holds during the first extinction period, while all groups remained in the instructed condition. The control group produced significantly more EDSFs than the other two groups in both the first ($p < .05$) and the second ($p < .01$) five first-extinction trials. Following the termination of hypnosis, there was a significant ($p < .005$) increase in EDSF production for the hypnotized group (change from the last five first-extinction trials to the first five second-extinction trials). No such change occurred in the control group.

The data on EDSF changes during hypnosis and between hypnosis and awake comparison groups is among the most consistent in the physiological response literature. While the same consistency is available in the basal skin resistance studies of the relaxation response, no report of EDSFs from Benson or his coworkers has appeared. It is very reasonable to assume that a similar reduction of EDSFs would be reported had EDSFs been tabulated. The data reported in Chapter 7 will strengthen this assumption. For the time being, it remains clear that hypnosis produces precisely the type of EDSF data expected from an individual who is highly relaxed.

CONCLUSION

In this chapter I have tried to demonstrate, by analogy rather than by direct comparison, that the induction of hypnosis produces various physiological changes in human beings that strongly mimic those changes seen in conditions of relaxation and sleep. In both hypnosis and relaxation the data are not totally

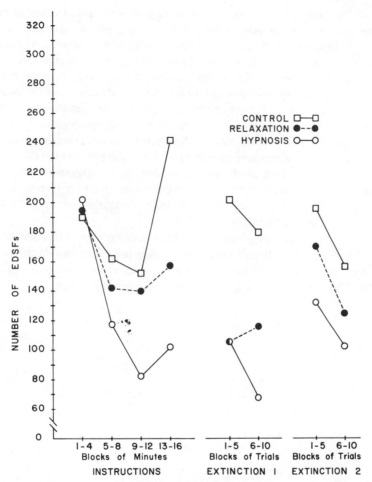

Figure 6.7.   Total number of SFs for each group over blocks of trials during the first and second extinction periods and four-minute blocks of time during the instructional period. (From Edmonston, 1968. Copyright © American Society of Clinical Hypnosis. Reprinted by permission.)

consistent. For each physiological response system there are studies that seem to run counter to the thesis of an equation of hypnosis and relaxation. But the reader should be aware that such inconsistencies are the rule, not the exception, in any area of scientific endeavor. Each of the studies reviewed had its own particular set of variables and degrees of those variables. Very few of the studies in each response category can be adequately and fully compared to any other measuring the same physiological parameter. Any review of the sort carried out above suffers from overgeneralization in a number of directions.

Essentially, what I have done is to reenter a diverse and at times disparate literature with a different perspective, or set, and apply this perspective to a reevaluation of old data. In a sense, I have started with a theoretical bias and asked if the data already available could be interpreted in a manner different from the way it may have been originally interpreted. In most cases there has been no need to reinterpret, only a need to call to the reader's attention that the data also produced evidence for a *similarity* between hypnosis and relaxation as well as a *difference* between hypnosis and various control manipulations. Where the original data did not seem compatible with a hypnosis-relaxation equation, I have openly speculated on alternative interpretations that suggest that the discrepancy between those data and my thesis was not as great as the original interpretations may have made them seem. How convincing these arguments have been is in the reader's eye, but I hope they have at least made the reader rethink the physiological response literature.

Despite the few apparently discrepant studies in this review, I feel that there is, in this chapter alone, sufficient data to reconsider the hypnosis-relaxation-sleep continuum, and specifically to consider relaxation as the basic foundation of hypnosis. The next chapter will make this conclusion imperative.

CHAPTER 7

Hypnosis and Relaxation: Relaxation Control Group Studies

The initial development of any science is the process of refining our ability to distinguish one thing from another, to be able to discriminate one event from another, one phenomenon from another. Thus we know one thing by knowing many. It is only as we compare one thing with another more carefully that the first object of our observation becomes more sharply defined. In this sense, then, definition is guided by comparison. So it is in our study of hypnosis.

Thus far I have argued by analogy: that is, I have pointed out studies wherein the products of hypnosis are similar to the products of relaxation, both with respect to physiological measurement and clinical outcomes. From these comparisons I have drawn the tentative conclusion that hypnosis and relaxation share a sufficient number of properties and effects as to be considered highly similar, if not identical. But this is a conclusion based on an indirect interlacing of investigations from disparate parts of the literature and history. It is now time to answer the question posed in the title of Plapp, Edmonston, and Lieberman's 1972 symposium: "To what should hypnosis be compared? The problem of appropriate experimental controls."

A number of methodological control strategies have been used by investigators of hypnosis. Historically, the most prevalent type of control group has been the awake control, used predominantly to demonstrate that measurements in hypnosis compare favorably, thus "demonstrating" that hypnosis is more like the waking condition than sleep and supposedly putting to rest the hypnosis-sleep hypothesis. A variation on the waking comparison group is the time-control group in which the subjects are instructed to sit (or lie) quietly, without further instruction, for a time period equal to that consumed by the hypnotic induction. In addition, some investigators have filled such time controls with "nonemotional" (translated "dull") passages from textbooks or short stories. Such variations on waking controls constituted the main ones used in the studies reviewed in chapter 6.

In the last two decades, two other types of comparison groups have appeared in the literature: (a) task-motivated and (b) simulating subjects. In the former, subjects are urged and encouraged to perform the suggested challenges to the best of their ability either as their own controls or as a separate control group. In the latter, individuals who have not had or are not capable of having hypnotic experiences are instructed to act as if, pretend to be hypnotized.

The early 1960s saw a controversy within the ranks of investigators utilizing task-motivation as a comparison technique to hypnosis. Weitzenhoffer and Sjoberg (1961), investigating the necessity of hypnotic induction for enhancing responsiveness to hypnotic suggestions, found that a hypnosis group yielded significant gains over nonhypnotized controls on a 17 test-suggestion scale in a test-retest format. They concluded that the induction of hypnosis was crucial and that the induction "brings about a change in the state of the individual which is subsequently reflected in his behavior with respect to suggestions" (p. 215). Other studies also showed that performance improves with motivational instructions only when they are paired with a hypnotic induction (Rosenhan and London, 1963; Slotnick and London, 1965; Smith, 1969). "The hypnotic condition somehow functions to make a subject more receptive than he has previously been to *certain kinds* of maximum performance instructions" (Slotnick and London, 1965, p. 45).

Barber and his colleagues think otherwise. Although Barber and Glass (1962) produced data that confirmed the facilitation of suggestibility through hypnotic induction, Barber and Calverley (1962, 1963b) argued for an equated effectiveness of hypnotic induction and task-motivational instructions. Generally, what Barber has shown was that motivational instructions were *as* effective as standard (relaxation) hypnotic inductions, *not* that the hypnotic induction was ineffective or even that task-motivation was more effective. Barber made this clear in two later studies (Barber and Calverley, 1965a,b) in which relaxation-sleep suggestions facilitated performance on the BSS. Thus both motivation and relaxation instructions were shown to be "effective, when isolated, in producing heightened objective and subjective responses to test suggestions . . ." (Barber and Calverley, 1965b, p. 262).

However, the argument of equivalent effectiveness of the two instructional conditions (task-motivation and relaxation-hypnosis) did not go unchallenged. Hilgard (1965), Hilgard and Tart (1966), and Edmonston and Robertson (1967), using *intrasubject* change scores (Barber et al. used *intersubject* differences), found a small but statistically significant advantage in responsiveness for relaxation-hypnosis over motivational instructions. Although Spanos and Chaves (1970) contended that Hilgard's studies were not comparable to Barber's because different motivating instructions were used, the same criticism could not be applied to my work with Robertson (1967), as the task-motivational instructions of Barber and Calverley (1962, 1963b) were used verbatim. Our conclusions paralleled those of Hilgard and Tart (1966). Relaxation hypnotic induction facilitates response to certain tasks significantly more than motivational instructions alone.

The curious point is that such a conclusion is not at all out of line with Barber's own earlier work. In an attempt to develop a parsimonious explanation of hypnosis, Barber (1965) analyzed the induction into several basic variables, one of which was suggestions of relaxation, drowsiness, and sleep. Investigating the effectiveness of this variable, Barber and Hahn (1963) found that hypnotic inductions were no more effective in producing physiological concomitants of relaxation (heart rate, respiratory rate, and palmar conductance changes) than were instructions to sit quietly. In fact, Barber and Calverley (1965a,b) produced data indicating that adding suggestions of relaxation, drowsiness, and sleep to defining the situation as hypnosis increased the levels of performance above those for defining the situation alone. Thus the relaxation factor was as effective as the combination of both motivating instructions *and* defining the suggestions as easy to carry out. Even the work on task-motivation as a control procedure foretold of the need to use a nonhypnotic relaxation control for investigating the basic nature of hypnosis.

Simulation, as a comparison device, has been the main thrust of much of Orne's work. (See Orne, 1972, 1979.) The technique involves, as stated above, using a control group in experimentation that has two characteristics: (a) they are instructed at the outset of an experiment to behave as though they were a subject capable of entering "deep hypnosis," and (b) they have proven to be unhypnotizable through repeated efforts to hypnotize them. While the former instruction makes this particular type of control group very adequate in studies of the "transcendent" qualities of hypnotic behavior, unwilling compliance, and deception, the latter characteristic forms a pitfall not easily overcome without additional control groups. In order to avoid the criticism that control subjects really "slip into hypnosis" without being aware of it when their performances match those of a hypnotized group, Orne deliberately chose to use proven unhypnotizable subjects as simulators.

It is somewhat a puzzle, however, why investigators and practitioners, in particular, consider the hypnotized subject so volatile. To assume that control subjects will fool us by slipping in and out of trances while performing suggested behaviors must then be counterbalanced by the assumption that the hypnotized subject is moving in and out of trances during experimental and clinical sessions as well. Carrying out that logic one step further, any data obtained from an experimental hypnotized subject that looks like waking performance must be interpreted not to mean that hypnosis is akin to the waking condition but that the subject is coming out of hypnosis when he or she performs and back "in" when he or she is "dormant." The futility of such reasoning should be obvious, because it assumes that the experimenter's instructions to enter hypnosis are effective and those not to enter hypnosis are ineffective. Frankly, the logic behind such an assumption is not apparent.

Unfortunately, by avoiding one supposed confound (slipping "in" and "out"), yet another was maximized in the simulation model. Hypnotic susceptibility factors confound the results of studies using only a single simulating control group, as defined. What the model has done is to help amplify the subjective quality of hypnotic performance, in that, while both a hypnotized and a simulating group of subjects may perform the same challenges (so too will task-motivated subjects), their reasons for so doing are different.

Curiously, simulation does not seem to be a two-way thoroughfare. Although trained investigators of hypnosis appear unable to discriminate "real" from "simulating" subjects when the latter are imitating hypnosis, the reverse does not hold. Reyher (1973), in a delightful study and replication, has shown that deeply hypnotized (somnambulistic) subjects cannot simulate being awake in a manner that goes undetected. Pointing out that the way to understand the effectiveness of intoxication is not by having a sober individual act drunk (analogous to Orne's simulator model), but to have an inebriated individual act sober, Reyher instructed eight hypnotized subjects to simulate wakefulness in the presence of another investigator and an unhypnotized subject. It was considered that the degree of success of the simulators would be a far more accurate picture of the effect of the treatment (alcohol, drugs, or hypnosis) than the degree of successful performance of Orne's simulators. The second investigator (not knowing which subject was which) had no difficulty selecting the hypnotized, simulating-wakefulness subjects in seven of the eight pairings and only minor difficulty with the eighth. A replication using five pairs of subjects, in which one was awake but entered hypnosis on a cue word, while the other was hypnotized and simulating wakefulness but terminated hypnosis on the same cue word, yielded the same results. Reyher concluded that the results "support the inference that the simulation of an altered state while S is in the waking state is not as sensitive to differences between the two states as is the simulation of the waking state while S is in an altered state" (1973, p. 35).

The "difference" that occurs in hypnosis is relaxation, but none of the above experimental models (waking, task-motivation, and simulation controls) is geared to test that notion directly. In the midst of the controversies over task-motivation and simulation models of investigation, we seem to have overlooked the most significant datum. Most of the studies testing the models used a relaxation-type induction procedure, yet the lack of an appropriate control group precluded the experimental separation of the relaxation component as the hypnotic element.

In my own laboratories a nonhypnotic relaxation control group was not used until the late 1960s, and even then the interpretation given the results was not what it is today. So intent was I upon discovering what it is that is unique about hypnosis that when hypnotic performance did not differ from a control group (nonhypnotic relaxation or otherwise), the focus of interpretation was on the concept that the response being measured was not unique to hypnosis, rather than on it not being different from that obtained in the control group (nonhypnotic relaxation). This is a crucial change of focus. The point is *not* that hypnosis is not unique, but that it is *not different* from the control group utilized. Rather than dispelling the notion of hypnosis being a unique state or yielding unique responses, such data present us with what hypnosis *is,* not what it is not. This simple reorganization of our perception of the data is critical to understanding hypnosis.

The examples of this changing perception will make clear its importance. In 1968 I presented data on the influence of hypnotic induction on conditioned electrodermal responses (see below for a complete description), in which measures of electrodermal spontaneous fluctuations (EDSFs) were also taken. One group used was instructed to relax but not to become hypnotized. When it was found that the number of EDSFs during and immediately following the instruction period (hypnosis or relaxation) did not differ between the two groups, the following interpretation was offered:

Contrary to previous reports in the literature, hypnotic induction instructions do not produce in Ss a state marked by the reduction of EDSFs. More precisely, if a "state" is produced, it is not distinguishable (by this measure) from that in Ss who received merely abbreviated instructions to relax. (Edmonston, 1968, p. 22)

Notice how what we look for shapes our perception. The primary interpretation (first sentence) reports that the data are in conflict with the previous literature. That is only because previous studies did not use a relaxation control group. A crucial phrase should have been added to the first sentence: "when compared with a group that is relaxed but not hypnotized" (as I then interpreted hypnosis). However, since my intent was to look for a response unique to hypnosis, I was content only to report what hypnosis was not. Only in the second sentence of the above quote did I pay deference to what now, in retrospect, seems so obvious—that the experimental group (hypnosis) did not differ from the control (relaxation) on this measure (EDSF), and *therefore* the two were *alike.*

A second example is warranted. In 1969 Weitzenhoffer published an article proposing a relationship between "passive hypnosis" and slow eye movement (SEMs) and SEM cones. These responses were considered essentially unique to hypnosis. In 1974 Dunwoody and I compared these same responses in hypnosis with SEMs and SEM cones in nonhypnotic relaxation (see below) and discovered no basic difference. Although we did make note that the data indicated the "similarity, if not identity, of hypnosis and relaxation" (Dunwoody and Edmonston, 1974, p. 273), the majority of other investigators with whom I talked, including Weitzenhoffer, interpreted our findings to indicate that SEMs and SEM cones are not unique to hypnosis. The point is not that these responses are not unique to hypnosis but that they, like other responses discussed below, are similar to those obtained in nonhypnotic relaxation, and that because the responses are similar in the two conditions there is the strong hint that the two conditions are basically the same. Control conditions such as waking, task-motivation, simulation, and others do not address themselves to the proper condition for comparison with hypnosis.

THE COLGATE STUDIES

For a number of years, beginning in 1965, I was engaged in a series of studies intended to clarify some of Pavlov's hypotheses regarding the relationships among hypnosis and various degrees of sleep. In particular, interest focused on the influence of neutral hypnotic instructions on a graded series of conditioned responses calculated to test the Pavlovian proposition that as hypnosis progresses, there is increasing loss of the motor (voluntary) response components and very little change in visceral responses. (See chapter 2 for a detailed discussion.) These studies are reported fully in Edmonston (1972 b, 1979). Following investigations measuring a conditioned finger withdrawal and a conditioned eyelid response, a series of studies were conducted on conditioned electrodermal responses. In the context of these latter studies a nonhypnotic relaxation control group was introduced.

The same basic methodological steps were used in all of the investigations. Following the habituation of the electrodermal response (EDR) to the stimuli to be used as the conditioned response (CR; a tone), 20 conditioning trials (pairing of the conditioned stimulus with the unconditioned stimulus, a mild shock) ensued. Then came the experimental instructions. For one group these entailed 17 minutes of tape-recorded hypnotic induction instructions modeled on the Stanford Hypnotic Susceptibility Scale, Form B (SHSS:B); for another the instructions were to: "let yourself become very deeply relaxed, but do not allow yourself to enter hypnosis; allow yourself to become deeply relaxed, but do not become hypnotized." These instructions were presented five times during a 17 minute period (time equivalent to the hypnotic induction). A second control group sat uninstructed in the experimental room for 17 minutes, and a second experimental group received, in addition to the hypnotic induction, information regarding the experimenter's expectations. This latter group was used to test the influence of subjects' desires to please on the response measures. After the instructions or time-control, 10 extinction trials (conditioned stimulus alone) were presented. Between this series of extinction trials and a second 10-trial set, the termination of the experimental instructions was accomplished. For the hypnosis groups this consisted of standard arousal instructions; for the nonhypnotic relaxation group, instructions to become fully alert. Thus the groups used were as follows: Group 1—hypnotic induction; Group 2—intermittent relaxation instructions; Group 3—no instruction, time-control; Group 4—hypnotic induction and expected outcome information. Groups 1, 2, and 4 were equated for hypnotic susceptibility (Harvard Group Scale of Hypnotic Susceptibility [HGSHS]); Group 3 consisted of low-susceptibility subjects. All groups contained 15 subjects.

Upon reevaluating the data, it was not the original response designated for investigation—the conditioned EDR—but the EDSFs that seemed to offer the most exciting finding. Although Pessin, Plapp, and Stern (1968) interpreted their findings of reduced EDSFs in hypnosis (*when compared with a waking control*) as evidence for a focused attention interpretation of hypnosis, my comparison with relaxation controls suggests that, if there is a focusing of attention away from extraneous external and internal stimuli, it is due to the relaxation component inherent in hypnosis (see also chapter 6). Figure 7.1 presents the EDSF data during the instruction period and the two extinction periods. (The data for the habituation and conditioning trials are omitted here; as they have been published elsewhere and are less pertinent to the present discussion.)

At the beginning of the instruction period all four groups were equated with respect to EDSFs. As the instructions (or time in the case of Group 3) continued there appears a decided separation of the four groups, which has become quite apparent by the third block of minutes (9—12) and quite significant by the last block (13—16). The overall significant change is due to differences between the experimental subjects (Groups 1 and 4) and the time-control subjects (Group 3) ($t = 2.38, p < .03$, for example, between Group 1 and Group 3). No difference was found between the nonhypnosis relaxation and the hypnotized subjects (e.g., $t = 1.43$, n.s., between Group 1 and Group 2). Thus when subjects are compared during the instruction period with one group receiving a hypnotic induction and the other receiving intermittent nonhypnotic relaxation instructions, no differences are found. With regard to EDSF, hypnosis and relaxation do not differ during the instruction period.

After the instruction period the situation is the same. Inspection alone of the first extinction period in figure 7.1 makes it apparent that the hypnotized groups are producing fewer EDSFs than the time-control group and that the former do not differ from the relaxation group. Covariance analysis between the last four minutes of the instruction period and the first five first extinction trials indicated that the hypnotized group and the relaxation group each yielded significantly fewer EDSFs than the control group ($F = 4.11, p < .05$), but did not differ from one another. Group 4 followed a similar pattern. Covariance analysis also demonstrated significant differences in the second five extinction trials of the first extinction period ($F = 5.87, p < .01$). These differences were due to significant differences between the hypnosis group and the time-control subjects ($t = 2.92, p <. 01$). The hypnosis group did not differ from the relaxation group in EDSF production ($t = 1.23$, n.s.), nor did the latter differ from the control ($t = 1.34$, n.s.). Again Group 4 patterned itself after the other hypnosis group.

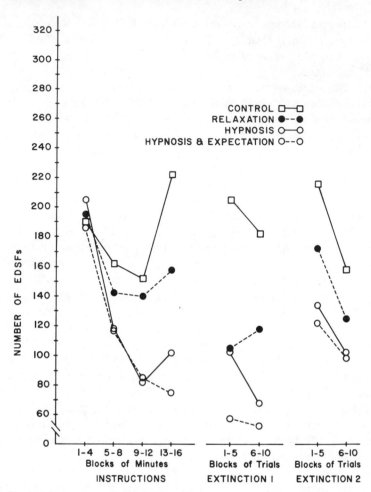

Figure 7.1. Total number of EDSFs for each group over 4-minute blocks of time during instructional period and blocks of trials during first and second extinction periods. (From Edmonston, 1979. Copyright © 1979 by Erika Fromm and Ronald E. Shor. Reprinted with permission from Hypnosis: Developments in Research and New Perspectives (New York: Aldine Publishing Company.)

Finally, looking at the EDSF production during the first five trials of the second extinction period, which followed arousal instructions, we note that the hypnosis group produced a significant increase in EDSFs over the last five first-extinction trials ($t = 2.66$, $p < .005$), while Group 2, the nonhypnotic relaxation group, yielded a similar but not significant trend ($t = 1.37, p < .08$).

The above data were replicated in the contest of studying the effects of neutral hypnosis on conditioned heart-rate (see Edmonston, 1972b, 1979). This time 20 subjects were equally divided between two groups, one receiving standard relaxation hypnosis instructions and the other receiving nonhypnotic relaxation instructions as above (five times in 17 minutes). The groups were equated on the HGSHS. Figure 7.2 presents the EDSF data for these groups during the instruction and two extinction periods. (The lack of a data point for the last four minutes of instruction for the relaxation group was due to experimental error. The trend, however, indicates that if available, it would have shadowed that of the hypnosis group very closely.) Except for the last five trials of the second extinction period the EDSFs produced by the two groups are virtually identical. During instructions EDSFs become fewer in both groups. Following instructions

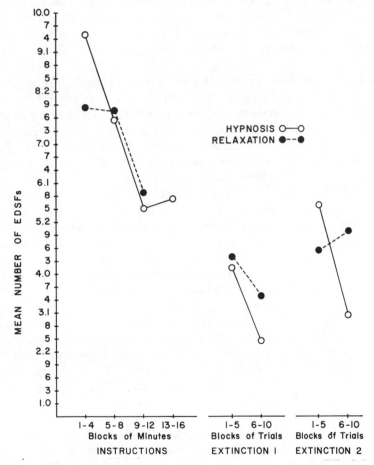

Figure 7.2. Mean number of EDSFs for each group over 4-minute blocks of time during instructional period and blocks of trials during first and second extinction periods. (From Edmonston, 1979. Copyright © 1979 by Erika Fromm and Ronald E. Shor. Reprinted with permission from Hypnosis: Developments in Research and New Perspectives (New York: Aldine Publishing Company.)

there is a further significant decrease in EDSFs in both groups (first five trials of first extinction period), and after the termination of instructions (arousal) both groups yield increasing numbers of EDSFs. The apparent differences between the groups in the EDSF trend from the first five to the second five second extinction trials may simply be due to the intermittent nature of the relaxation instructions.

Combining the data from figures 7.1 and 7.2 brings out even more clearly the differences and similarities among the groups with respect to EDSF production during and after the instruction period. Figure 7.3 depicts these combined data. The hypnosis group is composed of the two hypnosis groups (one with and one without knowledge of experimenter expectations) from the first study outlined above and the hypnosis group from the heart-rate study, making 40 subjects in all. The 25 subjects of the relaxation group are from the two studies also, and the 15 control (no instruction, time-control) subjects are from the EDR conditioning study.

Once again, at the beginning of the instruction period there is no EDSF production difference among the three groups. As time and the instructions progress, the three groups separate, the hypnosis and relaxation groups producing lesser amounts of EDSFs than the control, with the relaxation group falling between the hypnosis and the control groups. The hypnosis group produces significantly less EDSFs than the control, but not less than the nonhypnotic relaxation group. The difference between the hypnosis and the control group and the close similarity between the hypnosis and the nonhypnotic relaxation group is greatly magnified and apparent in the extinction period following the instructions. After the termination of hypnosis and relaxation (between the first and second extinction periods), there is a significant increase in EDSF production.

Although it could be argued that the difference in yields between the control group and the other two groups was due to a susceptibility factor, I am inclined to discount that argument as the whole basis for the results. Unlike Orne's simulator subjects, the ones who served in the control group were not totally insusceptible. They had achieved scores of 2, 3, and 4 on the HGSHS. In fact, had I used a pure simulator design, I suspect the differences among groups would have been even greater. But the major point is not what the time-control group was doing but the obvious similarity between the hypnotized and the nonhypnotic relaxation groups. Few would argue that there are individual differences with regard to susceptibility, but the point is that those who perform in hypnosis to a certain level of susceptibility will also perform to a similar level when presented with nonhypnotic relaxation instructions, and will thereby demonstrate the similarity between the two conditions, regardless of what special talents (or lack of talent) the individual subjects bring to the situation in the first place. What the EDSF data point to is the degree of relaxation of the hypnotic subject that allows him or her to exclude the influence of extraneous stimuli. The same degree of reduced responsiveness appears in the nonhypnotically relaxed subject.

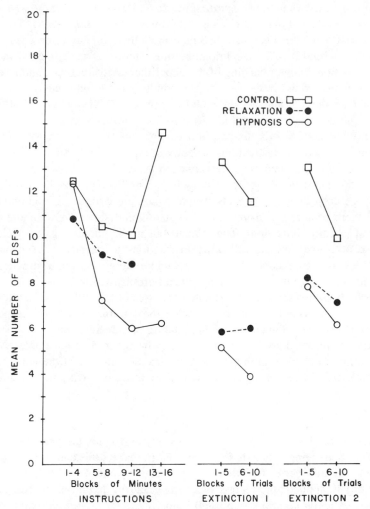

Figure 7.3. Mean number of EDSFs for combined groups (Figures 7.1 and 7.2) over 4-minute blocks of time during instructional period and blocks of trials during first and second extinction periods. (From Edmonston, 1979. Copyright © 1979 by Erika Fromm and Ronald E. Shor. Reprinted with permission from Hypnosis: Developments in Research and New Perspectives (New York: Aldine Publishing Company.)

Heart Rate

As indicated above, some of the electrodermal measures were obtained during a study on the influence of neutral hypnosis on conditioned heart-rate (HR) responses. The heart-rate response studies were part of the larger research program of Pavlov's notions regarding the fate of conditioned responses during hypnosis described above and elsewhere (Edmonston, 1972b, 1979). The same basic format was used here also: habituation to the stimulus to be used as the conditioned stimulus (CS), conditioning, introduction of experimental instructions, extinction, countermanding of the experimental instructions, and a second set of extinction trials. In the case of HR conditioning a light-intensity increase was used as the CS and an automobile horn as the unconditioned stimulus (UCS). The latter is a meaningful startle stimulus in our society.

Twenty subjects equally divided into two groups (hypnosis instructions and nonhypnotic relaxation instructions, as above), equated for hypnotic responsiveness on the HGSHS, were used. Heart-rate, in beats per minute, was noted before and after the instructions. As reported in chapter 6, the hypnotized group showed an average drop in HR of 8 beats/minute following hypnotic induction. Upon arousal there occurred an increase of 5 beats/minute (still 3 beats/minute under the rate preceding induction). The relaxed but not hypnotized group yielded a decrease of 5 beats/minute following instructions to become relaxed but not hypnotized and an increase of 2 beats/minute upon alerting instructions (3 beats/minute under the rate preceding relaxation instructions).

Thus both groups showed appreciable decreases in HR following instructions. This trend was partially reversed following the termination of their respective instructions. Considering the intermittent nature of the "relax but do not become hypnotized" instructions, these changes can be taken as comparable. Again, direct comparisons between hypnosis and relaxation show that the changes that occur in HR during hypnosis are mimicked by those occurring in relaxation.

Body Temperature

As noted in the last chapter, some controversy surrounds the changes, or lack thereof, in body temperature during hypnosis. In reality, this controversy focuses the thesis of this book, for when an appropriate control group (nonhypnotic relaxation) is applied, the reports of changes during hypnosis (in comparison with the particular control group used) pale.

Both Reid and Curtsinger (1968) and Timney and Barber (1969) reported significant increases in body temperature measured orally during hypnosis. As discussed in chapter 6, it is not clear to what degree Reid and Curtsinger's control group ("instructed to relax") could be considered comparable to the nonhypnotic relaxation groups now in use. Timney and Barber's control group, as you will recall, was engaged in taking parts of the Wechsler-Bellevue Intelligence Scale, Form II, and Jackson, Barkley, and Pashko (1976) compared their neutral hypnosis group to one group that was task-motivated and one that "read quietly." That there were significant increases in oral temperature within the hypnosis groups but not the control groups is evident, but the interpretation of these changes depends on the comparison group condition. What happens when the control group is clearly a nonhypnotic relaxation group?

Cogger and I (1971) reexamined the question of body temperature during hypnosis in a group setting. Twenty paid volunteer college students were divided equally into two groups: (a) hypnotic induction and (b) relaxation instructed. We used the hypnotic induction of Reid and Curtsinger (1968) for both groups. For the control group, the verbalizations were changed to reduce references to hypnosis; for example, "you may fall into hypnotic sleep" was changed to "do not let yourself fall into hypnotic sleep," and the word relaxation was substituted for the word trance. In order to ascertain that the subjects in the control group knew what they were not to allow themselves to "fall into" (hypnosis), all received one administration of the hypnosis induction without change. Temperatures were measured orally seven times during each two-hour experimental session, and all subjects participated in four sessions.

The results of this study did not confirm those of Reid and Curtsinger (1968) and Timney and Barber (1969). In fact, those nonsignificant temperature changes that did occur in the hypnotized group were in the opposite direction (a reduction in temperature). Two considerations seemed to account for the discrepancy between this study and those of Reid and Curtsinger and Timney and Barber: (a) our study was conducted in the late afternoon, when body temperature is at its natural peak, and (b) the measurements analyzed were a composite of a number of trials in the experimental sessions. Regarding the first consideration, the law of initial value dictates that the subjects' temperatures could not have risen appreciably because they were already at their natural peak and the latitude of nonpathological change in oral temperature is highly restricted. Regarding the second point, we suspect that the natural apprehension of the subjects in the other two studies may have accounted for a portion of the reported rise in temperature. In fact, Timney and Barber themselves showed that additional hypnotic sessions were accompanied with less of a temperature rise than the initial session. Thus repeated experience with the same situation reduces apprehension and its physiological concomitants.

The more important finding of Cogger's and my work (1971) is in the comparison of the hypnotic group with the nonhypnotic relaxation group. No significant differences in oral temperature changes were noted between the two groups. With respect to oral temperature, the group receiving hypnotic induction instructions showed the same pre- and post-instruction pattern as the group receiving nonhypnotic relaxation instructions. According to this study, oral temperature measurements do not differentiate between hypnosis and nonhypnotic relaxation.

Reaction Time

In his dissertation, Plapp (1967) found that reaction time (RT) was the only variable measured that showed a significant change during hypnosis. Hypnotized subjects yielded a significantly slower RT and failed to show the progressive reduction of RTs that characterized nonhypnotized nonrelaxed subjects. Plapp suggested that this finding was due to the suggestions of relaxation inherent in most hypnotic induction procedures.

Another study from my laboratories makes the same point very clearly (Ham and Edmonston, 1971). Thirty male undergraduates, equated on the BSS, were equally divided among three groups: (a) relaxation-hypnosis induction, (b) nonhypnosis relaxation instructions, and (c) alert induction. The hypnosis induction was adapted from the Stanford Hypnotic Susceptibility Scale, Form A (SHSS:A) (Weitzenhoffer and Hilgard, 1959); the nonhypnotic relaxation instructions were suggestions of relaxation, including instructions not to become hypnotized and not to fall alseep; the alert induction was patterned after that developed by Liebert, Rubin, and Hilgard (1965), which will be discussed more fully in chapter 8.

Reaction times were measured by having each subject press a telegraph key to the tape-recorded instruction, ''Ready.'' Thirty-five test trials followed three practice trials, the intertrial intervals varying between 20 and 40 seconds. Figure 7.4 dramatically depicts the findings, which showed significant differences among the experimental conditions ($F = 3.979, p < .05$) and across trials ($F = 2.909, p < .05$). The RTs for the alert group were significantly faster ($\bar{X} = 357$ msec) than those for both the hypnosis group ($\bar{X} = 629$ msec) and the nonhypnotic relaxation group ($\bar{X} = 621$ msec). The RTs for the hypnosis and the relaxation control subjects *did not differ*. When presented with instructions to relax, with or without indications of hypnosis, subjects yield slower RTs overall and demonstrate a progressive decrease in responsiveness over time. The motor inhibition exhibited following a hypnotic induction appears to be more related to suggestions of relaxation than to a specific hypnotic ''trance state.''

Not only did this study demonstrate, in yet another measurement area, the similarities between hypnosis and relaxation, but it also demonstrated the differences between traditional neutral hypnosis and the so-called ''alert trance.'' This is a very important consideration when trying to sort out the basic nature of hypnosis from the other reported varieties of trance and hypnoticlike phenomena. More detailed attention will be paid to both the alert condition and ''trance'' as a concept in the ensuing chapters.

Eye Movements

Another area of investigation that has come under consideration in my laboratories is that of eye movement during hypnosis. When one looks at the heavy emphasis placed on the eyes in both modern and ancient induction techniques, it is surprising to find as few reports on eye movements and conditions during hypnosis as there are in the literature. Strosberg and Vics (1962), in one of the only investigations of the physical and physiological

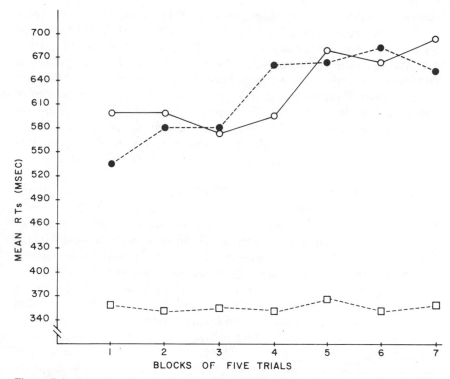

Figure 7.4. Mean reaction times of relaxation control (solid circle, dashed line), relaxation induction (open circle, solid line) and alert induction (squares, dashed line) groups. (From Edmonston, 1979. Copyright © 1979 by Erika Fromm and Ronald E. Shor. Reprinted with permission from Hypnosis: Developments in Research and New Perspectives (New York: Aldine Publishing Company.)

condition of the eyes during hypnosis, concluded that the reductions of blood supply, the reluctance of the arcades, changes in cornea curvature, and the engorging of the scleral vessels were brought about by the relaxation inherent in hypnosis.

There have been a few more studies of eye movements during hypnosis. Amadeo and Shagass (1963), for example, reported a "consistent reduction of REM rates during hypnosis" (p. 144), undercutting the interpretation of hypnosis as increased and/or focused attention noted in chapter 6. The work of Antrobus, Antrobus, and Singer (1964) also relates decreased eye movement to a condition of passivity and lessened attention.

Recently, slow eye movements have received more attention in the literature. In 1969 Weitzenhoffer noted that SEMs were associated with highly susceptible subjects and thought that they might be characteristic of deep hypnotic conditions. In particular, he showed that high susceptibles produced pendular (sinusoidal) SEMs similar to those found in Stage 1 of light sleep. These waveforms increased during hypnosis (Weitzenhoffer, 1971), and have been proposed as unique involuntary indicators of hypnosis (Weitzenhoffer, 1969, 1971; Weitzenhoffer and Brockmeier, 1970). Lorens and Darrow (1962) and Weitzenhoffer (1971) also investigated SEMs for patterns that might differ with different phases of the deepening of hypnosis. In addition to his discussion of pendular SEMs, Weitzenhoffer (1971) reported a conical pattern of SEMs that appear upon the induction of hypnosis, immediately following eye closure. These 'SEM cones'' were thought to indicate not only the deepening upon induction but neurophysiological changes underlying the induction phase of hypnosis.

While it is clear from Weitzenhoffer's (1971) data that SEMs occur during hypnosis, his data did not establish the uniqueness of SEMs to hypnosis. Weitzenhoffer reported data only on hypnotized subjects, without benefit of control group comparisons. As he noted, the SEMs were similar to those found in Stage 1 sleep, and thus he suggested that hypnosis might share similar neurophysiological changes to early sleep and relaxation, but beyond that, the data did not allow for a clear statement of the underlying nature of hypnosis. (It has been pointed out elsewhere—Dunwoody and Edmonston, 1974—that SEM cones are a measurement artifact created by the natural transition from waking, high-frequency, low-amplitude electrooculograms (EOG) to resting, low-frequency, high-amplitude wave forms.) What was needed for a fuller interpretation of the SEM data was a control group comparison with a nonhypnotic relaxation condition.

In 1974 Dunwoody and I compared the SEM productivity of eight high-susceptible subjects (Harvard Group Scale of Hypnotic Susceptibility [HGSHS], 9−12) and eight low-susceptible subjects (HGSHS, 0−3) under two instructional conditions, hypnosis and nonhypnotic relaxation. Each subject participated in both conditions. SEMs appeared in 28 of the 32 experimental sessions with the subjects, and indicated no difference either between conditions (hypnosis and relaxation) or between susceptibility groups (high and low). SEMs do not appear to be unique to hypnosis either in the frequency of occurrence or their time of onset—they begin with eye closure in both relaxation and hypnosis. Dunwoody and I concluded that SEMs and SEM cones "seem to be more associated with relaxation (loss of muscular tension) and/or the deepening phase of Stage 1 sleep than they are with the various stages of hypnosis" (p. 274).

Although the foregoing is an accurate interpretation of the experimental data on SEMs, the full impact of that conclusion was not exploited. As described above, our perception was narrowed, if not tunneled, by the notion that the data showed that a particular response (in this case, SEMs) was not unique to hypnosis. The emphasis should have been more on what hypnosis was not different from—relaxation. The point was not that the response was not unique to hypnosis, but that it was the same as in nonhypnotic relaxation. When the appropriate relaxation control group is used, no response is unique to hypnosis. Rather, hypnosis and relaxation are one and the same condition.

OTHER RELAXATION CONTROL GROUP STUDIES

My laboratories are not the only ones to produce increasing amounts of data pointing to the similarity of hypnosis and relaxation. Although little was produced before the 1970s, one earlier study is worth reviewing. In the second of two studies into the attitudes of college students toward hypnosis, Dorcus, Brintnall, and Case (1941) compared a group of 20 hypnotized students with a group of 25 students told "to lie on a cot, close their eyes and relax" (p. 220) on the amount of the time they took to arise and prepare to leave the experimental room after the experimenter had been called away. The original data indicated that the time distributions for the two groups were comparable, ranging from 0 to 30 minutes for 55% of the hypnotized subjects and 84% of the relaxed subjects. Barber (1979), in his account of this study, reported that the mean time for the hypnosis group was 28 minutes and that for the relaxed group, 23 minutes.

Here, then, was an early behavioral comparison between hypnosis and relaxation in which a degree of comparability between the two conditions was found. Dorcus et al.'s subjects remained passive, with their eyes closed, for about the same amount of time regardless of whether they had been hypnotized or simply instructed to relax. While the authors dwelt on the potential reasons behind the similar behavior (similar attitudinal factors), the lack of a clear difference in the behavior of these two groups would imply not only that people behave similarly in the two situations (hypnosis and relaxation) but that they do not make attitudinal distinctions between the two.

More recent comparisons between hypnosis and relaxation have arisen in the context of evaluating different aspects of behavior therapy. In 1969 Paul reported a study in which he compared Jacobson's progressive relaxation, Kline's hypnotic relaxation, and self-instructions to relax but not to sleep. Much of Paul's earlier work concerned systematic desensitization therapy, and this study was intended to test the Wolpeian notion that abbreviated relaxation was a basic requirement of such behavior therapies. Noting that the progressive relaxation of desensitization therapy and hypnotic inductions share common factors, he assigned 20 female undergraduate students to each of the three groups noted above. As a measure of anxiety, the focal symptom toward which systematic desensitization is directed, Paul used a self-report anxiety scale—the Anxiety Differential—before and after each treatment procedure. Physiological arousal measures included HR, respiration rate, muscle tension (EMG), and skin conductance. As an indicator of hypnosis, he used the challenge of arm immobilization, which 90% of the hypnotized group "passed" during the first experimental session and 85% during the second.

Two identical experimental sessions were used for each group. During the first session, relaxation produced significant changes in all systems except skin conductance. Hypnosis changed only the anxiety measure and the respiration rate. No changes were noted in the control group. However, during the second session both the hypnosis and relaxation groups produced changes significantly different from the control group, although the relaxation group maintained its superiority over the hypnosis group in HR and EMG. Again, skin conductance did not differentiate among the three groups.

What Paul (1969a) had shown then was that both relaxation training and hypnotic induction were effective in reducing tension, anxiety, and stress whether measured subjectively by self-report or physiologically. That the hypnosis group needed a second session to produce changes similar to those of the relaxation group in the physiological measures Paul attributed to a training effect. However, as indicated in the discussion of Cogger's and my work (1971) on body temperature, anxiety engendered by our cultural views of hypnosis during the subjects' first encounter could also explain the results over the two sessions. Initial anxiety over the experimental treatment itself (hypnosis) could have kept the subjects of that group in a prolonged state of apprehension during the first session. Only when the subjects learn through experience that hypnotic procedures per se are not to be feared can they relax physiologically as well as subjectively. As many therapists will attest, patients will often agree to "be relaxed" when they refuse to "be hypnotized" for treatment purposes. This reality of our culture and the reality of a hypnotic-relaxation equation raises some interesting ethical and legal problems to be discussed in chapter 9. Be that as it may, Paul's (1969a) results added to the growing body of literature suggesting a close if not identical relationship between hypnosis and nonhypnotic relaxation.

In the context of the above study, Paul (1969b) also obtained personality data including the Wolpe and Lang (1964) Fear Survey Schedule (FSS), a self-rating scale of anxiety-provoking items. In addition, during the two experimental sessions all subjects were asked to visualize a scene that they had individually checked as "much or very much disturbing" from the FSS. All four of the physiological measures (HR, respiration rate, EMG, and skin conductance) were reduced to a composite score using techniques described by Lacey (1956) and compared among groups from pre- to post-visualization. A significant interaction among groups from pre- to post-imagery is shown in figure 7.5 ($F = 4.496, p < .05$). Both relaxation and hypnosis reduced the physiological response to stressful imagery significantly when compared to the self-instructed control, but the two experimental groups' responses did not differ from one another. While Paul (1969a, b) prefers relaxation training to hypnosis for achieving therapeutic relaxation (mainly because of the first versus second session differences), he

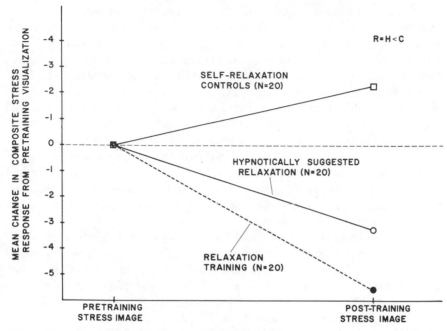

Figure 7.5. Mean change in composite physiological lability scores from stressful visualization before training to stressful visualization after two training sessions. (From Paul, 1969a. Copyright 1969 by the American Psychological Association. Reprinted by permission.)

does point out that the manner of producing relaxation "does not appear to strongly influence the suppression of physiological responses to stressful imagery" (1969b, p. 255). I might emphasize that the manner of producing relaxation results in no appreciable outcome differences whether the method is by nonhypnotic relaxation or by hypnotic induction.

Paul (1969a) explained the inability of the skin conductance measure to differentiate among the three groups in the first study on the basis of the possibility of an interaction between peripheral blood flow and skin conductance. The highly aroused individual has a high skin conductance; as he or she relaxes, the skin conductance may remain the same because of the action of the parasympathetic nervous system brought into play by the relaxation process. That is, the increasing regnance of the parasympathetic system over the sympathetic as relaxation ensues brings about a concomitant increase in peripheral blood flow (vasodilatation), which in turn, because of "water load," tends to maintain the conductance levels that were originally measured in the aroused sympathetic state. Thus while the subjective report of the subject changes, this particular measure may not, and high conductance levels are maintained for different physiological reasons.

In addition, the limits imposed by Wilder's (1967) Law of Initial Value may also be operating in Paul's data. For example, McAmmond, Davidson and Kovitz (1971), studying stress reactions in dental situations, found a differential effect in skin conductance measures to pain depending upon original baseline measures. In subjects whose baseline conductance was initially high, both relaxation and hypnosis produced a decrease in response to pain. However, as the baseline itself was reduced, the effect disappeared. Regardless of how one understands the lack of differences in skin conductance, Paul's investigations (1969a,b) represent some of the few studies prior to 1970 that directly compared hypnosis with nonhypnotic relaxation. By 1970, then, these few studies gave strong indication of what later data and the studies reviewed below further confirmed: that when hypnosis and nonhypnotic relaxation are directly compared within a given investigation, the two conditions produce the same results, regardless of the measure chosen.

Since 1970 there has been a small but growing interest in relaxation as an appropriate control group in hypnotic investigations. aside from my work (Edmonston, 1972a,b, 1979; Dunwoody and Edmonston, 1974; Cogger and Edmonston, 1971; Ham and Edmonston, 1971) and that of McAmmond, Davidson, and Kovitz (1971), studies by Bullard and DeCoster (1972), Reyher and Wilson (1973), Peters and Stern (1973), Mather and Degun (1975) (with a rejoinder by Wagstaff [1976]), Tebēcis et al., (1975), Morse et al. (1977), Benson et al. (1978), and Coleman (1976) have appeared. Most of these papers report findings commensurate with the hypnosis-relaxation equation; where they do not, methodological and/or statistical conditions dictate caution in data interpretation.

In a study of behavioral compliance and vividness, Bullard and DeCoster (1972) used differences in pre- and post-treatment measures on the BSS as a compliance score and a composite of the BSS subjective score as a vividness of experience estimate. Comparing an abbreviated version of the Wolpe and Lazarus (1967) procedure for relaxation with a "standard hypnotic induction," the authors reported no significant differences between the two procedures with respect to the vividness of the subjects' reported experiences. Thus from the subjective standpoint the two procedures obtain the same results. However, the more objective scores (compliance) did indicate that hypnosis was more effective. These data may be seen as analogous to those reported by Paul (1969a), in that the subjective measures (self-reported anxiety scale) demonstrated no differences between hypnosis and relaxation, while some differences were noted initially in more objective measures (physiological response). These differences disappeared, you will recall, upon repeating the session, indicating, I feel, the contribution of subject apprehension during the first session. A similar phenomenon could be operating in Bullard and DeCoster's data, in that the concept of hypnosis creates a more aroused condition and thereby better compliance in the one experimental session they conducted. Although it is mere conjecture, a second repeated session with their hypnotic subjects may also have obviated the initial differences between hypnosis and relaxation on the compliance measure.

Reyher and Wilson (1973) were also concerned with the maladaptive consequences of subject apprehension and anxiety toward hypnosis as manifested in the subject's (patient's) inability to enter into the hypnotic condition freely and comfortably. Initial apprehension of hypnosis is a pragmatic concern for the clinician, just as it is a theoretical concern for the laboratory investigator. In an attempt to find data justification for indirect induction procedures, the authors tested two hypotheses: (a) that procedures designated "relaxation" would be less anxiety provoking than identical situations labeled "hypnosis," and (b) that susceptibility to the induction would be greater when the procedure is labeled "relaxation" than when it is labeled "hypnosis."

After prefacing an abbreviated version of Jacobson's progressive relaxation method and a version of the SHSS:A, altered to exclude references to "hypnosis," with instructions that the experiment involved either relaxation or hypnosis, the authors measured 20 subjects on the number of galvanic skin responses (GSRs; 2000 ohms or greater) elicited, the 12 SHSS challenge items, and a self-report, post-experiment questionnaire. Using GSRs as an indication of anxiety level, Reyher and Wilson found that subjects do indeed have a higher anxiety level when procedures are presented as "hypnosis" rather than "relaxation" ($t = 13.84$, $p < .001$). In addition, their performance on the SHSS is significantly more variable under the "hypnosis" label than under that of "relaxation."

These data do not speak directly to the thesis of my book, but they do indicate that culturally predisposed attitudes toward the word hypnosis may operate in the initial phases of studies comparing relaxation and hypnosis. Subject apprehension may give rise to data that indicate differences in initial comparisons but that show no differences in repeated measurement sessions. Timney and Barber (1969) reported such differences between initial measures of body temperature and those taken in subsequent sessions. Cogger and Edmonston (1971) found the same progression of change in the data comparing hypnosis and relaxation on body temperature, as did Paul (1969a) in a number of physiological measures. The basic nature of hypnosis is relaxation, but a clear indication of this equation may, with respect to some measures, require repeated comparisons.

Peters and Stern's study (1973) was presented briefly in chapter 6. Using subjects that scored either 8 of 8 on the BSS or 10 of 11 on the HGSHS:A, the authors measured skin temperature and peripheral blood flow in 20 subjects during the relaxation hypnotic induction used by Reid and Curtsinger (1968) and instructions to "sit and relax." (Two groups of 10 each were counterbalanced for instruction sequence.) Just as in the Reid and Curtsinger data, a significant increase in body temperature (skin temperature, in this case) during neutral hypnosis was found, *but,* and this is crucial, a similar significant increase in body temperature was also found in the relaxation control group. The same was true of peripheral blood flow; peripheral vasodilatation increased significantly in *both* hypnosis and relaxation. As Peters and Stern interpreted their data: "the observed increase in skin temperature [and pulse volume] for the hypnotic session cannot be attributed to anything other than the relaxed state of the control session" (p. 106). Yes, hypnosis differs from the waking condition on these measures (Reid and Curtsinger, 1968; Timney and Barber, 1969), but not from the relaxation condition (Peters and Stern, 1973), a rather critical point made clear only by the use of the appropriate control group.

In 1975 Mather and Degun presented data that seemed in part to support the equation of hypnosis with relaxation and in part to echo those of Bullard and DeCoster (1972). Six subjects served in both the hypnotized (by a process involving eye closure and arm and hand responses) and the relaxed conditions. Relaxation in this study, however, involved only telling the subject to lie down and relax; prolonged relaxation instructions were not given. Heart-rate and responsiveness to three suggestions (to dream on a specified topic, to awaken at a specified time, and to carry out a specified act the following night) were measured, the former during the treatment conditions and the latter by a self-report scale (0 to 5) upon awaking from the following night's sleep.

As expected from previous data comparing hypnosis and relaxation, HR decreased significantly during the time of hypnosis and relaxation, with no significant differences being found between the two conditions (see figure 7.6). On the other hand, the authors reported that the subjective reports differed between the two conditions, with hypnosis yielding higher ratings (more suggestions carried out) than relaxation.

While the latter finding struck me as very similar to the differences reported by Bullard and DeCoster (1972) with respect to compliance and may suffer from the same initial subject apprehension confounding as discussed above, Wagstaff (1976) posed more serious statistical objections. He criticized Mather and Degun's (1975) work on two grounds. First, he argued that the scaling technique used to measure compliance with suggestions was ordinal in character, and therefore the parametric analysis of variance used to evaluate the data was inappropriate. Second, he felt that the data reported were so easily prone to distortion by the subjects (whether deliberate or inadvertent) that the subjects' performance could not be adequately assessed. To strengthen this argument, Wagstaff points out that the relaxed subjects awoke from sleep at the specified time with an accuracy equal to the hypnotized subjects. It was only on the reports of dreaming and carrying out a specific act that the two groups differed—those measures most easily distorted by a subject.

It is also noticeable that no differences in heart-rate were found betweens the conditions of hypnosis and relaxation. Thus, the only two measures which a role-playing subject would have found difficult to control [heart-rate and awaking on time] failed to differentiate the two conditions. (Wagstaff, 1976, p. 300)

Tebēcis, Provins, Farnbach, and Pentony (1975) also compared an experimental group both in hypnosis and relaxed but not hypnotized. Although the authors mislabeled the relaxation condition as "awake" (see chapter 6), they found that electroencephalogram theta production did not differ between the two conditions but was significantly greater than that found in another truly "awake" control group. These data not only indicated the similarity between hypnosis and nonhypnotic relaxation, but also showed the relationship of both to Stage 1 sleep, as denoted by theta activity.

More recently, three studies have reported results of direct comparisons between hypnosis techniques and meditation-induced relaxation. One (Benson et al., 1978) has already been described in detail in chapter 5. Briefly, the authors compared a self-hypnosis and a meditation relaxation technique in the treatment of 32 patients suffering from anxiety neurosis. Pre- and post-treatment measures by psychiatric assessment, self-assessment, and physiological techniques revealed no difference on any measure with respect to therapeutic effectiveness.

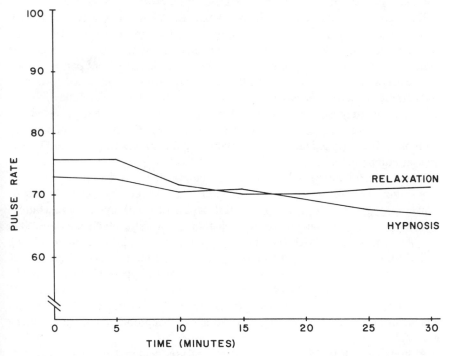

Figure 7.6.   Pulse rate over time during hypnosis and relaxation. (From Mather and Degun, 1975. Copyright 1975 by the British Psychological Society. Reprinted by permission.)

Not only were there no differences on the more subjectively oriented assessments (the self-assessment and the psychiatric interview), but, keeping in mind Wagstaff's (1976) criticism of Mather and Degun's (1975) work, no differences were found on all save one of the physiological measures. Oxygen consumption, heart-rate, and systolic blood pressure did not differ between the two groups, while the hypnosis group did show a significant decrease in diastolic blood pressure that was not present in the meditation group. (This point has been discussed in chapter 5.) Essentially, what these data provide is yet another instance—this time in the context of a clinical study—of the failure of data to reveal a difference between nonhypnotic relaxation and hypnosis as traditionally practiced.

Walrath and Hamilton (1975) also presented data directly comparing meditation-induced autonomic responses with those during autohypnosis and a relaxation control. All 30 subjects (10 in each group) were initially screened for hypnotic susceptibility, each scoring at least 10 on the SHSS:A. Heart-rate, respiratory rate, skin conductance, and discrete GSRs were measured during an initial baseline period; during meditation, hypnosis, or relaxation; and during a final baseline period.

The results were the same in all four measures. While there was a significant change in all groups from the first baseline period to the treatment period in the predicted direction (decrease), there were *no differences among the groups*. The same was true for the physiological changes from the treatment periods to the post-test period (final baseline). In this case, all measures increased to a level comparable to the initial baseline levels. The only subjects not following this pattern completely were those in the meditation group, whose HR persisted at a lower level even during the final baseline period. From the standpoint of autonomic arousal, meditation, autohypnosis, and instructions to relax all reduce arousal comparably.

Morse, Martin, Furst, and Dubin (1977) found essentially the same similarities when they compared six conditions—(a) alert state, (b) hetero-hypnosis-relaxation-type, (c) hetero-hypnosis-task-type, (d) auto-hypnosis-relaxation-type, and (e) meditation—on respiration rate, pulse rate, blood pressure, skin resistance, EEG, and EMG. Based on a thorough review of the literature relating to TM relaxation and non-TM relaxation that led to the conclusion that "there appears to be similarities between TM and relaxation hypnosis" (Morse et al., 1977, p. 307), 48 subjects were divided into four groups (trained in the TM procedure, trained in autohypnosis, trained in both, and trained in neither) for monitoring under the six conditions noted above. Appropriate counterbalancing was used.

Although much of Morse et al.'s data analysis centered on skin resistance, none of the physiological measures differentiated among the various forms of relaxation (meditation, autohypnosis, heterohypnosis) including task-motivated hypnosis. What was shown was that measures taken during all forms of relaxation were significantly different from the measures taken during an alert state. The basal skin resistance in the alert state was significantly lower (indicating arousal) than in the relaxation conditions. By the same token, pulse and respiration rates, both systolic and diastolic blood pressure, muscle artifacts in the EEG, and nonspecific fluctuations in skin resistance (EDSFs in chapter 6), were all higher in the alert state than in any of the relaxation states. Synchronous alpha activity was less in the alert condition.

The authors did note one difference among the various forms of relaxation. In the subjective reports with respect to effortlessness of induction, the subjects reported that meditation and relaxation-hypnosis were superior to simple relaxation. Morse et al. concluded from this datum and the physiological data that "relaxation-hypnosis and meditation can be considered similar on both physiological and subjective levels" (p. 321). Duff (1977) drew a similar conclusion when he attempted to enhance hypnotic susceptibility. Neither progressive relaxation nor hypnosis practice (nor alpha biofeedback) differentially influenced HGSHS scores.

COLEMAN STUDY

Coleman's dissertation at Brigham Young University (1976) represents one of the more thoroughgoing investigations of the relationships between hypnosis and relaxation. It was his avowed purpose to compare the behavioral process—relaxation—with hypnosis, using physiological indices (EEG and EMG), responses to suggestion, and self-reports of individual subjective experiences as measures. His initial orientation—"that the only difference between relaxation procedures and hypnotic induction procedures is the name given them" (p. 13)—turned out to be his final conclusion as well.

Coleman used three self-report scales in his study, one to assess responsivity to suggestion and two to assess the subjective experiences in either hypnosis or relaxation. The first, the responsivity scale (RS) consisted of 10 standard suggestions gleaned from various scales of hypnotic susceptibility. The scale consisted of hand lowering, finger lock, verbal inhibition, recall of a meal, fly hallucination, anosmia to ammonia, taste hallucination, hand analgesia, post-treatment suggestion, and postsuggestion amnesia. The two experience scales were made of 38 statements to which the subjects responded true or false regarding their subjective impressions. Typical statements were: "Time stood still"; "I tried to resist, but could not"; "My mind seemed empty." Whenever the word hypnosis appeared in a statement, it was retained for the hypnosis groups and replaced by "relaxation" for the other groups.

Four groups of seven males and females each were treated in the following manner: (a) subjects in one group were individually hypnotized through the SHSS:A eye-closure induction, (b) those in another group were relaxed through the Wolpe and Lazarus (1967) relaxation procedure, while (c) those in another (the contrast-training group) received the same relaxation procedure with the descriptive language removed. In other words, the latter group was merely instructed "forehead, tight," "loose," "crease your brow, tight," "loose." Thus muscle groups were tightened or relaxed, as in Wolpe and Lazarus's procedure, but without the surrounding context indicating the goal of relaxation. The subjects in the fourth group (d) were told to remain in a chair but otherwise allowed freedom of choice as to their mental activity.

The responsivity scale measure was taken following the "inductions," while the experiential scale measures were obtained after the instructions had been countermanded. EEG and EMG were recorded throughout the inductions and the responsivity testing. Following the experiment proper, a second group session was conducted in which all subjects were presented with the HGSHS. This measure was used to demonstrate that the groups did not differ with respect to hypnotic susceptibility, which they did not.

Using four different multivariate analyses, Coleman's data revealed that neither alpha production nor muscle tension distinguished among the groups, with the exception that the experimental groups yielded increased EMG during their respective instruction periods, whereas the control group did not. Coleman considers this finding indicative of relaxation, in either form, being an "active" process. However, a look at the simple methodological differences among the groups may be more revealing. The control group received no instructions, while verbal instructions were presented to the other three. Whether the latter three groups were actively entering relaxation or not may not be as important as the fact that they were being bombarded with auditory stimulation, and thus the mere act of listening, actively or passively, may be accompanied with increased EMG. What is more important, however, is that EEG and EMG measurements during relaxation and hypnosis do not reveal a clear difference between the two.

Coleman's analysis of the two experiential scales for the groups (one for hypnosis and one for the other groups) revealed that the subjectively reported experiences of the hypnotized subjects and the nonhypnotic relaxation subjects were the same overall. Since an overall analysis showed no differences between the relaxation (hypnosis and relaxation) groups and the control (contrast training and control) groups, the responses of each group were factor analyzed separately. Qualitative differences were noted in the factors underlying the responses of each group, particularly the primary ones. Not surprisingly, these data reveal the same relationship between subjects in hypnosis and those in relaxation on a one-time experimental basis that was discussed in relation to the findings of Cogger and Edmonston (1971) and Bullard and DeCoster (1972). Subjects entering hypnosis for the first time are more apprehensive than those entering "relaxation" for the first time. Coleman found that the prime factor in the experiential scale for the hypnotized subjects was one of alertness and amazement, while the prime factor for the relaxed group subjects was one of feelings of withdrawal, mental haziness, and mental inactivity. For the contrast-training control group the experience was one of cautious relaxation, while the uninstructed control group reported resistance and defensiveness as exemplifying their experience. These data seem to offer some support for the EMG data, indicating more muscle tension in the experimental groups. Coleman's summary of his data regarding the number of times a given subject has been hypnotized is pertinent: "the first and second times a person is hypnotized may produce more feelings of amazement and vigilance than later induction, even though all of the hypnosis sessions produce overall feelings which have been associated with hypnosis" (p. 162).

Perhaps what are of more interest in Coleman's study than his replication of the finding that nonhypnotic relaxation and hypnosis do not differ from one another on physiological and self-report measures are his data regarding the responsiveness of the various groups to suggestion. The suggestions used for the responsivitiy scale were essentially standard challenges offered to hypnotized individuals.

Both the hypnotized and the nonhypnosis relaxation groups scored significantly higher on the responsivity scale than the control group, and did not differ from one another. In addition, a comparison of those subjects who associated the relaxation and control procedures with hypnosis and those who did not revealed that being told or suspecting that an investigation involves hypnosis does not affect responsivity to suggestions. This finding, which runs somewhat counter to those of Dorcus, Brintall, and Case (1941) and Barber, Spanos, and Chaves (1974), seems to indicate that what is more important in the situation is the particular set of instructions offered the subjects, rather than any preconceived anticipations about hypnosis they may acquire either directly or indirectly from the situation. Whether they suspect hypnosis to be a part of the procedure or not does not affect their performance to suggestions, although it may affect their retrospective self-report of their experiences. (See Evans studies, chapter 3.)

Much of the literature of hypnosis attempts to define the condition as "responsiveness to suggestion" (see, e.g., Bernheim, 1888; Hull, 1933). In Coleman's study, both the relaxation and the hypnotized groups responded to hypnotic suggestions equally well and significantly better than the control groups.

If hypnosis can be defined as increasing responsivity to suggestion, then this particular relaxation procedure can be said to produce hypnosis. This idea implies that perhaps the relaxation procedure, when used in desensitization, produces a state of increased suggestibility or hypnosis. . . . (Coleman, 1977, p. 141)

This "particular relaxation procedure," it should be remembered, is a standard relaxation procedure used widely by behavior therapists. This one finding alone has far-reaching consequences for our perception of hypnosis and relaxation from the therapeutic and investigative standpoints.

CONCLUSION

In this chapter I have reviewed the literature that directly compares hypnosis with nonhypnotic relaxation. The mounting evidence is becoming clearer and clearer. From the standpoint of history, induction procedures, clinical practice, physiological measurement, and direct comparison, the equation of hypnosis with relaxation becomes more and more tenable. Coleman's data, particularly with respect to responsivity to suggestion, furthers the conviction, leaving but one final set of data to be explored before we can rest comfortably with the hypnosis-relaxation equation.

CHAPTER 8

Hypnosis, Relaxation, and the "Alert" Trance

The first response of most colleagues to the proposition that neutral hypnosis is relaxation is: "What about the alert trance?" or "Doesn't the alert trance demonstrate that hypnosis is not relaxation?" It is to these sorts of questions that the present chapter is addressed. Specifically, we will explore the data on alert and waking hypnosis and show that, while they do not abrogate the idea of hypnosis being relaxation, they do raise some interesting questions with respect to our conceptualizations of the general term trance.

The concept of an active or alert hypnotic condition did not, as many today suppose, begin with White's (1937) signal article, but was noted as far back as de Puységur's times. It will be recalled from earlier discussions (chapters 1 and 3) that de Puységur's most famous case, Victor Race, demonstrated at least two phases of the mesmerism de Puységur instructed. *Initially* Race was passive, in a sleep-appearing condition (which led to de Puységur's credit for the passivity and relaxation that is hypnosis), but upon instruction, *during mesmerism*, Race became alert, carrying out various suggestions, and, in fact, taking on personality characteristics that seemed most unlike him. He was no longer the dull peasant but an alert, intelligent, challenging equal of the Marquis himself.

De Puységur made a distinction between two types of alertness in the general context of mesmerism. First, there was a type of alertness or arousal of the nervous system brought about by the particular form of induction used with the patient—reminiscent of the crisis, hysteria-like behavior of Mesmer's patients. Second, there was an alertness that occurred within the mesmeric trance itself, which allowed the patient to carry out suggestions that would be difficult, if not impossible, to perform in the general lethargy of mesmerism per se. This is an important distinction to attend to in the ensuing discussion of "alert trance," because there is little disagreement today, or in the past, that the carrying out of hypnotic suggestions involves subjects becoming more alert than they are upon induction. De Puységur's second type is easily illustrated in the study by Dudley, Holmes, Martin, and Ripley (1963) noted in chapter 6. The authors found respiratory hyperfunction (increased alveolar ventilation, oxygen uptake, and decreased carbon dioxide concentration) upon suggested anger, anxiety and/or exercise during hypnosis. These changes were significant compared to resting measures during hypnosis alone.

Moll (1889), for example, described active and passive types of hypnosis, although from his description he seemed to be dealing more with what occurs during the hypnotic condition (de Puységur's second type) than what happens upon induction. Subjects in passive hypnosis could not be sufficiently aroused to respond to various suggestions of the hypnotist, while subjects in active hypnosis were able to follow post-induction instructions and respond to questions. To Moll, it was the presence or absence of muscular relaxation that denoted the type of hypnosis obtained. "The passive form has a great external likeness to natural sleep, while the active might be taken for a normal state on superficial observation" (Moll, 1889, p. 78). (We know now, of course, upon detailed observation that hypnotized subjects cannot satisfactorily simulate wakefulness [Reyher, 1973].) What gives us the clue that Moll's active hypnosis is de Puységur's second type of alertness (wherein the subject becomes relatively aroused to carry out some suggestion) is his notation that: "Hynposis often shows itself as passive at the beginning . . ." (Moll, 1889, p. 78). However, arousal for the purpose of responding to further suggestions is not what we are concerned with as the "alert trance."

There have been earlier descriptions of de Puységur's first type of alertness. As I indicated in chapter 3, Braid (1843) and Binet and Féré (1888) made note of a period during hypnosis when the patient was alert—usually preceding the deepest, somnambulistic phase. Walden (1900–01) also informed us that Tamburini and Seppelli (1882) described two conditions of hypnosis through plethysmographic measures, a lethargic condition in which forearm dilation was noted and a cataleptic one in which constriction occurred. Walden did point out that Tamburini and Seppelli only measured the immediate effects of the hypnotic induction and did not take prolonged measurements as he did. Walden, in fact, found initial decreases in peripheral blood flow (vasoconstriction) upon induction, followed by signs of increasing peripheral flow as time continued. He was of the following opinion: "The division of hypnotic sleep into two states, the lethargic and the cataleptic, does not seem necessary" (Walden, 1900–01, p. 153).

All of these notations of a degree of alertness in the patients or subjects at the outset are strikingly reminiscent of initial subject apprehension created by the social connotations of the term hypnosis in western culture. This apprehension is not too unlike individuals' natural response to any new situation. This particular point has been discussed in the last two chapters with respect to the work on body temperature and hypnosis and Bullard and DeCoster's (1972) work.

While the alert trance, sometimes called "waking hypnosis," has been mentioned throughout the history of hypnosis (see, e.g., Wells, 1924), there have been relatively few studies of it. Wells (1924), after discussing the merits of the presence or absence of amnesia or dissociation as the signal for the presence or absence of hypnosis, offers a narrative description of "experiments on several hundred subjects." The experiments consist more of testimonial statements of the merits of waking hypnosis procedures than comparison data with traditional relaxation hypnosis. Of his method of induction we know little, other than that it starts with the methods of Wingfield and Coué, followed with an explanation of dissociation, and may have involved ideomotor action and various motor catalepsies. In his description of autohypnosis, he did indicate that he started with eye closure, followed by limb contractures and then analgesias, essentially avoiding, it seems, the usual induction. Work with one subject is described in fair detail, including automatic writing and amnesia for various events and suggestions. The evaluation of the subject's responses was, as was the rest of the article, vague: "The genuineness of his surprise and interest may be easily imagined" (Wells, 1924, p. 403). While such descriptive phrases were perfectly acceptable five decades ago and are the fuel that led to many present investigations, present-day experimentation is made of sterner stuff. For the most part, Wells seems to be saying that waking and sleeping hypnosis are the same, in that similar results are obtained from the two procedures. Others, such as Davis and Kantor (1935), found otherwise.

Davis and Kantor provided more replicable data in their study of skin resistance during hypnosis (see also chapter 6). Fifty-six subjects were divided among four groups: those receiving passive then active suggestions, active then passive, passive alone, and active alone; and skin resistance measurements were made from the palmar surfaces and the fingertips. No difference was found between the two measurement sites. Later, Davis and Kantor looked at the data for subgroups of subjects who either carried out only the active suggestions or did not respond to either active or passive suggestions. The passive induction consisted of suggestions of relaxation coupled with finger strokes over the eyes; the active induction consisted of what is now used either as challenges to estimate hypnotizability or depth of hypnosis: arm and leg catalepsies and verbal aphasias. These two inductions were meant to replicate Tamburini and Seppelli's lethargic and cataleptic conditions.

By and large the data for the direction of change of skin resistance followed what one might expect; namely, under conditions of suggested relaxation it rises and under conditions of alertness it falls. The crucial finding was the comparison between the lethargic and cataleptic conditions, which revealed: "a real difference between skin resistance changes under conditions of 'sleep' and catalepsy" (Davis and Kantor, 1935, p. 73). Stated differently, "The active state of hypnosis resembles, in resistance behavior, the waking state. The quiescent condition resembles the sleep states . . ." (Davis and Kantor, 1935, p. 77). The authors go on to express, in much the same vein as proposed by Pavlov (see chapter 2), the opinion that, physiologically at least, there are all possible gradations between sleep and wakefulness. Dividing hypnosis into active and passive does not seem to add to our understanding, according to Davis and Kantor, particularly since their data indicated a decided difference between the active and passive conditions. In essence the control group against which they compared the traditional relaxation induction was one to whom a set of activating instructions were presented. Such a comparison shows hypnosis, as traditionally and historically understood, to differ from an active condition, but not (as was pointed out in the last chapter) from a nonhypnotic relaxation control condition. These experimentally demonstrated conclusions were available as early as 1935.

A slight detour in the history of the behavior of subjects given different types of induction instructions (alerting and relaxing) occurred in 1937 with the publication of White's noted article on "two types of hypnotic trance." In this article White is not describing differences in subjects' behavior due to different instructional sets, but rather differences in performance of different subjects given the same instructions. White, then, writes of *two different types of subjects,* not two different types of trance except as behavior is dependent upon the personality types of the subjects. Obviously, this is a difficult point of separation, but it is important for understanding relaxation as the fundamental property of hypnosis.

The active subject behaves as if he were in a completely submissive state. He seems to fall in eagerly with the hypnotist's assertion(s). . . . The passive subject seems bent on immobility. He can be made to move, or to wake, only by urgent efforts on the part of the hypnotist. (White, 1937, p. 283)

White tested 11 of 28 subjects who responded with a score of 1.75 or higher on Barry, MacKinnon, and Murray's (1931) scale of hypnotizability for various needs as described by Murray (see chapter 3). The five subjects White designated as "active" scored high on nDeference and nAffiliation, while the five "passive" subjects scored high on nCounteraction and nInfavoidance. The basic criterion for separating the two groups of subjects behaviorally was "the absence or presence of a delay and difficulty in making movements when it has been suggested that they will occur easily" (White, 1937, p. 288).

More recently, Kratochvíl and Shubat (1971) also presented data demonstrating individual differences in hypnotic behavior based on an activity-passivity dimension. Using two psychomotor tasks, speed of tapping and speed of circle drawing, 12 subjects were tested under hypnotic (Revised Stanford Profile Scale of Hypnotic Susceptibility, Form II) and awake conditions, properly counterbalanced. The speed of tapping was highly correlated between the conditions, although hypnosis reduced the absolute speed significantly from that attained in wakefulness. Speed of circle drawing results were nonsignificant for both analyses. The authors interpreted their results as indicating that the activity or passivity differences noted in hypnosis are at least in part a function of the "normal activity-passivity" levels of the subjects. In other words, the individual differences of the subjects, along this activity-passivity dimension, influence the degree of activity-passivity achieved during hypnosis.

More important, Kratochvíl and Shubat's findings regarding the absolute levels of tapping in the two conditions—that hypnosis significantly lowered the speed from the waking level—confirms hypnosis as a state of relaxation within which individual subjects perform at different levels of activity or passivity. White's 1937 thesis and Kratochvíl and Shubat's 1971 data do not confirm active and passive trance conditions, but deal with subject matter more accurately belonging under the topic of individual differences in responses *during* hypnosis. It is not the sort of alert-relaxed hypnosis denoted by de Puységur's second category of ease (or difficulty) of responding during the trance and studied by Davis and Kantor (1935) and others described below.

It is clear that the distinction being made here is a fine one, and not all readers will agree with the categorization. However, keep in mind that the purpose of this book is to attempt to filter out relaxation as the essence of hypnosis as we have come to know it historically, clinically, and experimentally. Saying that different individuals respond to the same instructions differently is not the same as saying that different individuals respond to different instructions differently. Both should be obvious, and neither detracts from the proposed relaxation-hypnosis equation.

Curiously, even White himself did not dwell long on the individual differences he noted in 1937. His 1941 description of the hypnotized person offers no hint of the dichotomy he suggested four years earlier:

The hypnotized person lacks alertness and humor; he is literal and serious in his execution of the operator's wishes, seems to have lost all sense of the ludicrous, pursues one goal with disproportionate intensity, and pays little attention to matters and impressions which lie outside this purpose. He seems to have a contracted frame of reference, and above all he lacks initiative, lying perfectly quiet and even dropping off to sleep if the operator stops proposing lines of action. (pp. 495–496)

Not only does White describe essentially a relaxed individual, who under further instructions carries out various suggestions, but he even suggests that when alerted the subject would perform poorer than a fully alert, awake individual. "It may well be that suitable tests of performance demanding alertness, decisions, and quick complex judgments would outline a sphere of achievement in which hypnotized persons made reliably poorer scores" (p. 496).

Finally, when he came to discuss induction procedures, White recognized "relaxation and the reduction of sensory input" as one of the two near universal features of hypnosis (the other being the presence of an operator). "It can be safely stated that nine out of ten hypnotic techniques call for reclining posture, muscular relaxation, and optical fixation followed by eye closure" (p. 498). (See also chapter 3.) White even takes issue with Wells's (1924) notion of "waking hypnosis," pointing out that while Wells avoided suggestions of drowsiness and sleep, "the subjects are instructed to close their eyes and to attend carefully to the operator" (p. 498). Thus by 1941 White seems to have played down the two types of hypnotic subjects in favor of placing relaxation in a more central position in an attempt to understand hypnosis. "There would appear to be enduring value, nevertheless, in the hypothesis of lowered functioning, of activity a little removed from the alert, wide-awake, self-conscious level which we ordinarily consider the best of all possible mental states" (White, 1941, p. 502). Investigating this "moderate degree of disinhibition" (along with motivation) was, for White, "the direction in which the scientific caravan should move."

RECENT LITERATURE

In the context of discussing "the hypnotic state," Hilgard (1977) calls attention to the idea that while the vast majority of individuals experiencing hypnosis report feelings of general relaxation, "hypnotic states can be produced without any suggestions of relaxation" (p. 165). This observation rests on two assumptions: (a) that an agreed-upon definition of hypnosis is available, against which to compare the effect of a variety of instructional sets, and (b) that the phrase trance state is synonymous with "hypnosis" or "hypnotic-like states." The former point is what I aim to establish with this book, and the latter will be dealt with in the concluding chapter. For the present it is sufficient to note that another orientation might be that hypnosis should be considered one type of trance and that the term trance be used as an overall, all-encompassing designation under which a variety of altered states be included.

Nonetheless, Hilgard (1977) cites various "spontaneous" trance states such as occur in religious gatherings and tribal ceremonies. He also points to whirling dervishes or Balinese dancing as being trance inducing. On this basis, and on data from his work with Leibert and Rubin (1965) and Banyai (1976), he offers active-alert hypnosis, whether induced following a relaxation induction (de Puységur's second type) or directly by instructions to be hyperalert (de Puységur's first type), as evidence that the equation of hypnosis and relaxation is limiting. The more recent literature on alert hypnosis is as sparse as the older literature, and studies directly comparing alert and relaxation inductions even more so.

Although Oetting (1964) and Vingoe (1968, 1969, 1973) discuss and present alert inductions, neither compared the results of their techniques with those of the usual hypnotic induction or of a nonhypnotic relaxation procedure. Oetting , for example, offers a brief set of instructions regarding concentration while studying, intended to keep the subject alert for that purpose. Although the author proclaims that this technique of "alert trance" induction has advantages over "classical" techniques, no data are offered on which to evaluate such an opinion.

Vingoe, on the other hand, developed a Group Alert Trance Scale (GAT) (1968), which urges the subjects to be mentally alert but physically and muscularly relaxed, harking back to Rachman's (1968) distinction between cognitive and physical relaxation and their relative effectiveness in behavioral therapies (see chapter 5). Those subjects who scored high on the self-report of the Harvard Group Scale of Hypnotic Susceptibility, Form A (HGSHS:A) tended to score high on the GAT as well ($r = .64$).

When one looks at the detail of Vingoe's GAT, it is not difficult to understand why individuals scoring high on its five-point scale should also score high on the HGSHS:A. Although admonishing the subject to be mentally alert, the following instructions are also included:

Let the muscles in your toes relax . . . your ankles . . . your feet . . . relax your calf muscles . . . let your thighs relax . . . relax the muscles of your back . . . of your shoulders . . . relax the muscles of your neck . . . let all your facial muscles relax . . . relax your forehead . . . all the muscles of your head. . . . Just relax all over, but as you've relaxed in body your mind has become very alert. Just relax your body all over, just relax your body all over. (pp. 123–124)

Instead of putting the horse (hypnotic induction) before the cart (suggestions to carry out some task calling for alertness and movement), Vingoe has mixed the two. As with Oetting (1964), the author claims that such a procedure is advantageous for education and experimentation, particularly in the realm of facilitating learning, but he has presented no data to support that contention. At any rate, presenting a set of instructions labeled "alert trance" neither establishes the condition nor abrogates relaxation as the fundamental basis of traditional hypnosis. It merely adds to the long list of instructional sets used to arouse subjects to perform certain tasks *during* hypnosis.

Of the studies that have compared alerting with relaxing techniques, Ludwig and Lyle's (1964) is often taken as a modern-day starting point. A number of mental and/or physically active procedures were presented to nine "post-addict" patients, after which standard hypnotic suggestions (e.g., arm rigidity, hallucinations, amnesia, etc.) were presented. The "alert induction" involved having the subjects rapidly pace the floor; spin around, sweeping the room with their eyes; do knee-bends, rotate their heads (while seated), and tense various muscle groups. During these activities suggestions were presented intended to create muscular rigidity and immobility in the muscles used in the activity. In addition, the subject was "continually bombarded with statements telling him he was 'keyed up,' 'on edge,' 'nervous' " (p. 72).

Following the alerting procedures—without benefit of the usual counterbalancing of instructions—hypnosis and "waking hypnosis" inductions were presented and the same measures taken. The hypnosis procedure consisted of an eye-closure induction with the usual suggestions of relaxation, while the "waking hypnosis" control consisted of misinforming the subjects that the study had nothing to do with hypnosis and asking for their cooperation by not allowing themselves to become drowsy and by performing the tasks suggested. Since these two instructions followed the alerting experience, it is difficult to assess the degree to which the subjects believed the latter instructions. Although the authors report that suggestibility, as measured in the alert condition, did not differ from that in hypnosis, the lack of a counterbalanced design, which obscures the possible effects of the interaction of repetition with treatment, and the rather select and unusual pool of subjects generally noted for their expertise of manipulation of other individuals make the results very difficult to interpret.

In addition, and perhaps more germane to the thesis of this book, is their description of the subjects' general behavior:

All but two subjects broke down and cried, and behavior such as holding their hands over their ears to shut out the rapid verbal statements, spontaneous tremors and gross shaking in the extremities, occasional writhing movements, neck muscle spasm, short periods of hyperventilation, gross clinical signs of anxiety and discomfort, heavy sweating, and angry retorts during questioning were commonly found in one or more subjects. (Ludwig and Lyle, 1964, p. 72)

While this description may accurately describe *a* trance, recalling the great mesmeric crises that de Puységur found so abhorrent, it does not describe hypnosis as investigators through the last two centuries have come to know it. Hypnosis, particularly neutral hypnosis, is not a painful experience; in fact, much of its therapeutic value lies in its being just the opposite.

Hilgard's laboratories have produced two studies that bear on the matter of alert hypnosis. In the first (Liebert et al., 1965) 15 subjects served as their own controls in a paired associate learning task (word-number pairs). Waking baseline scores were obtained from each subject before introducing one of three treatments (waking repeat, *traditional* hypnosis, and "alert hypnosis") and remeasuring on an equivalent list of word and number pairs. The *traditional* hypnosis induction was the Stanford Hypnotic Susceptibility Scale, Form A (SHSS:A); the alert induction was the same set of instructions modified to eliminate all references to sleep or relaxation. Both error scores and failures to respond indicated that the alert induction enhanced learning significantly over the *traditional* induction. The former produced fewer errors and fewer failures to respond than the latter, thus indicating that alerting instructions produce a condition that is *different* from that produced by a *traditional* induction in so far as paired associated learning is concerned. As with Davis and Kantor (1935), Bartlett, Faw, and Libert (1967), Ham and Edmonston (1971), and Gibbons

(1974, 1975, 1976), instructions to be alert produce a condition that is different, as measured, from hypnosis. On the other hand, the comparison of hypnosis with other relaxation instructions produces results that are similar, as measured (see chapter 7).

The second study from the Stanford laboratories, however, does give us pause in the progressive demonstration of differences between alert and hypnotic conditions. Banyai and Hilgard (1976) measured 50 subjects serving as their own controls on eight items of the SHSS:A and SHSS:B, following either *traditional* hypnotic or alerting instructions, properly counterbalanced. Besides the differences in the instructions given the subjects, the two conditions also differed in the subjects' general activity. During alerting instructions the subjects rode a Monark bicycle ergometer, but during the *traditional* hypnosis they were seated comfortably with their eyes closed. Comparing the mean scores on their eight-point scale, the authors found "that the two induction procedures were equivalent in their influence on responsiveness to hypnotic test items" (p. 220). Considering the large difference between the two treatment configurations, this is a rather startling finding, one that would not have been expected on the basis of Liebert, Rubin, and Hilgard's (1965) work in which the alert subjects performed better.

Banyai and Hilgard (1976) do indicate that, despite the results on the mean scores, some differences between the inductions may be seen in responsiveness to the eight individual items. They note that some slight advantage for the *traditional* induction may be present, although the statistical significance of this notation is in doubt. It is not until we look at what the authors have called the "secondary consequences of induction" and some of the subjective differences between the conditions that there is a hint that even in this study we may still be dealing with two related, but different, phenomena when we speak of trance and hypnosis in the same context. As one would expect, postural and motoric differences appear in the subjects under the different conditions. They were calm and relaxed and moved slowly and laboriously following *traditional* hypnosis, and displayed a tense posture, with rapid motor responsiveness, following the alerting instructions.

Since the similarity of the mean scores on the eight test items was the main finding of this study, note should be taken of the method of assessing the performance of the subjects. Assessment of the adequacy or inadequacy of response to suggestion was done by the experimenters themselves. Obviously, such a procedure is potentially confounding, since it was these same investigators who presented the two instructional sets to the subjects in the first place. Even if that had not been the case, the fact that the two physical settings during the different instructions (alert—on a bicycle; *traditional*—seated in a chair) were so different would have given any observer information as to which set of instructions had been administered, and thus brought the observers' preconceived expectations into play. The mean score similarities become suspect, then, due to the subjective nature of the behavior ratings and their possible confounding by observers, who were not naive to the experimental condition of the subjects. Unlike the simulator model (see chapter 7), there is no way in which assessments of the effects of the two instructional sets could have been obtained independent of prior knowledge of the condition of the subjects.

Although Hilgard is quite correct when he points out that such assessment procedures are the generally accepted format,* such a consensus does not set aside the methodological considerations, particularly when they can be partially met by the presence of an independent observer or similarities in testing environments. Furthermore, when the details of the reports of the subjects themselves are inspected, the interpretation of mean performance score similarities becomes more unclear.

The subjective reports are more enlightening. Although Liebert, Rubin, and Hilgard (1965) reported that their subjects maintained the feeling of being hypnotized, despite the differences in the learning scores, Banyai and Hilgard (1976) reported a mixture of subjective similarities and diffrences. Noting that 28 subjects reported similarities between the two conditions, they also found 21 who outlined differences, the major difference being in level of alertness, which 43 of the subjects reported. Although the authors attribute this difference to situational factors (activity and instructions), it is when we look at the dichotomy of those subjects who preferred the *traditional* over the alert instructions (and vice versa) that we get some hint that, at least for certain individuals, the *traditional* relaxation induction is the more effective instruction. "Those who preferred the traditional induction *were, in general, higher scorers than those who preferred the alert induction,* but they scored even higher following the traditional induction" (Banyai and Hilgard, 1976, p. 222, italics added). Again we seem confronted with the problem of individual differences, in that neither the ceiling effect of the scale used nor the relaxation inherent in the traditional induction inhibited their responsiveness.

In addition, the authors themselves touch upon another point that is crucial in the distinction to be made between alerting and hypnotic instructions. Discussing their results, they opine that through their "active-alert hypnotic induction" they can produce "a state in which all the important characteristics of hypnosis occur [subjective report of altered state, trancelike appearance, response to susceptibility tests], *except the resemblance to sleep*" (Banyai and Hilgard, 1976, p. 223, italics added). As the case has developed in the preceding chapters, without the relaxation that is historically, clinically, and experimentally inherent in the word hypnosis, defining alerting instructions as "alert hypnosis" may only be adding further confusion to an already chaotic literature that attempts to define the essence of hypnosis. That alerting instructions may produce trancelike behavior

*Personal communication.

does not necessarily assure us that these instructions produce *traditional* hypnosis.

To date, Banyai and Hilgard (1976) have produced the only study in which the measurements used do not clearly distinguish between the effects of alerting instructions and hypnosis. However, the impact of their data is reduced by the methodological considerations of the many roles played by the experimenters. The other studies reported above and those to be discussed all demonstrate a difference between the two conditions. Gibbons (1974, 1975, 1976), for example, compared an induction procedure based on instructions of alertness with a *traditional* hypnotic induction including suggestions of drowsiness and sleep, and found the performance of his "hyperempiria" group significantly better than the hypnosis group on the self-report HGSHS:A. He, unlike Banyai and Hilgard (1976), concluded that "hyperempiria is discriminably different from hypnosis" (Gibbons, 1976, p. 834), or that alerting instructions produce different results from relaxation-hypnosis inductions.

Bartlett, Faw, and Liebert (1967), just two years after Liebert had reported differences between the two conditions with Rubin and Hilgard, produced data on pupillary size in a single subject after alerting instructions and hypnosis (relaxation) instructions. The findings, depicted in figure 8.1, show clearly the differential influence of the two instructions. Under alerting conditions the subject's pupil was significantly larger in diameter than during hypnosis. The authors attributed this change to the "characteristics of the instructions used rather-than to stable characteristics of the 'state' of hypnosis" (p. 191). Once again, when subjects are presented with alerting instructions, they act accordingly and in a manner different than when they are hypnotized.

Kratochvíl (1970) found the same relationship between "waking" and "sleep hypnosis." "Waking hypnosis" was defined to his subjects as a condition wherein the individual acts as if in the normal, awake state, reacting quickly and purposively to suggestions, walking, standing, and so forth. On the other hand, "sleep hypnosis" was defined as a condition similar to sleep wherein the subject is drowsy, tired; slow to react, speak, and think; and generally passive and without normal initiative. By inducing these two types of "hypnosis" through prearranged signals ("somnus" and "vigilia") in six female subjects carefully selected from a group of 100 for somnambulistic ability, Kratochvíl tested the hypothesis that the drowsiness, inhibition, and sleeplike qualities of hypnosis are artifacts rather than "substantial characteristics" of hypnosis. Using 11 test suggestions especially developed to reflect both active and passive qualities as criteria measures, the author tested each subject under each condition twice while subjects were being observed by two judges who were unaware of the type of instruction given the subject (alert or passive). The judges rated the subjects' behavioral performances on a one to seven scale for each suggestion, one indicating most active and seven indicating most passive.

Five of the six subjects yielded ratings of greater behavioral passivity during

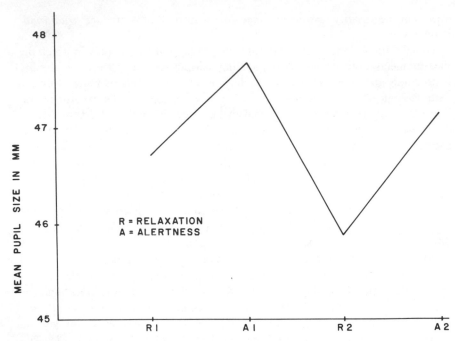

Figure 8.1. Pupil size after relaxation and alertness suggestions. (From Bartlett, Faw, and Liebert, 1967. Reprinted from the October, 1967 International Journal of Clinical and Experimental Hypnosis. Copyrighted by the Society for Clinical and Experimental Hypnosis, October, 1967.

"sleep hypnosis" than during "waking hypnosis," and the two conditions compared statistically yielded $t = 3.27$, $p < .05$. "In sleep hypnosis significantly more manifestations of behavioral inhibition and passivity were present than in waking hypnosis" (Kratochvíl, 1970, p. 36). As in the cases cited above (Davis and Kantor, 1935; Liebert et al., 1965; and Bartlett et al., 1967), when alerting instructions (alert trance, waking hypnosis, alert hypnosis) are compared with traditional induction techniques the results are consistent in demonstrating that behaviorally and physiologically the two conditions differ from one another.

However, Kratochvíl (1970), whose data clearly showed a significant difference in the behavioral performance of his subjects under the two conditions of hypnosis and "waking hypnosis," concluded: "As far as the central hypothesis of the study is concerned, the results demonstrated that deeply hypnotized Ss need not necessarily show the behavioral characteristics associated with a sleep-like state" (p. 37). That is not the conclusion I would draw from his data. His two groups differed significantly from one another, the hypnotized group being rating significantly more inhibited and passive. In addition, the author also concluded that "the behavioral prediction about hypnosis drawn from the present

Russian writings can be regarded as not confirmed'' (p. 37). Since he himself predicted (from the Pavlovian position) that hypnosis as partial sleep would lead to passivity and a lowering of reactivity with increasing depth, and his subjects were, indeed, significantly more passive when hypnotized, this interpretation also is not what I would have expected. The results did indeed show that a hypnotic induction couched in terms of relaxation and sleep (the *traditional* mode) creates behavioral passivity, as predicted by the Russian literature and consistently attested to throughout this book. Thus, while in this study Kratochvíl appears to view his data as supporting an ''expected deficiency of the sleep theory as a complete explanation of hypnosis'' (p. 30), on the basis of his own results the opposite is true.

As with most authors writing about ''alert hypnosis,'' there seems to be an insistence upon labeling the behavior attending alerting instructions ''alert hypnosis'' just because the instructions are presented in the context of an experiment the investigator has designated ''hypnotic.'' Such a procedure is acceptable provided that: (a) the behavior the subjects engage in is uniformly accepted as hypnotic behavior, and (b) the subjects perform in the same manner under the differing sets of instructions; that is, alerting and hypnotic. Most studies have met the first provision, with the notable exception of Ludwig and Lyle (1964). However, none of the studies of ''alert trance'' have been able to meet the second standard, with the possible exception of Banyai and Hilgard's (1976), and I have already reviewed the difficulties inherent in that experimental design. Despite the overwhelming findings that the behavior elicited by the two instructions is different either in kind or degree, authors continue to conclude that inhibition and relaxation do not play a crucial role in hypnosis. Frankly, such a conclusion does not seem warranted by the data.

Only one study has compared a *traditional* hypnotic induction with both alerting instructions (*á la* Liebert et al., 1965) and nonhypnotic relaxation. This study has already been described in chapter 7, but it bears some review here. In brief, Ham and I (1971) measured simple reaction times and found that the nonhypnotic relaxation control and the hypnotic relaxation induction groups *did not* differ from one another, but did differ from the alerted group. Figure 8.2 reproduces these results. The two relaxation groups had progressively increasing and significantly longer reaction times (RTs) than those of the alert group. No doubt the retarded motor responsivity noted in the hypnosis and the relaxed groups was partially due to the nature of the instructions—that is, to relax—but these instructions are the traditional instructions of hypnosis. The nature of the induction in part defines the condition, but this does not allow one license to label arbitrarily any procedure ''hypnosis'' and then proclaim that the fundamental nature of the condition (relaxation) has been proven to be not what two centuries of clinical and experimental investigation have shown it to be. When you compare alerting instructions with *both a traditional* hypnotic induction *and*

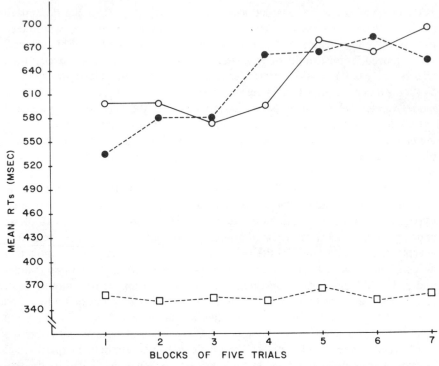

Figure 8.2. Mean reaction times of relaxation control (solid circle, solid line), relaxation induction (open circle, solid line) and alert induction (open circle, dashed line) groups. (From Edmonston, 1979. Copyright © 1979 by Erika Fromm and Ronald E. Shor. Reprinted with permission from Hypnosis: Developments in Research and New Perspectives (New York: Aldine Publishing Company.)

nonhypnotic relaxation instructions, the alerting instructions yield a different result from the other two, which, in turn *do not* differ from one another.

CONCLUSION

The experimental evidence is clear. Virtually all of the investigations to date show that whether the measures used are motivational (White, 1937), cognitive (Liebert et al., 1965), physiological (Davis and Kantor, 1935; Bartlett et al., 1967) or behavioral (Kratochvíl, 1970; Kratochvíl and Shubat, 1971; Ham and Edmonston, 1971; Gibbons, 1974, 1975, 1976), alerting instructions produce a condition that is different from *traditional* hypnosis.

The answer to the question asked at the beginning of this chapter—doesn't the alert trance demonstrate that hypnosis is not relaxation?—is simply no. What the concept of an alert trance docs show is our proclivity for cluttering up the conceptual framework within which investigators of hypnosis attempt to work. That alerting instructions (or any instructions, for that matter) produce a modified condition in the human listener is granted. That they produce hypnosis in the traditional sense is not. The studies reviewed in chapter 7 made it clear that experimental comparisons between hypnosis and nonhypnotic relaxation produce results making the equation of the two conditions evident. Those reviewed in chapter 8 have made it clear that experimental comparisons between alerting instructions and hypnosis produce results making the equation of those two conditions untenable. The one study that compared all three conditions (Ham and Edmonston, 1971) made the relationship among the three even clearer. The equation of hypnosis and relaxation must be more seriously entertained than it has been in the recent past. The clinical and experimental evidence of such an equation is there; it will not go away.

CHAPTER 9

Conclusions, Ethics, and Nomenclature

Neutral hypnosis is relaxation. No matter where we turn—to the history of hypnosis, to the induction procedures commonly used, to the clinical studies of the applications of hypnosis, to the experimental data—the message is the same. *Traditional* hypnosis, from the time of de Puységur and before, is basically and fundamentally relaxation. Even those who least endorse relaxation as the fundamental of hypnosis persist in labeling relaxation-hypnosis *traditional* hypnosis. Why? Because it *is*, historically, clinically, and experimentally. The literature reviewed in the preceding eight chapters repeatedly attests to the fact.

But the demonstration of the hypnosis-relaxation correspondence is only a beginning to our search for understanding hypnosis. Unfortunately, some readers will perceive the viewpoint indicated by the data set forth herein as running counter to many of the theories of hypnosis. Such is not the case. The relaxation of hypnosis is *prerequisite* to all of the theories in the field. The relaxation precedes, must come first, *before* the various theoretical explanations can begin to weave their hypothetical webs. It is the empirical *how* that predates the theoretical explanations. It is the mechanism for the disinhibition; the hyper-suggestibility; the circumventing of the ego mechanisms; the regressions in the ego's service; the effectiveness of the attitudes, motivations, and the role-playing of the subjects and the "demand characteristics" of the situations; the dissociations and the dividing of the consciousness; and, yes, the production of the so-called hypnotic phenomena themselves.

For one thing, there is very little theoretical about the hypnosis-relaxation correspondence. I do not intend its statement as a theoretical position; it is an empirical report of what, on balance, are the data as presented. There is very little theory about it; the experimental and clinical reports, when seen collectively, are very clear. These are the facts of the matter.

Obviously, the data can be seen to relate to the theory of hypnosis as partial sleep and cortical inhibition, as outlined in chapter 2 on Pavlov. Relaxation forms the initial cortical (and subcortical) inhibition of hypnosis, following which there is a disinhibition of certain areas (through the various rapport zones) for the purpose of carrying out the suggestions of the hypnotist. The similarity of the disinhibitions (which are secondary to the primary inhibition—relaxation) of

Pavlov to the second type of alertness noted by de Puységur (see chapter 8) is clear, but it is the primary inhibition of the relaxation fundamental to hypnosis that relates most easily to Pavlov's theory.

This relationship—the relaxation of hypnosis as prerequisite to what follows—is apparent in other theoretical positions as well. For example, it is hard to imagine the operation of the primary process or ego receptivity of the psychoanalytic viewpoint (see Fromm, 1979) without considering some mechanism for their emergence. The relaxation of hypnosis provides that mechanism, as suggested by the data and in Fromm's notion of a continuum of depth to altered states of consciousness. In her terms, the deeper the hypnosis (light, medium, deep), the more primary-process thinking emerges and is allowed into consciousness by the reduced ego strength. Thus the relaxation fundamental to hypnosis may be the mechanism through which effective psychoanalytically based therapy may be implemented. The same, of course, is true of autogenic training and behavior therapy as therapeutic approaches. The great emphasis that is placed on the early "exercises," which essentially relax the patient as a prerequisite to the eventual therapeutic effectiveness of autogenic training, certainly draws our attention to the primary step of relaxation (Schultz and Luthe, 1959). It is this relaxation that allows what follows to be effective, in much the same way that it allows the disinhibitions and the primary-process flow. Despite the controversy over the necessity of relaxation (see chapter 5), the vast majority of behavior therapists begin with relaxation exercises.

Hilgard's (1977, 1979) revival and elaboration of Janet's dissociation hypothesis clearly acknowledges the debt owed to hypnotic procedures in laying the groundwork for dissociation experiences. In his interpretation, these procedures aid, in part, by disrupting ongoing memory patterns and thus disorienting the subject and, in part, by reducing muscular feedback needed for special orientation. "The altered background for receiving suggestions, the state of hypnosis, is one of felt changes from normal in that the usual orientation to reality has been disturbed, and familiar reality testing does not go on" (Hilgard, 1977, p. 227). This altered background is the relaxation inherent in hypnosis.

Thus hypnosis would seem to emerge as a two-step phenomenon, as noted in chapter 1. The first stage is the induction of neutral hypnosis (relaxation) and the second is the disinhibitions, the emergent primary-process, the dissociations, the hypersuggestibility, or whatever the particular theorist considers important. But is this necessarily the case? Certainly it is logical that disinhibitions might follow an inhibition condition (relaxation) and we might see more of what the psychoanalists call primary-process thinking and awareness. The discontinuities of orientation predicted by the dissociationists and the Hullian hypersuggestibil-ity may also appear, but are these secondary phenomenon what give constancy to the term hypnosis, or is it the primary step, the relaxation? The number of different but related factors on which the various theorists have dwelt would imply that none alone is constant in hypnosis. The only phenomenon that is constant in the literature is the primary factor—relaxation. Relaxation pervades the literature, clinical and experimental, whenever one studies hypnosis. The only thing that hypnosis consistently relates to is the relaxation inherent in its production. In fact, the studies reviewed in chapter 7 reveal that under conditions not labeled hypnosis but consisting of its fundamental—relaxation—results indistinguishable from hypnosis-labeled relaxation are obtained. All of the phenomena considered important by the various theorists in the field can be obtained through the process of nonhypnotic relaxation.

For example, Hull considered the essence of hypnosis to be a relative increase in suggestibility. Yet the same degree of increased responsivity that follows a hypnotic induction has been obtained following nonhypnotic relaxation. Recall, if you will, the Evans (1967) studies reviewed in chapter 3. While not arranged to measure an *increase* in suggestibility, his work demonstrated that the distribution of responses from subjects receiving instructions only to relax (omitting any reference to the concept of hypnosis) was the same as that which would be expected from subjects given a *traditional* hypnotic induction, and that the subjects responded to significantly more of the test items (chosen from traditional hypnotic phenomena) than a group of subjects serving as an uninstructed control group.

Coleman's (1976) experience was identical. He too found that whether or not the subjects knew or suspected that the experience involved hypnosis did not affect their responsivity (see chapter 7). Both of his hypnosis and nonhypnotic relaxation groups were significantly more responsive to hypnotic phenomena suggestions (finger lock, fly hallucination, etc.) than the control group and did not differ from one another. Responsiveness to suggestions of hypnotic phenomena is not a factor constant to hypnosis but to its essence, relaxation. Hypnotic phenomena are producible through relaxation, whether it is designated hypnosis or not and whether the individuals involved perceive the relaxation to be hypnotic or not. Neutral hypnosis is *not* a two-step phenomenon. There is but one step, the relaxation. All else is secondary to that one fundamental characteristic.

But, the reader may think, doesn't the fact that Orne's simulators can deceive skilled professionals by pretending to act hypnotized indicate that relaxation is not a neccessary condition for hypnosis? Doesn't the simulator model and Sarbin's role-taking theory of hypnosis indicate that "true" relaxation is unnecessary, since mere pretense will suffice to delude an observer into reporting the presence of hypnosis in the simulator or role-player? No, it does not, because (a) from the traditional standpoint there is no hypnosis without relaxation, and (b) pretense and reality *are* distinguishable if the experimental design and the observational methods are properly sensitive. Reyher (1973) has made the latter point very cogently (see chapter 7). By asking deeply hypnotized subjects to simulate being awake, he found that independent observers had no difficulty differentiating those who were simulating wakefulness from those who were not. Once the relaxation of hypnosis has been achieved, wakefulness cannot be adequately represented until the relaxation has been terminated. And this was on an observational basis alone. Had one measured the covert responsiveness of the simulating subjects (e.g., their physiology) or some more precise behavioral response (e.g., reaction time), the differences may have been even more apparent.

Another example may help clarify further the import and the impact of a change in the state of the organism (relaxation) that not only defines hypnosis but is not surmountable by simulation or conscious role-playing. Recognizing that sleep is not a uniform condition, that there are gradations within the concept, and that the precise demarcation between sleep and wakefulness is not sharply defined, individuals, be they actors or not, can pretend to be asleep to a degree that the casual observer would attest to their being alseep. *However,* an individual who is asleep cannot pretend to be awake. Not only can they not feign wakefulness to the satisfaction of an observer, they cannot do it at all! Within the difficulties of precise definition noted above, when one is asleep, one is asleep and cannot be otherwise. The mechanisms of sleep are so overpowering that the pretense of wakefulness is out of the question, short of actually becoming awake.

So it is with the fundamental of neutral hypnosis—relaxation. When one is relaxed, one is relaxed; no amount of feigning or pretending or simulating will achieve another condition (e.g., wakefulness) short of its actual production. Once neutral hypnosis (relaxation) has been produced, the credible simulation of a more alert condition is out of the question. During hypnosis some change comes about that cannot be reversed by mere pretense alone. That change is relaxation, with all of its behavioral, physiologic, and attitudinal concomitants.

What this means, of course, is that we have somewhat more latitude in our behavior during wakefulness than during neutral hypnosis (relaxation). We can pretend to be other than what we are when we are awake. Neutral hypnosis, on the other hand, is more limiting. Our focus of attention is narrowed. Our motor and physiological responsiveness is altered. There is a functional irreversibility to the hypnotic condition that cannot be overcome without producing actual arousal. There is a change that takes place in the organism at all levels when neutral hypnosis is induced, and that change is the activation of the relaxation mechanisms with their concomitant behavioral and physiologic changes. Whether these mechanisms are activated through direct intervention, as with Hess's (1957) cats, or indirectly through verbal suggestions, which in turn activate the mechanism through meaning and symbolism, the effect is the same, a functionally irreversible condition that is discernible in retrospect by the individual involved as relaxation.

The latter point, that of the subjective experience of hypnotic subjects being recognized and reported as relaxation, was made clear in my questionnaire data (Edmonston, 1977) on patients being treated during hypnosis (see chapter 5). If you will recall, the overwhelming spontaneous description offered of hypnosis was relaxation. Coleman (1976) reported similar findings (see chapter 7). In addition to physiological and behavioral measures not distinguishing between relaxation and hypnosis, the self-reports of his subjects were essentially the same between the two conditions. Repeatedly the literature calls to our attention the identity of relaxation with neutral hypnosis, historically, clinically, motorically, physiologically, behaviorally, and attitudinally. It is this last attribute—the attitudes of patients, subjects, practitioners, and investigators—that highlights one of the issues that the recognition of the relaxation-neutral hypnosis correspondence raises. That issue is one of ethics and legalities, to which the field will eventually have to address itself.

ETHICAL AND LEGAL ISSUES

As noted in chapter 7, Coleman (1976) opines that if hypnosis is considered a condition of increased suggestibility, then hypnosis is produced by relaxation procedures. The implications of this notation, of course, are rather broad. As Coleman points out, relaxation as used in behavioral therapies (e.g., desensitization) produces a state of hypnosis, a state of increased suggestibility. Put another way, behavior therapists are producing hypnosis in their patients, whether defined by its fundamental, *relaxation*, or by an increasing suggestibility. Reyher and Wilson (1973) made this point very explicit:

The effectiveness of the Jacobson method of progressive relaxation in inducing hypnosis implies that its use in other situations such as desensitization therapy also produces hypnosis. . . . The implication of these considerations is that hypnosis occurs unwittingly in situations wherein passive compliance is produced by relaxation procedures and S's attention is directed by the operator. (p. 233)

While we are aware that there is some controversy among behavior therapists as to the importance of relaxation for therapeutic benefit (see chapter 5), Coleman's point is that relaxation (hypnosis) produces increased susceptibility to suggestions, and when the suggestions are therapeutic, they benefit the patient. There is little doubt among clinicians of any persuasion that increasing the suggestibility of the patient increases the therapist's chances of manipulating the effectiveness of whatever therapy is applied, be it behavioral, psychological, surgical, or pharmacological. The attitudes of the patient toward the proposed or applied treatment can be crucial to the patient's response to treatment, and many clinicians view enhancing the patient's positive attitudes to be as critical as the direct treatment itself.

The ethical point that these observations and Coleman raise is: If a patient refuses hypnosis as part of treatment, is it ethical to substitute relaxation techniques, considering that we now recognize relaxation as the fundamental, defining characteristic of hypnosis? Is it professionally appropriate for the practitioner to say to the patient: "All right, I won't use hypnosis in your treatment, I'll just teach you how to relax"? Has our knowledge of the relationship of relaxation to hypnosis placed us in the ethically awkward position of having to deceive, "for their own good," patients who are resistive to the use of hypnosis? Are we now forced to an "end justifies the mean" position, in which the practitioner must live with a sin of omission (not informing the patient of the relationship between the treatment refused—hypnosis—and the treatment proposed—relaxation) in order to benefit the patient? Of course not. The problem is one of education and nomenclature, not ethics and legalities.

In the first place, we must recognize that legality is basically the binding acceptance by the general public of a subgroup's particular code of moral conduct, and that the two issues, ethical and legal, are intricately intertwined. For example, most of the major professional organizations devoted to the study and understanding of hypnosis, applied or experimental, are continually pressing for legal restrictions on the use of hypnosis by individuals who are not members of the health professions at the doctoral level. These organizations have developed committees that both stay informed on the state of legislation regarding hypnosis and act as advocate bodies where appropriate. A very clear indication of how closely the codes of ethics of these groups tie in with proposed restrictive legislation is seen in a recent resolution passed by both a national and an international organization. The resolution pertains to the increasing use of hypnotic techniques by individuals in police and other law enforcement or investigative bodies whom the professional society feels are not adequately trained either in hypnosis or a broader range of psychological variables, or both. The ethical restriction, which is incumbent upon the members of the professional society, is that the organization considers it "unethical for its members to train lay individuals in the use of hypnosis, to collaborate with laymen in the use of hypnosis, or to serve as a consultant for laymen who are utilizing hypnosis" (Society for Clinical and Experimental Hypnosis, 1979, p. 452). Without regard to the appropriateness of such a dictum, it should be clearly recognized that such ethical statements are preliminary to pressing for restrictive legislation in the same vein. In many instances the ethical codes of organizations, originally presented as a statement of the degree of self-discipline within the profession, become the initial steps to obtaining restrictive legislation with regard to the performance of some service or set of behaviors.

The legal question raised by the data presented herein is similarly related to the ethical one. Not only are we confronted by the ethics of substituting the essence (relaxation) of one procedure (hypnosis) for that procedure refused, but we are confronted with the question of restrictive legislation for the essence. To wit, should any legislation that would restrict the use of hypnosis include its fundamental, relaxation, as well? Should the various other procedures for producing relaxation be legislatively restricted, because the condition produced (relaxation) is the fundamental characteristic of hypnosis, which the legislation set out to restrict in the first place? Obviously, this is an extremely complicated affair and it is unlikely that any single solution will satisfy all concerned.

Coleman's (1976) solution to the ethical problem is the same as mine for the problem of restrictive legislation as a general concept (Edmonston, 1973). His is more individual, mine more broadly based. As stated above, the problem is one of education and nomenclature, not ethics and legality. Coleman's solution is one of the proper education of the individual patient with regard to the potentials of the procedures used. Thus the patient is provided with virtually the same knowledge of the procedure as the practitioner in an effort to allay anxieties and fears engendered by the misconceptions our society attributes to the word hypnosis. In this manner the anxieties of the patient, which may disrupt the treatment process, can be converted into excitement, which Reyher and Wilson (1973) view as facilitory. The ethical difficulty is resolved by making the patient or subject a partner in the program, actively participating in his or her treatment, rather than being an object of someone else's manipulations. But it should now be apparent that relaxation techniques will have to be thoroughly reported to the patient or subject as producing that condition that many people in the past have characterized as hypnosis. The findings reviewed in this book no longer allow the practitioner the unfettered privilege of substituting "relaxation" for "hypnosis."

While we may agree that more complete disclosure of our procedures to individual people in the confines of the treatment room will solve the ethical dilemma created by our awareness of the relaxation-hypnosis equation, there is some doubt that professionals working in the field of hypnosis are ready to embrace *Veritas Vos Liberabit* as a general principle, much less desist from urging that the practice of hypnosis (relaxation) be restricted to certain individuals possessing superior education and knowledge. The effect of the passage quoted above from the resolution concerning law enforcement uses of hypnosis is not just to restrict the behavior of the organization's members, but to disallow one form of knowledge to the populace at large.

Just as Coleman's suggested solution to the ethical dilemma was the education of the individual patient, so has my solution to the legal dilemma created by the relaxation-hypnosis concomitance been education. An educated, knowledgeable populace is better able to make a well-reasoned choice than one held in relative ignorance, whether by ethical codes of organizations of individuals providing services or by restrictive legislation that places the care of the many in the hands of the few. In 1973 I formally put forth the principle of education rather than legislation with regard to restricting the uses of hypnosis. The awareness of

relaxation as the fundamental characteristic of hypnosis in no way restricts that
point of view. The dilemma of whether or not to include the many procedures for
producing relaxation in legislation on hypnosis is not a dilemma at all. If you are
to have such legislation, then the data suggest that it must also take into account
relaxation. If, however, one is willing to challenge the legislative view and
substitute education for legislation, then relaxation must be included in an
educational program.

NOMENCLATURE

There are several issues here. The first is the confusion of the terms trance and
hypnosis and the second is the accurate labeling of what we have been calling
hypnosis since the 1840s. The confusion of terms most recently grew out of the
literature on "alert trance" and the "accurate labeling" problem grew out of
the recognition of the meaning of the data reviewed in the preceding chapters.

One of the difficulties with the contention that "alert trance" contradicts the
notion of hypnosis being essentially relaxation, besides the lack of a data base for
that contention, is the use of the terms hypnosis and trance interchangeably.
Whether the authors recognize it or not, the consistency of this supposed
interchangeability is quite apparent. For example, the juxtaposition of discussing
the trances of religious gatherings, tribal rituals, whirling dervishes, and the like
with hypnosis, without some disclaimer that the two terms, trance and hypnosis,
are not necessarily the same (differing at least in the mode of induction) tends to
lead the reader down a conceptual path that is not warranted. Such an equation,
particularly without substantiating data other than rather global observations that
individuals act or feel "strange," "different," "altered," confuses rather than
clarifies attempts to understand what is fundamental to any of the processes that
produce such "altered states."

Anthropologists and sociologists have certainly documented trances—altered
states—in a variety of cultures, both primitive and civilized; but whether this
means that all trances, regardless of their origins, must be considered hypnosis
has not been established. That alerting instructions or various forms of social or
individual rituals may create an altered state of consciousness may be true, but
that does not necessarily imply that such procedures and their outcomes qualify
for the title of hypnosis or hypnotic inductions. There are gradations within the
generic notation trance, and such concepts as hypnosis and alert trance should be
considered but subclasses of trance, each different from the other in definable
ways. What defines hypnosis as a type of trance different, say, from alert trance
is the relaxation inherent in its production, form, and substance.

The recognition of that one point alone relieves us from what is in reality a
very restrictive categorization schema. Many have seemed to consider hypnosis

the generic term and trance the subclass. In this way, any behavior designated as trance or trance inducing is supposed to be a form of hypnosis, so that the definition of hypnosis is so broadened as to encompass all forms of altered states of consciousness; thus the definition is meaningless. Neutral hypnosis is but a rung on the ladder of consciousness, altered from other forms of consciousness through its fundamental characteristic, relaxation. The induction of *traditional,* neutral hypnosis (relaxation) creates only one of a number of possible alterations of consciousness subsumed under the more generic term trance. All trances are not hypnosis; hypnosis is only one form of trance.

Anesis

A second nomenclature problem was highlighted again by Coleman (1976) when he noted "that the only difference between relaxation procedures and hypnotic induction procedures is the name given them" (p. 13). The problem of accurate labeling is not new. Braid, of course, was one of the early investigators to concern himself with the nomenclature of hypnosis. As we know, this concern led directly to the change of the phrase animal magnetism to the term hypnosis. Even within the term hypnosis Braid perceived difficulties of precision, which he at first attempted to deal with by further definining the different parts of speech derived from the word.

Let the term *hypnotism* be restricted to those cases alone in which, by certain artificial processes, oblivious sleep takes place, in which the subject has no remembrance on awaking of what occurred during his sleep, but of which he shall have the most perfect recollection on passing into a similar stage of hypnotism thereafter.

Hypnotic coma, Braid suggested, would

denote that still *deeper* stage of the sleep in which the patient seems to be quite unconscious at the time of all external impressions, and devoid of voluntary power, and in whom no idea of what had been said or done by others during the said state of *hypnotic coma* can be be remembered by the patient on awaking, or at *any* stage of *subsequent* hypnotic operations. (Braid, 1855, pp. 370–371)

Thus Braid's definitions hinged on behavioral phenomena, in particular amnesias. He reserved one term, hypnotism, for that condition in which memories could be recovered at some future time, and the other form, hypnotic coma, for the condition in which total amnesia occurs. It was only when Braid was satisfied that the processes he described were the result of "mental impressions" that he began to develop yet another nomenclature based on the term monoideism. Curiously, despite the general support of the later writings of such individuals as Bernheim and Janet and Hull, which reasserted the regnancy of suggestion in the process of hypnosis, the term monoideism and its attendant variation (monoideology, monoideiser, monoideo-dynamics, etc.) never came into popular use. No matter how the various modern theorists describe either the condition or the processes leading to the condition, such descriptions continue to be couched in terms of hypnosis.

Braid's efforts at relabeling were in the interest of more accurate description. Animal magnetism, to Braid, did not describe what was going on in the process of using this relatively new therapy with patients. A new, more accurate term was needed, and he supplied it by choosing the Greek word for sleep, *hypnos*. Although the sleep notation has been energetically contested through the years (see chapter 2), none of the investigators in the field have been sufficiently convinced of the inaccuracy of the term hypnosis to discard it for another. The data presented in this book do, however, raise the issue of whether or not we are at a crossroads much like that faced by Braid in the 1840s. Today we have no lack of definitions of hypnosis, often intimately integrated with the various methodologies used to investigate the condition and the phenomena derived therefrom (see Sheehan and Perry, 1976). Perhaps what is needed now, as in the days of Braid, is not so much a confrontation of theorists as a relabeling of neutral hypnosis.

One problem in the field of hypnosis today is that the majority of what is done under the title of hypnotism does not fit Braid's 1855 definition of the term. How many practitioners or experimental investigators have observed spontaneous, nonsuggested amnesia for the hypnotic condition? Reversible, nonsuggested amnesias are a rarity today and nonreversible amnesias are virtually nonexistent. The reasons why we do not observe hypnotism as described over a century ago are unknown, but the fact remains that we are not dealing with the same phenomena that Braid described then, except in those few rare cases such as Hilgard describes with his hidden-observer technique.

Hilgard's (1977) hidden-observer data and his conceptual comparisons between his notions of divided consciousness and Freudian repression (between the amnesic and the repressive barriers) very closely parallel Braid's distinction between *hypnotism* and *hypnotic coma*. The behavior of the subjects who reported the hidden-observer phenomenon fits very well that described by Braid in his definition of hypnotism. In fact, Braid also considered a division of consciousness during hypnotism: " *'Hypnotism'* will comprise those cases only in which what has hitherto been called the double-conscious state occurs" (1855, p. 371). The dissociations are maintained by an amnesic barrier, which can be penetrated or circumvented subsequently.

The barrier of repression, described by the psychoanalysts, lends itself to the interpretation of Braid's *hypnotic coma*. What makes this comparison of Braid's *hypnotism* with Hilgard's application of divided consciousness to hypnosis even more arresting is the fact that Hilgard's data base is extremely small, composed of data on only 30 subjects who responded appropriately to the hidden-observer technique. In addition, the subjects who do respond to such a procedure constitute only about half of those individuals on whom the procedure is attempted! Hidden-observer phenomena are rare, although now that the technique has been described, we will no doubt be reading more and more reports about them. Perhaps Braid's 1855 definition of *hypnotism* should be retained and some new term found to describe what the majority of *traditional* hypnosis studies are about.

Both Braid's definition of hypnotism and Hilgard's hidden-observer data describe the rarity, the seldom observed, the obscure; not the commonplace, the usual hypnosis as applied by clinicians and investigators. The most prevalent condition of hypnosis is not an amnesic-bound double consciousness, but the relaxation attested to historically, clinically, and experimentally. If we retain Braid's definition of hypnotism, it should not be for *traditional* hypnosis but rather for an extremely rare condition, explorable only through extraordinary and indirect means. We should reserve for another label all of the techniques and investigative procedures presently associated with *traditional* hypnosis.

A relabeling, based on the data presented in this book, would offer greater accuracy to the terms we use to describe what we, as investigarors and practitioners, do. There is a need for a label that is at one and the same time accurately descriptive and a direct statement of the basic nature of the condition (relaxation). Wherever we turn, whether it is to the history of hypnosis or to the more recent clinical and experimental data, we are confronted with the fact that neutral hypnosis is equated with relaxation. *Traditional* history, *traditional* induction procedures, and data directly comparing these *traditional* inductions with nonhypnotic relaxation instructions all lead us to consider that hypnosis, as only one of many forms of trance, is basically and fundamentally relaxation. Rather than continue to use the dichotomy of "hypnosis" and "nonhypnotic relaxation," or even the phrase neutral hypnosis, a single, unifying term is needed, one that can encompass what practitioners and experimental investigators of various persuasions call hypnosis.

Since the reason for relabeling is accuracy, the word *anesis* (pronounced, 'ænʌsəs) will serve us very well. *Anesis* is the noun form of the Greek verb *aniesis*—to relax, to let go*—and by its simple, straightforward meaning implies nothing more than what hypnosis is. *Hypnosis* (from the Greek "to sleep"), you will recall, led us into the mire of studies seeking an equation with deep sleep. *Anesis* is a data-based label clearly stating what it is that happens in what I have otherwise called neutral hypnosis. In addition, the term *anesis* extricates us from the occult and magical connotations that the older term has absorbed over the years. *Anesis* is not simply a label change; it is a new beginning for studying

---

*I am very grateful to Professor Roberl L. Murray, Chairman of the Classics Department of Colgate University, for bringing this Platonic term to my attention.

phenomena that have heretofore been so entangled in inaccurate connotations as to drive many respectable investigators away (Hull, for example) because of the potential legal actions by a misinformed public and, worse yet, the ridicule of their professional colleagues. The associated meanings of hypnosis have reduced our effectiveness in investigation and in understanding, and our ability to provide patients with another procedure that may be of benefit. Changing the label of hypnosis—perhaps retaining the term only for such rare phenomena as described by Braid—serves both accuracy and practicality.

Labels *are* important, for they are our means of communication both within and without the professional ranks. If our scientific endeavor is the accurate understanding and knowledge of the phenomena around us, then we must begin with categories that accurately group these phenomena and labels that accurately communicate these categories. What has traditionally passed for hypnosis over the centuries is fundamentally and basically relaxation. To continue to use the label hypnosis or even neutral hypnosis, as we have in the past, is to perpetuate meanings, categories, and connotations that the data just do not support. If our investigations and applications are to be data-based—as any scientific exploration should be—then hypnosis better deserves to be called *anesis*.

References

Aaronson, B. S. ASĆID trance, hypnotic trance, just trance. *American Journal of Clinical Hypnosis,* 1973, **16,** 110–117.

Amadeo, M. & Shagass, C. Eye movements, attention, and hypnosis. *Journal of Nervous and Mental Disease,* 1963, **136,** 139–145.

Anderson, J. A. D.; Basker, M. A.; & Dalton, R. Migraine and hypnotherapy. *International Journal of Clinical and Experimental Hypnosis,* 1975, **23,** 48–58.

Andreychuk, T. & Skriver, C. Hypnosis and biofeedback in the treatment of migraine headache. *International Journal of Clinical and Experimental Hypnosis,* 1975, **23,** 172–183.

Ansel, E. L. A simple exercise to enhance response to hypnotherapy for migraine headache. *International Journal of Clinical and Experimental Hypnosis,* 1977, **25,** 68–71.

Antrobus, J. S.; Antrobus, J. S.; & Singer, J. L. Eye movements accompanying daydreaming, visual imagery, and thought suppression. *Journal of Abnormal and Social Psychology,* 1964, **69,** 244–253.

August, R. V. Hypnosis: Viewed academically and therapeutically. *American Journal of Clinical Hypnosis,* 1967, **9,** 171–180.

Bailly, J. S. et al. Secret report on mesmerism or animal magnetism (Aug. 11, 1784). In Shor, R. E. & Orne, M. T. *The Nature of Hypnosis: Selected Basic Readings.* New York: Holt, Rinehart & Winston, Inc., 1965. Pp. 3–7.

Bakal, D. A. Headache: A biopsychological perspective. *Psychological Bulletin,* 1975, **82,** 369–382.

Banyai, E. & Hilgard, E. R. A comparison of active-alert hypnotic induction with traditional relaxation induction. *Journal of Abnormal Psychology,* 1976, **85,** 218–224.

Barabasz, A. F. Treatment of insomnia in depressed patients by hypnosis and cerebral electrotherapy. *American Journal of Clinical Hypnosis,* 1976, **19,** 120–122.

Barabasz, A. F. & McGeorge, C. M. Biofeedback, mediated biofeedback and hypnosis in peripheral vasodilation training. *American Journal of Clinical Hypnosis,* 1978, **21,** 28–37.

Barber, T. X. Physiological effects of "hypnosis." *Psychological Bulletin,* 1961, **58,** 390–419.

Barber, T. X. Experimental analysis of "hypnotic" behavior: A review of recent empirical findings. *Journal of Abnormal Psychology*, 1965, **70**, 132−154.

Barber, T. X. Physiological effects of hypnosis and suggestions. In Barber, T. X. *LSD, Marihuana, Yoga & Hypnosis*. Chicago: Aldine Publishing Co., 1970. Pp. 133−203.

Barber, T. X. Physiological effects of hypnosis and suggestion. In Barber, T. X. et al., eds. *Biofeedback and Self-Control, 1970*. New York: Aldine-Atherton, 1971. Pp. 188−256.

Barber, T. X. Suggested ("hypnotic") behavior: The trance paradigm versus an alternative paradigm. In Fromm, E. & Shor, R. E. eds. *Hypnosis: Developments in Research and New Perspectives*. New York: Aldine Publishing Co., 1979. Pp. 217−271.

Barber, T. X. & Calverley, D. S. "Hypnotic behavior" as a function of task motivation. *Journal of Psychology*, 1962, **54**, 363−389.

Barber, T. X. & Calverley, D. S. "Hypnotic-like" suggestibility in children and adults. *Journal of Abnormal Psychology*, 1963a, **66**, 589−597.

Barber, T. X. & Calverley, D. S. The relative effectiveness of task-motivating instructions and trance-induction procedures in the production of "hypnotic-like" behavior. *Journal of Nervous and Mental Disease*, 1963b, **137**, 107−116.

Barber, T. X. & Calverley, D. S. Empirical evidence for a theory of "hypnotic" behavior. Effects on suggestibility of five variables typically induced in hypnotic induction procedures. *Journal of Consulting Psychology*, 1965a, **29**, 98−107.

Barber, T. X. & Calverley, D. S. Empirical evidence for a theory of "hypnotic" behavior. The suggestibility-enhancing effects of motivational suggestions, relaxation-sleep suggestions, and suggestions that the subject will be effectively "hypnotized." *Journal of Personality*, 1965b, **33**, 256−270.

Barber, T. X. & Coules, J. Electrical skin conductance and galvanic skin response during "hypnosis." *International Journal of Clinical and Experimental Hypnosis*, 1959, **7**, 79−92.

Barber, T. X.; Dalal, A. S.; & Calverley, D. S. The subjective reports of hypnotic subjects. *American Journal of Clinical Hypnosis*, 1968, **11**, 74−88.

Barber T. X. & DeMoor, W. A theory of hypnotic induction procedures. *American Journal of Clinical Hypnosis*, 1972, **15**, 112−135.

Barber, T. X. & Glass, L. B. Significant factors in hypnotic behavior. *Journal of Abnormal and Social Psychology*, 1962, **64**, 222−228.

Barber, T. X. & Hahn, K. W., Jr. Hypnotic induction and "relaxation": An experimental study. *Archives of General Psychiatry*, 1963, **8**, 295−300.

Barber, T. X.; Spanos, N. P.; & Chaves, S. F. *Hypnotism: Imagination and Human Potentialities*. New York: Pergamon Press, 1974.

Barker, W. & Burgwin, S. Brain wave patterns accompanying changes in sleep and wakefulness during hypnosis. *Psychosomatic Medicine*, 1948, **10**, 317−326.

Barker, W. & Burgwin, S. Brain wave patterns during hypnosis, hypnotic sleep, and normal sleep. *Archives of Neurology and Psychiatry*, 1949, **62**, 412−420.

Barkley, R. A.; Hastings, J. E.; & Jackson, T. L., Jr. The effects of rapid smoking and hypnosis in the treatment of smoking behavior. *International Journal of Clinical and Experimental Hypnosis,* 1977, **25**, 7−17.

Barry, H.; MacKinnon, D. W.; & Murray, H. A., Jr. Studies on personality: A. Hypnotizability as a personality trait and its typological relations. *Human Biology,* 1931, **13**, 1−36.

Bartlett, E. S.; Faw, T. T.; & Liebert, R. M. The effects of suggestions of alertness in hypnosis on pupillary response: Report on a single subject. *International Journal of Clinical and Experimental Hypnosis,* 1967, **15**, 189−192.

Basker, M. A. Hypnosis in migraine. *British Journal of Clinical Hypnosis,* 1970, **2**, 15−18.

Bass, M. J. Differentiation of the hypnotic trance from normal sleep. *Journal of Experimental Psychology,* 1931, **14**, 382−399.

Baumann, F. Hypnosis and the adolescent drug abuser. *American Journal of Clinical Hypnosis,* 1970, **13**, 17−21.

Beahrs, J. O. & Hill, M. M. Treatment of alcoholism by group-interaction psychotherapy under hypnosis. *American Journal of Clinical Hypnosis,* 1971, **14**, 60−62.

Beary, J. F. & Benson, H. (with H. P. Klemchuk) A simple psychophysiologic technique which elicits the hypometabolic changes of the relaxation response. *Psychosomatic Medicine,* 1974, **36**, 115−120.

Bechterev, W. V. What is hypnosis? *Journal of Abnormal and Social Psychology,* 1906, **1**, 18−25.

Benson, H. *The Relaxation Response.* New York: Wm. Morrow & Co., 1975.

Benson, H.; Alexander, S.; & Feldman, C. L. Decreased premature ventricular contractions through use of the relaxation response in patients with stable ischaemic heart-disease. *The Lancet,* 1975, August 30, 308−382.

Benson, H.; Beary, J. F.; & Carol, M. P. The relaxation response. *Psychiatry,* 1974, **37**, 37−46.

Benson, H.; Frankel, F. H.; Apfel, R; Daniels, M. D.; Schniewind, H. E.; Nemiah, J. C.; Sifneos, P. E.; Crassweller, K. D.; Greenwood, M. M.; Kotch, J. B.; Arms, P. A.; & Rosner, B. Treatment of anxiety: A comparison of the usefulness of self-hypnosis and a meditational relaxation technique—an overview. *Psychotherapy and Psychosomatics,* 1978, **30**, 229−242.

Benson, H.; Greenwood, M. M.; & Klemchuk, H. P. The relaxation response: Psychophysiological aspects and clinical applications. *International Journal of Psychiatry in Medicine,* 1975, **6**, 87−98.

Benson, H.; Klemchuk, H. P.; & Graham, J. R. The usefulness of the relaxation response in the therapy of headache. *Headache,* 1974, **14**, 49−52.

Benson, H.; Malvea, B. P.; & Graham, J. R. Physiologic correlates of meditation and their clinical effects in headache: An ongoing investigation. *Headache,* 1973, **12**, 23−24.

Benson, H.; Rosner, B. A.; Marzetta, B. R.; & Klemchuk, H. P. Decreased blood pressure in borderline hypertensive subjects who practice meditation. *Journal of Chronic Disease*, 1974*a*, **27**, 163–169.

Benson, H.; Rosner, B. A.; Marzetta, B. R. & Klemchuk, H. P. Decreased blood pressure in pharmacologically treated hypertensive patients who regularly elicit the relaxation response. *The Lancet*, 1974*b*, February 23, 289–291.

Benson, H. & Wallace, R. K. Decreased drug abuse with transcendental meditation—a study of 1862 subjects. In Zarafonetis, C. J. D., ed. *Drug Abuse: Proceedings of the International Conference*. Philadelphia: Lea & Febiger, 1972. Pp. 369–376.

Berillion, E. L'hypnotisme et la methode graphique. *Revue de l'Hypnose*, 1900, **17**, 3–10. (Cited in Jenness and Wible, 1937.)

Bernheim, H. *Hypnosis and Suggestion in Psychotherapy: A Treatise on the Nature and Uses of Hypnotism* (1884–1886). Translated by Christian A. Hertz. New Hyde Park, N.Y.: University Books, 1964.

Bertrand, A. *Traité du Somnambulisme et des Differentes Modifications qu'il Presente*. Paris: J. G. Dentu, 1823.

Bier, W. Beitrag zur Beeinflussung des Kreislaufes durch psychische Voränge. *Zeltschrift für Klinische Medizin*, 1930, **113**, 762. (Cited in Jenness and Wible, 1937.)

Bigelow, N.; Cameron, G. H.; & Koroljow, S. A. Two cases of deep hypnotic sleep investigated by the strain gauge plethysmograph. *International Journal of Clinical and Experimental Hypnosis*, 1956, **4**, 160–164.

Binet, A. & Féré, C. *Animal Magnetism*. New York: D. Appleton & Co., 1888.

Birk, L.; Crider, A. B.; Shapiro, D.; & Tursky, B. Operant electrodermal conditioning under partial curarizations. *Journal of Comparative and Physiological Psychology*, 1966, **62**, 165–166.

Bjorkhem, J. Alcoholism and hypnotic therapy. *British Journal of Medical Hypnotism*, 1956, **7**, 23–32.

Blake, H. & Gerard, R. W. Brain potentials during sleep. *American Journal of Physiology*, 1937, **119**, 692–703.

Blake, H.; Gerard, R. W.; & Kleitman, N. Factors influencing brain potentials during sleep. *Journal of Neurophysiology*, 1939, **2**, 48–60.

Blanchard, E. B. & Young, L. D. Clinical applications of biofeedback training: A review of evidence. *Archives of General Psychiatry*, 1974, **30**, 573–589.

Borkovec, T. D. & Fowles, D. C. Controlled investigation of the effects of progressive and hypnotic relaxation on insomnia. *Journal of Abnormal Psychology*, 1973, **82**, 153–158.

Borlone, M.; Dittborn, J. M.; & Palestini, M. Correlaciones electroencefalográficas dentro de una definición operacional de hipnosis sonambúlica: Connumicación preliminar. *Acta Hipnologica LatinoAmericana* (Buenos Aires), 1960, **1** (2), 9–19. (Seen in Dittborn & O'Connell, 1967.)

Brady, J. P. & Rosner, B. S. Rapid eye movements in hypnotically-induced dreams. *Journal of Nervous and Mental Disease*, 1966, **143**, 28–35.

Braid, J. *Satanic Agency and Mesmerism Reviewed*. Manchester: Sims & Dinham, 1842.

In Tinterow, M. M., ed. *Foundations of Hypnosis from Mesmer to Freud.* Springfield, Ill.: Charles C Thomas, 1970. Pp. 317−330.

Braid, J. *Neurypnology or, the Rationale of Nervous Sleep Considered in Relation with Animal Magnetism.* London: John Churchill, 1843. Reprinted New York: Arno Press, 1976.

Braid, J. *The Physiology of Fascination and the Critics Criticised.* Manchester, Eng.: Grant & Co., 1855. In Tinterow, M. M., ed. *Foundations of Hypnosis from Mesmer to Freud.* Springfield, Ill.: Charles C Thomas, 1970, Pp. 365−389.

Bramwell, J. M. *Hypnotism: Its History, Practice and Theory.* London: Grant Richards, 1903. Reissued New York: Julian Press, Inc., 1956.

Brown, W. Sleep, hypnosis and mediumistic trance. *Character and Personality,* 1935, **3,** 112−126.

Bullard, P. D. & DeCoster, D. T. The effects of hypnosis, relaxation and reinforcement on hypnotic behaviors and experiences. *American Journal of Clinical Hypnosis,* 1972, **15,** 93−97.

Byers, A. P. Training and use of technicians in the treatment of alcoholism with hypnosis. *American Journal of Clinical Hypnosis,* 1975, **18,** 90−93.

Cedercreutz, C.; Lähteenmäki, R.; & Tulikoura, J. Hypnotic treatment of headache and vertigo in skull injured patients. *International Journal of Clinical and Experimental Hypnosis,* 1976, **24,** 195−201.

Charcot, J. M. Essai d'une distinction nosographique des divers états compris sous le nom d' Hypnotisme. *Comptes rendus de l'Academie des Sciences* (1882). In Binet, A. & Féré, C. *Animal Magnetism.* New York: D. Appleton & Co., 1888. Pp. 154−163.

Charcot, J. M. The faith-cure. *New Review,* 1893, **8,** 18−31.

Chertok, L. Theory of hypnosis since 1889. *International Journal of Psychiatry,* 1967, **3,** 188−211.

Chertok, L. & Kramarz, P. Hypnosis, sleep and electroencephalography. *Journal of Nervous and Mental Disease,* 1959, **128,** 227−238.

Cogger, W. G., Jr. & Edmonston, W. E., Jr. Hypnosis and oral temperature: A re-evaluation of experimental techniques. *British Journal of Clinical Hypnosis,* 1971, **2,** 76−80.

Coleman, T. R. A comparative study of certain behavioral, physiological and phenomenological effects of hypnotic induction and two progressive relaxation procedures. Ph.D. dissertation, Brigham Young University, 1976. Ann Arbor, Mich.: University Microfilms, 1976.

Collison, D. R. Cardiological applications of the control of the autonomic nervous system by hypnosis. *American Journal of Clinical Hypnosis,* 1970, **12,** 150−156.

Conti, A. P. Heart rate conditioning in and out of hypnosis. Unpublished bachelor's thesis. Colgate University, 1968.

Crasilneck, H. B. & Hall, J. A. Physiological changes associated with hypnosis: A review of the literature since 1948. *International Journal of Clinican and Experimental Hypnosis,* 1959, **7,** 9−50.

Crasilneck, H. B. & Hall, J. A. Blood pressure and pulse rates in neutral hypnosis. *International Journal of Clinical and Experimental Hypnosis,* 1960, **8,** 137–139.

Crasilneck, H. B. & Hall, J. A. *Clinical Hypnosis: Principles and Applications.* New York: Grune & Stratton, 1975.

Daniels, L. K. The effects of automated hypnosis and hand warming on migraine: A pilot study. *American Journal of Clinical Hypnosis,* 1976, **19,** 91–94.

Daniels, L. K. Treatment of migraine headache by hypnosis and behavior therapy: A case study. *American Journal of Clinical Hypnosis,* 1977, **19,** 241–244.

Darnton, R. *Mesmerism and the End of the Enlightenment in France.* Cambridge, Mass.: Harvard University Press, 1968.

Darrow, C. W.; Henry, E. C.; Gill, M.; & Brenman, M. Interarea electroencephalographic relationships affected by hypnosis: Preliminary report. *Electroencephalography and Clinical Neurophysiology,* 1950, **2,** 231.

Darrow, C. W.; Henry, E. C.; Gill, M.; Brenman, M.; & Converse, M. Frontal-motor parallelism and motor-occipital in-phase activity in hypnosis, drowsiness and sleep. *Electroencephalography and Clinical Neurophysiology,* 1950, **2,** 355.

Das, J. P. The Pavlovian theory of hypnosis: An evaluation. *Journal of Mental Science,* 1958, **104,** 82–90.

Datey, K. K.; Deshmukh, S. N.; Dalvi, C. P.; & Binekar, S. L. "Shavason": A yogic exercise in the management of hypertension. *Angiology,* 1969, **20,** 325–333.

Davis, H.; Davis, P. A.; Loomis, A. L.; Harvey, E. N.; & Hobart, G. Human brain potentials during the onset of sleep. *Journal of Neurophysiology,* 1938, **1,** 24–38.

Davis, L. W. & Husband, R. W. A study of hypnotic susceptibility in relation to personality traits. *Journal of Abnormal & Social Psychology,* 1931, **26,** 175–182.

Davis, R. C. & Kantor, J. R. Skin resistance during hypnotic states. *Journal of General Psychology,* 1935, **13,** 62–81.

Deabler, H. L.; Fidel, E.; Dillenkoffer, R. L.; & Elder, S. The use of relaxation and hypnosis in lowering high blood pressure. *American Journal of Clinical Hypnosis,* 1973, **16,** 75–83.

Deleuze, J. P. F. Rules of magnetizing (1825). In Shor, R. E. & Orne, M. T., eds. *The Nature of Hypnosis, Selected Basic Readings.* New York: Holt, Rinehart & Winston, Inc., 1965. Pp. 24–29.

Deleuze, J. P. F. *Practical Instructions in Animal Magnetism* (1846). Quoted in Esdaile, J. *Mesmerism in India.* New York: Arno Press, 1976.

Dengrove, E. The uses of hypnosis in behavior therapy. *International Journal of Clinical and Experimental Hypnosis,* 1973, **21,** 13–17.

Deutsch, F. & Kauf, E. Psycho-physische Kreislaufstudien. *Zeltschrift für die Gesamte experimentelle Medizin,* 1923, **32,** 197–216. (Cited by Jenness and Wible, 1937.)

DiCara, L. V. & Miller, N. E. Long-term retention of instrumentally learned heart-rate changes in the curarized rat. *Community Behavioral Biology,* 1968, **2** (Part A), 19–23.

Dittborn, J. M.; Gutiérrez, O; & Godoy, L. M. Sleep suggestibility test. *Journal of Psychology*, 1960, **49**, 111–112.

Dittborn, J. M. & O'Connell, D. N. Behavioral sleep, physiological sleep, and hypnotizability. *International Journal of Clinical and Experimental Hypnosis*, 1967, **15**, 181–188.

Dorcus, R. M., ed. *Hypnosis and Its Therapeutic Applications*. New York: McGraw-Hill, 1956.

Dorcus, R. M.; Brintnall, A. K.; & Case, H. W. Control experiments and their relation to theories of hypnotism. *Journal of General Psychology*, 1941, **24**, 217–221.

Doupe, J.; Miller, W. R.; & Keller, W. K. Vasomotor reactions in the hypnotic state. *Journal of Neurology, Neurosurgery and Psychiatry*, 1939, **2**, 97–106.

Dudley, D. L.; Holmes, T. H.; Martin, C. J.; & Ripley, H. S. Changes in respiration associated with hypnotically induced emotion, pain and exercise. *Psychosomatic Medicine*, 1963, **26**, 46–57.

Duff, J. L. A comparison of procedures for enhancing hypnotic susceptibility. Ph.D. dissertation, University of Kansas, 1977. Ann Arbor, Mich.: University Microfilms, 1979.

Dunwoody, R. C. & Edmonston, W. E., Jr. Hypnosis and slow eye movements. *American Journal of Clinical Hypnosis*, 1974, **16**, 270–274.

Dynes, J. B. Objective method for distinguishing sleep from the hypnotic trance. *Archives of Neurology and Psychiatry*, 1947, **57**, 84–93.

Edmonston, W. E., Jr. Stimulus-response theory of hypnosis. In Gordon, J. E., ed. *Handbook of Clinical and Experimental Hypnosis*. New York: Macmillan Co., 1967. Pp. 345–387.

Edmonston, W. E., Jr., Hypnosis and electrodermal responses. *American Journal of Clinical Hypnosis*, 1968, **11**, 16–25.

Edmonston, W. E., Jr. Clinical and experimental trance: Unity through methodology. *American Journal of Clinical Hypnosis*, 1970, **13**, 5–9.

Edmonston, W. E., Jr. A quantitative evaluation of relaxation and hypnosis. In Langen D., ed. *Hypnose und Psychosomatische Medizin*. Stuttgart: Hippocrates Verlag, 1972*a*. Pp. 56–62.

Edmonston, W. E., Jr. The effects of neutral hypnosis on conditioned responses. In Fromm, E. & Shor, R. E., eds. *Hypnosis: Research Developments and Perspectives*. Chicago: Aldine-Atherton, 1972*b*. Pp. 323–356.

Edmonston, W. E., Jr. Presidential address, American Society of Clinical Hypnosis. *American Society of Clinical Hypnosis Newsletter*, October, 1973.

Edmonston, W. E., Jr. Neutral hypnosis as relaxation. *American Journal of Clinical Hypnosis*, 1977, **20**, 69–75.

Edmonston, W. E., Jr. The effects of neutral hypnosis on conditioned responses: Implications for hypnosis as relaxation. In Fromm, E. & Shor, R. E., eds. *Hypnosis: Developments in Research and New Perspectives* (2nd ed.). New York: Aldine Publishing Co., 1979. Pp. 415–455.

Edmonston, W. E., Jr. & Grotevant, W. R. Hypnosis and alpha density. *American Journal of Clinical Hypnosis*, 1975, **17,** 221–232.

Edmonston, W. E., Jr. & Pessin, M. Hypnosis as related to learning and electrodermal measures. *American Journal of Clinical Hypnosis*, 1966, **9,** 31–51.

Edmonston, W. E., Jr. & Robertson, T. G., Jr. A comparison of the effects of task motivational and hypnotic induction instructions on responsiveness to hypnotic suggestibility scales. *American Journal of Clinical Hypnosis*, 1967, **9,** 184–187.

Eichhorn, R. & Tracktir, J. The relationship between anxiety, hypnotically induced emotions and gastric secretion. *Gastroenterology*, 1955, **29,** 417–421.

Ellenberger, H. F. Mesmer and Puységur: From magnetism to hypnotism. *Psychoanalytic Review*, 1965*a*, **52,** 137–153.

Ellenberger, H. F. Charcot and the Salpêtrière School. *American Journal of Psychotherapy*, 1965*b*, **19,** 253–267.

Elliotson, J. *Numerous Cases of Surgical Operations Without Pain in the Mesmeric State*. Philadelphia: Lea & Blanchard, 1843. Reprinted in Robinson, D. N., ed. *Significant Contributions to the History of Psychology, 1750–1920. Series A, Orientations, Vol. 10*. Washington, D.C.: University Publications of America, Inc., 1977.

Engstrom, D. R.; London, P.; & Hart, J. EEG alpha feedback training and hypnotic susceptibility. *Proceedings of the Annual Convention of APA*, 1970, **5** (Part 2), 837–838.

Erickson, M. H. Deep hypnosis and its induction. In LeCron, L. M., ed. *Experimental Hypnosis*. New York: Macmillan, 1952. Pp. 70–114.

Erickson, M. H. Further techniques of hypnosis—Utilization techniques. *American Journal of Clinical Hypnosis*, 1959, **2,** 3–21.

Erickson, M. H. Laboratory and clinical hypnosis: The same or different phenomena? *American Journal of Clinical Hypnosis*, 1967, **9,** 166–170.

Erickson, M. H. & Erickson, E. M. Concerning the nature and character of posthypnotic behavior. *Journal of General Psychology*, 1941, **24,** 95–133.

Esdaile, J. *Mesmerism in India and Its Practical Application in Surgery and Medicine*. London: Longman, Brown, Green, and Longmans, 1846. Reprinted New York: Arno Press, 1976.

Esdaile, J. *Natural and Mesmeric Clairvoyance, with the Practical Application of Mesmerism in Surgery and Medicine*. London: H. Baillière, 1852. Reprinted New York: Arno Press, 1975.

Estabrooks G. H. The psychogalvanic reflex in hypnosis. *Journal of General Psychology*, 1930, **3,** 150–157.

Evans, F. J. An experimental indirect technique for the induction of hypnosis without awareness. *International Journal of Clinical and Experimental Hypnosis*, 1967, **15,** 72–85.

Evans, F. J. Hypnosis and sleep: Techniques for exploring cognitive activity during sleep. In Fromm, E. & Shor, R. E., eds. *Hypnosis: Research Developments and Perspectives*. Chicago: Aldine-Atherton, 1972. Pp. 43–83.

Evans, F. J. Hypnosis and sleep: Techniques for exploring cognitive activity during sleep. In Fromm, E. & Shor, R. E., eds. *Hypnosis: Developments in Research and New Perspectives,* (2nd ed.) New York: Aldine Publishing Co., 1979. Pp. 139–183.

Faria, L'Abbé de. *Du Sommeil Lucide ou Étude de la Nature de l'Homme.* Reprint of the 1819 edition, preface and introduction by D. G. Dalgado. Paris: Henri Jouve, 1906.

Fehr, F. S. & Stern, J. A. The effect of hypnosis on attention to relevant and irrelevant stimuli. *International Journal of Clinical and Experimental Hypnosis,* 1967, **15,** 134–143.

Field, P. B. & Scott, E. M. Experiences of alcoholics during hypnosis. *American Journal of Clinical Hypnosis,* 1969, **12,** 86–90.

Ford, L. F. & Yeager, C. L. Changes in electroencephalogram in subjects under hypnosis. *Diseases of the Nervous System,* 1948, **9,** 190–192.

Frankau, G., ed. *Mesmerism by Doctor Mesmer (1779).* London: MacDonald, 1948.

French, A. P. & Tupin, J. P. Therapeutic application of a simple relaxation method. *American Journal of Psychotherapy,* 1974, **28,** 282–287.

Friedlander, J. W. & Sarbin, T. R. The depth of hypnosis. *Journal of Abnormal and Social Psychology,* 1938, **33,** 453–475.

Friedman, H. & Taub, H. A. The use of hypnosis and biofeedback procedures for essential hypertension. *International Journal of Clinical and Experimental Hypnosis,* 1977, **25,** 335–347.

Friedman, H. & Taub, H. A. A six-month follow-up of the use of hypnosis and biofeedback procedures in essential hypertension. *American Journal of Clinical Hypnosis,* 1978, **20,** 184–188.

Friend, M. B. Group hypnotherapy treatment. In Wallerstein, R. S., ed. *Hospital Treatment of Alcoholism: A Comparative, Experimental Study.* New York: Basic Books, 1957. Pp. 77–120.

Fromm, E. The nature of hypnosis and other altered states of consciousness: An ego-psychological theory. In Fromm, E. & Shor, R. E., eds. *Hypnosis: Developments in Research and New Perspectives.* (2nd ed.) New York: Aldine Publishing Co., 1979. Pp. 81–103.

Fromm, E. & Shor, R. E., eds. *Hypnosis: Research Developments and Perspectives.* Chicago: Aldine-Atherton, 1972.

Fromm, E. & Shor, R. E., eds. *Hypnosis: Developments in Research and New Perspectives,* (2nd ed.) New York: Aldine Publishing Co., 1979.

Galbraith, G.; London, P.; Leibovitz, M. P.; Cooper, L. M.; & Hart, J. EEG and hypnotic susceptibility. *Journal of Comparative and Physiological Psychology,* 1970, **72,** 125–131.

Geer, J. H. & Katkin, E. S. Treatment of insomnia using a variant of systematic desensitization: A case report. *Journal of Abnormal Psychology,* 1966, **71,** 161–164.

Gibbons, D. E. Hyperempiria, a new "altered state of consciousness" induced by suggestion. *Perceptual and Motor Skills,* 1974, **39,** 47–53.

Gibbons, D. E. Hypnotic vs. hyperempiric induction procedures: An experimental comparison. *Journal of the American Society of Psychosomatic Dentistry & Medicine,* 1975, **22,** 35–42.

Gibbons, D. E. Hypnotic vs. hyperempiric induction procedures: An experimental comparison. *Perceptual and Motor Skills,* 1976, **42,** 834.

Gill, M. & Brenman, M. *Hypnosis and Related States: Psycho-Analytic Studies in Regression.* New York: International Universities Press, 1959.

Gladston, I. Mesmerism and animal magnetism. *CIBA Symposium,* 1948*a,* **9,** 832–837.

Gladston, I. Hypnosis and modern psychiatry. *CIBA Symposium,* 1948*b,* **9,** 845–856.

Goldwyn, J. The effect of hypnosis on basal metabolism. *Archives of Internal Medicine,* 1930, **45,** 109–114.

Gorton, B. E. The physiology of hypnosis. I. A review of the literature. *Psychiatric Quarterly,* 1949*a,* **23,** 317–343.

Gorton, B. E. The physiology of hypnosis. II. A review of the literature. *Psychiatric Quarterly,* 1949*b,* **23,** 457–485.

Graham, G. W. Hypnosis and biofeedback as treatments for migraine headaches. *Dissertation Abstracts,* 1974 (November), **35 (5-B),** 2428–2429.

Graham, G. W. Hypnotic treatment for migraine headaches. *International Journal of Clinical and Experimental Hypnosis,* 1975, **23,** 165–171.

Graham, K. R.; Wright, G. W.,; Toman, W. J.; & Mark, C. B. Relaxation and hypnosis in the treatment of insomnia. *American Journal of Clinical Hypnosis,* 1975, **18,** 39–42.

Greenwood, M. M. & Benson, H. The efficacy of progressive relaxation in systematic desensitization and a proposal for an alternative competitive response—the relaxation response. *Behavior Research & Therapy,* 1977, **15,** 337–343.

Haley, J. *Advanced Techniques of Hypnosis and Therapy: Selected Papers of Milton H. Erickson, M. D.* New York: Grune & Stratton, 1967.

Hall, J. A. & Crasilneck, H. B. Development of a hypnotic technique for treating chronic cigarette smoking. *International Journal of Clinical and Experimental Hypnosis,* 1970, **18,** 283–289.

Ham, M. W. & Edmonston, W. E., Jr. Hypnosis, relaxation, and motor retardation. *Journal of Abnormal Psychology,* 1971, **77,** 329–331.

Hartland, J. *Medical and Dental Hypnosis and Its Clinical Applications,* (2nd ed.). London: Baillière, 1971.

Heidenhain, R. *Hypnotism or Animal Magnetism, Physiological Observations.* Translated by L. C. Woolridge. London: Kegan Paul, Trench & Co., 1888.

Heron, W. T., ed. *A Handbook of Therapeutic Suggestions.* Minneapolis, Minn.: American Society of Clinical Hypnosis-Education and Research Foundation, 1971.

Hershman, S. Hypnosis and excessive smoking. *International Journal of Clinical and Experimental Hypnosis,* 1956, **4,** 24–29.

Hess, W. R. *The Functional Organization of the Diencephalon.* Edited by J. R. Hughes. New York: Grune & Stratton, 1957.

Hilgard, E. R. *Hypnotic susceptibility.* New York: Harcourt Brace & World, 1965.

Hilgard, E. R. *Divided Consciousness: Multiple Controls in Human Thought and Action.* New York: John Wiley & Sons, 1977.

Hilgard, E. R. The Stanford Hypnotic Susceptibility Scales as related to other measures of hypnotic responsiveness. *American Journal of Clinical Hypnosis,* 1978/79, **21,** 68–83.

Hilgard, E. R. Divided consciousness in hypnosis: The implications of the hidden observer. In Fromm, E. & Shor, R. E., eds. *Hypnosis: Developments in Research and New Perspectives.* (2nd ed.) New York: Aldine Publishing Co., 1979. Pp. 45–79.

Hilgard, E. R.; Lauer, L. W.; & Morgan, A. H. *Manual for Stanford Profile Scales of Hypnotic Susceptibility, Forms I and II.* Palo Alto, Calif.: Consulting Psychologists Press, 1963.

Hilgard, E. R. & Tart, C. T. Responsiveness to suggestions following waking and imagination instructions and following induction of hypnosis. *Journal of Abnormal and Social Psychology,* 1966, **71,** 196–208.

Hilgard, E. R.; Weitzenhoffer, A. M.; Landis, J.; & Moore, R. K. The distribution of susceptibility to hypnosis in a student population: A study using the Stanford Hypnotic Susceptibility Scale. *Psychological Monographs,* 1961, **75,** 8, 1–22 (Whole No. 512).

Hilgard, J. R. Sequelae to hypnosis. *International Journal of Clinical and Experimental Hypnosis,* 1974, **22,** 281–298.

Hilgard, J. R.; Hilgard, E. R.; & Newman, M. F. Sequelae to hypnotic induction with special reference to earlier chemical anesthesia. *Journal of Nervous and Mental Disease,* 1961, **133,** 461–478.

Hoover, C. F. & Sollman, T. A study of metabolism during fasting in hypnotic sleep. *Journal of Experimental Medicine,* 1897, **2,** 405–411. (Cited in Whitehorn et al., 1932.)

Hull, C. L. *Hypnosis and Suggestibility: An Experimental Approach.* New York: Appleton-Century-Crofts, 1933.

Jackson, T. L., Jr.; Barkley, R. A., & Pashko, S. M. The effects of hypnotic induction versus high motivation on oral temperature. *International Journal of Clinical and Experimental Hypnosis,* 1976, **24,** 22–28.

Jacobson, E. *Progressive Relaxation.* Chicago, Ill.: University of Chicago Press, 1929.

Jana, H. Energy metabolism in hypnotic trance and sleep. *Journal of Applied Physiology,* 1965, **20,** 308–310.

Jana, H. Effect of hypnosis on circulation and respiration. *Indian Journal of Medical Research,* 1967, **55,** 591–598.

Jana, H. & Patel, S. Biochemical changes in blood during hypnotic trance. *Indian Journal of Medical Research,* 1965, **53,** 1000–1002.

Janda, L. H. & Cash, T. F. Effects of relaxation training upon physiological and self-report indices. *Perceptual & Motor Skills,* 1976, **42,** 444.

Jenness, A. & Wible, C. L. Respiration and heart action in sleep and hypnosis. *Journal of General Psychology,* 1937, **16,** 197–222.

Johnson, L. C. & Lubin, A. Spontaneous electrodermal activity during waking and sleeping. *Psychophysiology*, 1966, **3**, 8−17.

Kahn, M.; Baker, B. L.; & Weiss, J. M. Treatment of insomnia by relaxation training. *Journal of Abnormal Psychology*, 1968, **73**, 556−558.

Kamiya, J. Conditioned discrimination of the EEG alpha rhythm in humans. Paper presented at the Western Psychological Association meeting, 1962.

Kamiya, J. Operant control of the EEG alpha rhythm and some of its reported effects on consciousness. In Tart, C. T., ed. *Altered States of Consciousness*. New York: John Wiley & Sons, 1969. Pp. 507−517.

Katkov, Y. 1941. (Cited in Platonov, 1959.)

Kellogg, E. R. Duration and effects of post-hypnotic suggestions. *Journal of Experimental Psychology*, 1929, **12**, 502−514.

Kirschberg, H. Die Verander d. Blutviskosität während der Hypnose. *Zentralblatt für die Gesamte Neurologie und Psychologie*, 1925, Bd. 41. (Cited in Jenness and Wible, 1937).

Kline, M. V. The use of extended group hypnotherapy sessions in controlling cigarette habituation. *International Journal of Clinical and Experimental Hypnosis*, 1970, **18**, 270−282.

Korotkin, I. I. & Suslova, M. M. Investigation into higher nervous activity in subjects in the somnambulistic phase of hypnosis. *Zhurnal Vyssheĭ Nervnoĭ Deiâtel' nosti*, 1951, **1**, 617−622. (Cited in Das, 1958.)

Korotkin, I. I. & Suslova, M. M. Investigation into the higher nervous activity in some somnambulistic phase of hypnosis during different depths of hypnotic sleep. *Fiziologicheskii Zhurnal*, 1953, **39**, 423−431. (Cited in Das, 1958.)

Korotkin, I. I. & Suslova, M. M. About some characteristics of the reciprocal influence of signal system in hypnotic and post-hypnotic states. *Zhurnal Vysshei Nervnoĭ Deiâtel' nosti*, 1955a, **5**, 511−519. (Read in abstract only.)

Korotkin, I. I. & Suslova, M. M. Materials for the investigation into the nervous mechanism of post-hypnotic suggestion with hysterics. *Zhurnal Vyssheĭ Nervnoi Deiâtel'nosti*, 1955b, **5**, 697−707. (Read in abstract only.)

Korotkin, I. I. & Suslova, M. M. On the physiological mechanism of inhibitory action on stimuli inhibited by hypnotic suggestions. *Doklady Akademii Nauk, SSSR*, 1955c, **102**, 189−192. (Cited in Das, 1958.)

Korotkin, I. I. & Suslova, M. M. Changes in conditioned and unconditioned reflexes during suggested states in hypnosis. In *The Central Nervous System and Human Behavior—Translations from the Russian Medical Literature*. Bethesda, Md.: U.S. Department of Health, Education & Welfare, 1959. Pp. 653−670.

Korotkin, I. I. & Suslova, M. M. Comparative effects of suggestion in the waking state and in hypnosis. *Pavlov Journal of Higher Nervous Activity*, 1960, **10**, 185−192.

Korotkin, I. I. & Suslova, M. M. An attempt to change the localization of conditioned inhibition by verbal suggestion in the state of hypnosis. *Zhurnal vyssheĭ Nervnoĭ Deiâtel' nosti*, 1962, **12**, 778−787. (Read in abstract only.)

Koster, S. Experimental investigation of the character of hypnosis. *Journal of Clinical and Experimental Hypnosis*, 1954, **2**, 42−55.

Krafft-Ebing, R. von. *Eine Experimentalle Studie auf dem Gebiete des Hypnotismus*.

Stuttgart, 1889.

Kratochvíl, S. Sleep hypnosis and waking hypnosis. *International Journal of Clinical and Experimental Hypnosis*, 1970, **18,** 25–40.

Kratochvíl, S. & Shubat, N. Activity-passivity in hypnosis and in the normal state. *International Journal of Clinical and Experimental Hypnosis*, 1971, **19,** 140–145.

Kroger, W. S. *Clinical and Experimental Hypnosis*. Philadelphia: J. B. Lippincott Co., 1977.

Kubie, L. S. & Margolin, S. The process of hypnotism and the nature of the hypnotic state. *American Journal of Psychiatry*, 1944, **100,** 611–622.

Kuffler, S. W. Discharge patterns and functional organization of mammalian retina. *Journal of Neurophysiology*, 1953, **16,** 37–68;

Lacey, J. I. The evaluation of autonomic responses: Toward a general solution. *Annals of the New York Academy of Sciences*, 1956, **67,** 123–163.

Langen, D. Modern hypnotic treatment of various forms of addiction, in particular alcoholism. *British Journal of Addiction*, 1967, **62,** 77–81.

Lapides, J.; Sweet, R. B.; & Lewis, L. W. Role of striated muscle in urination. *Journal of Urology*, 1957, **77.**

Laudenheimer, R. Über d. Einwirkung d. hypnotischen Suggestion u.s.w. *Münchener medizinische Wochensehr*, 1925, **72,** 1843. (Cited in Jenness and Wible, 1937.)

Lenox, J. R. & Bonny, H. The hypnotizability of chronic alcoholics. *International Journal of Clinical and Experimental Hypnosis*, 1976, **24,** 419–425.

Levander, V. L.; Benson, H.; Wheeler, R. C.; & Wallace, R. K. Increased forearm blood flow during a wakeful hypometabolic state. *Federation of American Societies for Experimental Biology*, 1972, **31,** 405.

Levine, M. Electrical skin resistance during hypnosis. *Archives of Neurology and Psychiatry*, 1930, **24,** 937–942.

Liebeault, A.A. *Le Sommeil Provoque et les États Analogues*. Paris: Doin, 1889.

Liebert, R. M.; Rubin, N.; & Hilgard, E. R. The effects of suggestions of alertness in hypnosis on paired-associate learning. *Journal of Personality*, 1965, **33,** 605–612.

Livshits, L. S. The investigation of the higher nervous activity of man in hypnosis in relation to chronic alcoholism. *Pavlov Journal of Higher Nervous Activity*, 1959, **9,** 745–753.

London, P. *The Children's Hypnotic Susceptibility Scale*. Palo Alto, Calif.: Consulting Psychologists Press, 1962.

London, P.; Hart, J.; & Leibovitz, M. EEG alpha rhythm and susceptibility to hypnosis. *Nature*, 1968, **219,** 71–72.

Loomis, A. L.; Harvey, E. N.; & Hobart, G. Brain potential during hypnosis. *Science*, 1936, **83,** 239–241.

Lorens, S. A. & Darrow, C. W. Eye movements, EEG, and EKG during mental manipulation. *Electroencephalography and Clinical Neurophysiology*, 1962, **14,** 739–746.

Lovett Doust, J. W. Studies on the physiology of awareness: Oximetric analysis of emotion and the differential planes of consciousness seen in hypnosis. *Journal of Clinical and Experimental Psychopathology*, 1953, **14**, 113−126.

Luckhardt, A. B. & Johnston, R. L. Studies in gastric secretion: I. The psychic secretion of gastric juice under hypnosis. *American Journal of Physiology*, 1924, **70**, 174−182.

Ludwig, A. M. An historical survey of the early roots of mesmerism. *International Journal of Clinical and Experimental Hypnosis*, 1964, **12**, 205−217.

Ludwig, A. M. & Lyle, W. H., Jr. Tension induction and the hyperalert trance. *Journal of Abnormal and Social Psychology*, 1964, **69**, 70−76.

Ludwig, A. M.; Lyle, W. H.; & Miller, J. S. Group hypnotherapy techniques with drug addicts. *International Journal of Clinical and Experimental Hypnosis*, 1964, **12**, 53−66.

Luthe, W. Autogenic therapy: Excerpts on applications to cardiovascular disorders and hypercholesteremia. In Stoyva, J.; Barber, T. X.; DiCara, L.; Kamiya, J.; Miller, N. E.; & Shapiro, D.; eds. *Biofeedback and Self-Control, 1971*. Chicago: Aldine-Atherton, 1972. Pp. 437−462.

McAmmond, D. M.; Davidson, P. O.; & Korvitz, D. M. A comparison of the effects of hypnosis and relaxation training on stress reactions in a dental situation. *American Journal of Clinical Hypnosis*, 1971, **13**, 233−242.

McCranie, E. J. & Crasilneck, H. B. The conditioned reflex in hypnotic age regression. *Journal of Clinical and Experimental Psychopathology*, 1955, **16**, 120−123.

Maiorov, F. 1948. (Cited in Platonov, 1959.)

Marenina, A. 1952. (Cited in Platonov, 1959.)

Marenina, A. I. Further investigation on the dynamics of cerebral potentials in the various phases of hypnosis in man. In *The Central Nervous System and Human Behavior-Translations from the Russian Medical Literature*. Bethesda, Md.: U.S. Department of Health, Education & Welfare, 1959. Pp. 645−649.

Marks, R. W. *The Story of Hypnotism*. New York: Prentice-Hall, 1947.

Marmer, M. J. *Hypnosis in Anesthesiology*. Springfield, Ill.: Charles C Thomas, 1959.

Marquis, D. G. & Hilgard, E. R. Conditional lid responses to light in dogs after removal of the visual cortex. *Journal of Comparative Psychology*, 1936, **22**, 157−178.

Maslach, C.; Marshall, G.; & Zimbardo, P.G. Hypnotic control of peripheral skin temperature: A case report. *Psychophysiology*, 1972, **9**, 600−605.

Mather, M. D. & Degun, G. S. A comparative study of hypnosis and relaxation. *British Journal of Medical Psychology*, 1975, **48**, 55−61.

Mathews, A. M. & Gelder, M. G. Psycho-physiological investigations of brief relaxation training. *Journal of Psychosomatic Research*, 1969, **13**, 1−12.

May, J. R. & Edmonston, W. E., Jr. Hypnosis and a plethysmographic measure of two types of situational anxiety. *American Journal of Clinical Hypnosis*, 1966, **9**, 109−113.

Meares, A. *A System of Medical Hypnosis*. Philadelphia: W. B. Saunders & Co., 1961.

Melzack, R. & Perry, C. Self-regulation of pain: The use of alpha-feedback and hypnotic training for the control of chronic pain. *Experimental Neurology,* 1975, **46,** 452–469.

Miller, M. M. Treatment of chronic alcoholism by hypnotic aversion. *Journal of the American Medical Association,* 1959, **171,** 164–167.

Miller, N. E. Learning of visceral and glandular responses. *Science,* 1969, **163,** 434–445.

Moll, A. *The Study of Hypnosis* (1889). New York: Julian Press Inc., 1958.

Montgomery, I.; Perkin, G.; & Wise, D. A review of behavioral treatments for insomnia. *Journal of Behavior Therapy and Experimental Psychiatry,* 1975, **6,** 93–100.

Morse, D. R.; Martin, J. S.; Furst, M. L.; & Dubin, L. L. A physiological and subjective evaluation of meditation, hypnosis, and relaxation. *Psychosomatic Medicine,* 1977, **39,** 304–324.

Nemtzowa, O. L. & Schattenstein, D. I. The influence of the central nervous system on certain physiological processes during work. *Bull. Biol. Med. Exp. U.S.S.R.,* 1936, **1,** 144–145. (*Psychological Abstracts,* 1938, No. 2379.)

Nicassio, P. & Bootzin, R. A. A comparison of progressive relaxation and autogenic training as treatments for insomnia. *Journal of Abnormal Psychology,* 1974, **83,** 253–260.

Nuland, W. & Field, P. B. Smoking and hypnosis: A systematic clinical approach. *International Journal of Clinical and Experimental Hypnosis,* 1970, **18,** 290–306.

Nygard, J. W. Cerebral circulation prevailing during sleep and hypnosis. *Journal of Experimental Psychology,* 1939, **24,** 1–20.

O'Connell, D. N. & Orne, M. T. Bioelectric correlates of hypnosis: An experimental reevaluation. *Journal of Psychiatric Research,* 1962, **1,** 201–213.

O'Connell, D. N. & Orne, M. T. Endosomatic electrodermal correlates of hypnotic depth and susceptibility. *Journal of Psychiatric Research,* 1968, **6,** 1–12.

Oetting, E. R. Hypnosis and concentration in study. *American Journal of Clinical Hypnosis,* 1964, **7,** 148–151.

Ollendick, T. H. & Murphy, M. J. Differential effectiveness of muscular and cognitive relaxation as a function of locus of control. *Journal of Behavior Therapy & Experimental Psychiatry,* 1977, **8,** 223–228.

Orne, M. T. The nature of hypnosis: Artifact and essence. *Journal of Abnormal and Social Psychology,* 1959, **58,** 277–299.

Orne, M. T. On the simulating subject as a quasi-control group in hypnosis research: What, why, and how. In Fromm, E. & Shor, R. E., eds. *Hypnosis: Research Developments and Perspectives.* Chicago: Aldine-Atherton, 1972. Pp. 399–443.

Orne, M. T. On the simulating subject as a quasi-control group in hypnosis research: What, why, and how. In Fromm, E. & Shor, R. E., eds. *Hypnosis: Developments in Research and New Perspectives.* (2nd ed.) New York: Aldine Publishing Co., 1979. Pp. 519–565.

Paley, A. Hypnotherapy in the treatment of alcoholism. *Bulletin of the Menninger Clinic,* 1952, **16,** 14–19.

Paskewitz, D. A. & Orne, M. T. Visual effects on alpha-feedback training. *Science*, 1973, **181**, 360–363.

Patel, C. Yoga and biofeedback in the management of hypertension. *The Lancet*, 1973, November 10, 1053–1055.

Patel, C. Twelve-month follow-up of yoga and biofeedback in the management of hypertension. *The Lancet*, 1975, January 11, 62–64.

Patel, C. & North, W. R. S. Randomised controlled trial of yoga and biofeedback in management of hypertension. *The Lancet*, 1975, July 19, 93–95.

Pattie, F. A. Mesmer's medical dissertation and its debt to Mead's *De Imperio Solis ac Lunae*. *Journal of the History of Medicine and Allied Sciences*, 1956, **11**, 275–287.

Pattie, F. A. A brief history of hypnotism. In Gordon, J. E., ed. *Handbook of Clinical and Experimental Hypnosis*. New York: Macmillan Co., 1967. Pp. 10–43.

Pattie, F. A. & Griffith, R. M. The non-hypnotizability of Korsakoff patients. *American Journal of Clinical Hypnosis*, 1962, **5**, 61–62.

Paul, G. L. Physiological effects of relaxation training and hypnotic suggestion. *Journal of Abnormal Psychology*, 1969*a*, **74**, 425–437.

Paul, G. L. Inhibition of physiological response to stressful imagery by relaxation training and hypnotically suggested relaxation. *Behavior Research and Therapy*, 1969*b*, **7**, 249–256.

Pavlov, I. P. The identity of inhibition with sleep and hypnosis. *Scientific Monthly*, 1923, **17**, 603–608.

Pavlov, I. P. *Conditioned Reflexes, An Investigation of the Physiological Activity of the Cerebral Cortex*. London: Oxford University Press, 1927.

Pavlov, I. P. *Lectures on Conditioned Reflexes*. Translated by W. Horsley Gantt. New York: International Publishers, 1928*a*.

Pavlov, I. P. *Lectures on Conditioned Reflexes: Twenty-five Years of Objective Study of the Higher Nervous System Activity (Behavior) of Animals*. Translated and edited by W. Horsley Gantt. New York: Liveright Publishing Corp., 1928*b*.

Pavlov, I. P. *Lectures on Conditioned Reflexes, Vol. 2: Conditioned Reflexes and Psychiatry*. Translated and edited by W. Horsley Gantt. New York: International Publishers, 1941.

Pavlov, I. P. *Selected Works*. Moscow: Foreign Languages Publishing House, 1955.

Pederson, L. L.; Scrimgeour, W. G.; & Lefcoe, N. M. Comparison of hypnosis plus counseling, counseling alone, and hypnosis alone in a community service smoking withdrawal program. *Journal of Consulting and Clinical Psychology*, 1975, **43**, 920.

Pederson, L. L.; Scrimgeour, W. G., & Lefcoe, N. M. Variables of hypnosis which are related to success in a smoking withdrawal program. *International Journal of Clinical and Experimental Hypnosis*, 1979, **27**, 14–20.

Perkins, J. Hypnosis and migraine. *British Journal of Clinical Hypnosis*, 1975, **5**, 121–125.

Pessin, M.; Plapp, J. M., & Stern, J. A. Effects of hypnosis induction and attention direction on electrodermal responses. *American Journal of Clinical Hypnosis*, 1968, **10**, 198–206.

Peters, J. E.; Lundy, R. M.; & Stern, R. M. Peripheral skin temperature responses to hot and cold suggestions. *International Journal of Clinical and Experimental Hypnosis,* 1973, 21, 205–212.

Peters, J. E. & Stern, R. M. Peripheral skin temperature and vasomotor responses during hypnotic induction. *International Journal of Clinical and Experimental Hypnosis,* 1973, **21,** 102–108.

Plapp, J. M. Hypnosis, conditioning and physiological responses. Ph.D. dissertation, Washington University. Ann Arbor, Mich.: University Microfilms, 1967.

Plapp, J. M. & Edmonston, W. E., Jr. Extinction of a conditioned motor response following hypnosis. *Journal of Abnormal and Social Psychology,* 1965, **70,** 378–382.

Plapp, J. M.; Edmonston, W. E., Jr.; & Lieberman, L. R. To what should hypnosis be compared? The problem of appropriate experimental controls: A symposium. *American Journal of Clinical Hypnosis,* 1972, **14,** 209–235.

Platonov, K. I., ed. *The Word as a Physiological and Therapeutic Factor: Problems of Theory and Practice of Psychotherapy on the Basis of the Theory of I. P. Pavlov.* Translated from 2nd Russian edition (1955) by D. A. Myshne. Moscow: Foreign Languages Publishing House, 1959.

Povorinskii, Iu. A. Vliianie emotsial'nogo sostoianiia na sosudodvigadel'nye reaktsii. (The influence of an emotional condition on the vasodilatation reaction.) *Problemy kortiko-vistseral'noi Patologii,* 1949.

Puységur, LeComte Maxime de Chastenet de. *Rapport des Cures Opérées a Bayonne par le Magnétisme Animal* (Sept. 20, 1784). In Tinterow, M. M., ed. *Foundations of Hypnosis from Mesmer to Freud.* Springfield, Ill.: Charles C Thomas, 1970. Pp. 58–72.

Puységur, Marquis de. *An Essay of Instruction on Animal Magnetism.* Translated by J. King. New York: J. C. Kelley, 1837.

Rachman, S. The role of muscular relaxation in desensitization therapy. *Behavior Research and Therapy,* 1968, **6,** 159–166.

Ratner, S. C. Comparative aspects of hypnosis. In Gordon, J. E., ed. *Handbook of Clinical and Experimental Hypnosis.* New York: Macmillan Co., 1967. Pp. 550–587.

Ravitz, L. J. Electrometric correlates of the hypnotic state. *Science,* 1950, **112,** 341–342.

Ravitz, L. J. The use of DC measurements in psychiatry. *Neuropsychiatry,* 1951a, **1,** 3–12.

Ravitz, L. J. Standing potential correlates of hypnosis and narcosis. *AMA Archives of Neurology & Psychiatry,* 1951b, **65,** 413–436.

Ravitz, L. J. History, measurement and applicability of periodic changes in the electromagnetic field in health and disease. *Annals of the New York Academy of Sciences,* 1962, **98,** 1144–1201. In Wolf, W. ed. *Rhythmic Functions in the Living System.*

Reid, A. F. & Curtsinger, G. Physiological changes associated with hypnosis: The effect of hypnosis on temperature. *International Journal of Clinical and Experimental Hypnosis,* 1968, **16,** 111–119.

Reyher, J. Can hypnotized subjects simulate waking behavior? *American Journal of Clinical Hypnosis*, 1973, **16**, 31−36.

Reyher, J. & Wilson, J. G. The induction of hypnosis: Indirect vs. direct methods and the role of anxiety. *American Journal of Clinical Hypnosis*, 1973, **15**, 229−233.

Richet, C. *L'homme et l'Intelligence*. Paris: Alcan, 1884. In Hilgard, E. R. *Hypnotic Susceptibility*. New York: Harcourt, Brace & World, 1965. P. 73.

Rogers, S. L. Early psychotherapy. *CIBA Symposium*, 1947, **9**, 602−632.

Rosen, G. From Mesmerism to hypnotism. *CIBA Symposium*, 1948, **9**, 838−844.

Rosenhan, D. & London, P. Hypnosis in the unhypnotizable: A study in rote learning. *Journal of Experimental Psychology*, 1963, **65**, 30−34.

Sanders, S. Mutual group hypnosis and smoking. *American Journal of Clinical Hypnosis*, 1977, **20**, 131−135.

Sarbin, T. R. Physiological effects of hypnotic stimulation. In Dorcus, R. M., ed. *Hypnosis and Its Therapeutic Applications*. New York: McGraw-Hill, 1956. Pp. 4/1−4/57.

Sarbin, T. R. & Slagle, R. W. Hypnosis and psychophysiological outcomes. In Fromm, E. & Shor, R. E., eds. *Hypnosis: Research Developments and Perspectives*. Chicago: Aldine-Atherton, 1972. Pp. 185−214.

Sarbin, T. R. & Slagle, R. W. Hypnosis and psychophysiological outcomes. In Fromm, E. & Shor, R. E., eds. *Hypnosis: Developments in Research and New Perspectives*, (2nd ed.) New York: Aldine Publishing Co., 1979, Pp. 273−303.

Sargent, J. D.; Green, E. E.; & Walters, E. D. Preliminary report on the use of autogenic feedback training in the treatment of migraine and tension headaches. *Psychosomatic Medicine*, 1973, **35**, 129−135.

Schneck, J. M. The school of the Hospital de la Charité in the history of hypnosis. *Journal of the History of Medicine and Allied Sciences*, 1953, **7**, 271−279.

Schneck, J. M. Jean-Martin Charcot and the history of experimental hypnosis. *Journal of the History of Medicine and Allied Sciences*, 1961, **16**, 297−305.

Schultz, H. A. & Luthe, W. *Autogenic Therapy: A Psychophysiological Approach to Psychotherapy*. New York: Grune & Stratton, 1959.

Schwarz, B. E.; Bickford, R. G.; & Rasmussen, W. C. Hypnotic phenomena, including hypnotically activated seizures, studied with the electroencephalogram. *Journal of Nervous and Mental Disease*, 1955, **122**, 564−574.

Scott, H. D. Hypnosis and the conditioned reflex. *Journal of General Psychology*, 1930, **4**, 113−130.

Sears, A. B. The measurement of somatic changes occurring in the medium-trance-state of hypnosis as compared with relaxed "normal" state. Unpublished research report, University of Minnesota, 1953.

Sears, A. B. & Beatty, J. M. A comparison of the galvanic skin response in the hypnotic and waking state. *International Journal of Experimental and Clinical Hypnosis*, 1956, **4**, 49−60.

Shafii, M.; Lavely, R. A.; & Jaffe, R. D. Meditation and marijuana. *American Journal of Psychiatry*, 1974, **131**, 60−63.

Shafii, M.; Lavely, R. A.; & Jaffe, R. Meditation and the prevention of alcohol abuse. *American Journal of Psychiatry*, 1975, **132**, 942–945.

Sheehan, P. W. & Perry, C. W. *Methodologies of Hypnosis: A Critical Appraisal of Contemporary Paradigms of Hypnosis*. Hillsdale, N.J.: Erlbaum, 1976.

Shor, R. E. The fundamental problem in hypnosis research as viewed from historical perspectives. In Fromm, E. & Shor, R. E., eds. *Hypnosis: Research Developments and Perspectives*. Chicago: Aldine-Atherton, 1972. Pp. 15–40.

Shor, R. E. & Orne, E. C. *Harvard Group Scale of Hypnotic Susceptibility*. Palo Alto, Calif.: Consulting Psychologists Press, 1962.

Shpil'berg, P. I. Human electroencephalography during sleep and hypnosis. In *The Central Nervous System and Human Behavior—Translations from the Russian Medical Literature*. Bethesda, Md.: U.S. Department of Health, Education & Welfare, 1959. Pp. 671–684.

Slotnick, R. S. & London, P. Influence of instructions on hypnotic and non-hypnotic performance. *Journal of Abnormal Psychology*, 1965, **70**, 38–46.

Smith, W. H. The effects of hypnosis and suggestion on auditory threshold. *Journal of Speech & Hearing Research*, 1969, **12**, 161–168.

Smith-Moorhouse, P. M. Hypnosis in the treatment of alcoholism. *British Journal of Addiction*, 1969, **64**, 47–55.

Society for Clinical and Experimental Hypnosis. Resolution adopted October 1978. *International Journal of Clinical and Experimental Hypnosis*, 1979, **27**, 452.

Spanos, N. P. & Chaves, J. F. Hypnosis research: A methodological critique of experiments generated by two alternative paradigms. *American Journal of Clinical Hypnosis*, 1970, **13**, 108–127.

Spanos, N. P.; DeMoor, W.; & Barber, T. X. Hypnosis and behavior therapy: Common denominators. *American Journal of Clinical Hypnosis*, 1973, **16**, 45–64.

Spiegel, H. A single-treatment method to stop smoking using ancillary self-hypnosis. *International Journal of Clinical and Experimental Hypnosis*, 1970, **18**, 235–250.

Spiegel, H. *Manual for Hypnotic Induction Profile*. New York: Soni Medica, 1974.

Spiegel, H. & Bridger, A. A. *Manual for Hypnotic Induction Profile*. New York: Soni Medica, 1970.

Stambaugh, E. E. & House, A. E. Multimodality treatment of migraine headache: A case study utilizing biofeedback, relaxation, autogenic and hypnotic treatments. *American Journal of Clinical Hypnosis*, 1977, **19**, 235–240.

Stanton, H. E. A one-session hypnotic approach to modifying smoking behavior. *International Journal of Clinical and Experimental Hypnosis*, 1978, **26**, 22–29.

Stern, J. A.; Edmonston, W. E., Jr. Ulett, G. A.; & Levitsky, A. Electrodermal measures in experimental amnesia. *Journal of Abnormal and Social Psychology*, 1963, **67**, 397–401.

Strosberg, I. M. & Vics, I. I. Physiologic changes in the eye during hypnosis. *American Journal of Clinical Hypnosis*, 1962, **4**, 264–267.

Sutcliffe, J. P. "Credulous" and "skeptical" views of hypnotic phenomena. *International Journal of Clinical and Experimental Hypnosis*, 1960, **8**, 73–101.

Sutcliffe, J. P. "Credulous" and "skeptical" views of hypnotic phenomena: Experiments on esthesia, hallucination and delusion. *Journal of Abnormal and Social Psychology*, 1961, **62**, 189–200.

Talbert, G. A.; Ready, F. L. & Kuhlman, F. W. Plethysmographic and pneumographic observations made in hypnosis. *American Journal of Physiology*, 1924, **68**, 113.

Tamburini, A. & Seppelli, G. Contribution de l'étude experimentale de l'hypnotisme. *Archives of Italian Biology*, 1882, **2**, 273–277. (Cited by Jenness and Wible, 1937 & Walden, 1900–01.)

Tart, C. T. Hypnotic depth and basal skin resistance. *International Journal of Clinical and Experimental Hypnosis*, 1963, **11**, 81–92.

Tebecis, A. K. & Provins, K. A. Further studies of physiological concomitants of hypnosis: Skin temperature, heart rate and skin resistance. *Biological Psychology*, 1976, **4**, 249–258.

Tebecis, A. K.; Provins, M. A.; Farnbach, R. W.; and Pentony, P. Hypnosis and EEG. *Journal of Nervous and Mental Disease*, 1975, **161**, 1–17.

Teste, A. *A Practical Manual of Animal Magnetism*. Translated from 2nd ed. by D. Spillan. London: Hippolyte Baillière, 1843.

Timney, B. N. & Barber, T. X. Hypnotic induction and oral temperature. *International Journal of Clinical and Experimental Hypnosis*, 1969, **17**, 121–132.

Tinterow, M. M., ed. *Foundations of Hypnosis from Mesmer to Freud*. Springfield, Ill.: Charles C Thomas, 1970.

Travis, T. A.; Kondo, C. Y.; & Knott, J. R. Interaction of hypnotic suggestion and alpha enhancement. *Journal of Psychiatry*, 1973, **130**, 1389–1391.

Tsinkin, A. Objective signs of suggested sleep. 1930*a*. (Cited in Platonov, 1959.)

Tsinkin, A. Blood pressure in hypnosis (experimental investigation). *Psychoneurological Institute, Ukraine*, 1930*b*, **14**. (Cited in Platonov, 1959.)

Tsinkin, A. Pulse and respiration during normal waking and hypnosis (experimental investigation). *Psychoneurological Institute, Ukraine*, 1930*c*, **14**. (Cited in Platonov, 1959.)

Vingoe, F. J. The development of a group alert-trance scale. *International Journal of Clinical and Experimental Hypnosis*, 1968, **16**, 120–132.

Vingoe, F. J. Introversion-extroversion, attitudes toward hypnosis, and susceptibility to the alert trance. *Proceedings of 77th Annual Convention of APA*, 1969, 903–904.

Vingoe, F. J. Comparison of the Harvard Group Scale of Hypnotic Susceptibility, Form A and the group alert trance scale in a university population. *International Journal of Clinical and Experimental Hypnosis*, 1973, **21**, 169–179.

Von Dedenroth, T. E. A. The use of hypnosis with "tobaccomaniacs." *American Journal of Clinical Hypnosis*, 1964*a*, **6**, 326–331.

Von Dedenroth, T. E. A. Further help for the "tobaccomaniac." *American Journal of Clinical Hypnosis*, 1964*b*, **6**, 332–336.

Von Dedenroth, T. E. A. Some newer ideas and concepts of alcoholism and the use of hypnosis. *British Journal of Medical Hypnosis*, 1965, **16**, 27.

Von Dedenroth, T. E. A. The use of hypnosis in 1000 cases of "tobaccomaniacs." *American Journal of Clinical Hypnosis*, 1968, **10**, 194—197.

Von Eiff, A. W. Ueber die moglichkeit einer grundumsatzsenkung durch psychische beeinflussung. *Aertzliche Forschung*, 1950, **4**, 611. (Abstract in *The Annual Review of Hypnosis Literature, 1953*. New York: The Society for Clinical & Experimental Hypnosis, 1953. Pp. 30—32.)

Wagstaff, G. F. A note on Mather and Degun's "A comparative study of hypnosis and relaxation." *British Journal of Medical Psychology*, 1976, **49**, 299—300.

Walden, E. C. A plethysmographic study of the vascular conditions during hypnotic sleep. *American Journal of Physiology*, 1900—01, **4**, 124—161.

Wallace, R. K. Physiological effects of transcendental meditation. *Science*, 1970, **167**, 1751—1754. Also in Orme-Johnson, D. W. & Farrow, J. T., eds. *Scientific Research on the Transcendental Meditation Program, Collected Papers, Vol. 1.* Rheinweiler, West Germany: Maharishi European Research University Press & Livingston, N.Y.: Maharishi International University Press.

Wallace, R. K. & Benson, H. The physiology of meditation. *Scientific American*, 1972, **226**, 85—90.

Wallace, R. K.; Benson, H.; & Wilson, A. F. A wakeful hypometabolic physiologic state. *American Journal of Physiology*, 1971, **221**, 797—799.

Walrath, L. C. & Hamilton, D. W. Autonomic correlates of meditation and hypnosis. *American Journal of Clinical Hypnosis*, 1975, **17**, 190—197.

Watkins, H. H. Hypnosis and smoking: A five-session approach. *International Journal of Clinical and Experimental Hypnosis*, 1976, **24**, 381—390.

Weitzenhoffer, A. M. A note on the persistence of hypnotic suggestion. *Journal of Abnormal and Social Psychology*, 1950, **45**, 160—162.

Weitzenhoffer, A. M. *Hypnotism: An Objective Study in Suggestibility*. New York: John Wiley & Sons, 1953.

Weitzenhoffer, A. M. Hypnosis and eye movements. A possible SEM correlate of hypnosis. *American Journal of Clinical Hypnosis*, 1969, **11**, 221—227.

Weitzenhoffer, A. M. Ocular changes in passive hypnosis. *American Journal of Clinical Hypnosis*, 1971, **14**, 102—121.

Weitzenhoffer, A. M. Behavior therapeutic techniques and hypnotherapeutic methods. *American Journal of Clinical Hypnosis*, 1972, **15**, 71—82.

Weitzenhoffer, A. M. & Brockmeier, J. D. Attention and eye movements. *Journal of Nervous and Mental Disease*, 1970, **151**, 130—142.

Weitzenhoffer, A. M. & Hilgard, E. R. *Stanford Hypnotic Susceptibility Scale, Forms A and B*. Palo Alto, Calif.: Consulting Psychologists Press, 1959.

Weitzenhoffer, A. M. & Hilgard, E. R. *Stanford Hypnotic Susceptibility Scale, Form C*. Palo Alto, Calif.: Consulting Psychologists Press, 1962.

Weitzenhoffer, A. M. & Hilgard, E. R. *Stanford Profile Scales of Hypnotic Susceptibility, Forms I and II*. Palo Alto, Calif.: Consulting Psychologists Press, 1963.

Weitzenhoffer, A. M. & Sjoberg, B. M. Suggestibility with and without "induction of hypnosis." *Journal of Nervous and Mental Disease*, 1961, **132**, 204—220.

Wells, W. R. Experiments in waking hypnosis for instructional purposes. *Journal of Abnormal and Social Psychology*, 1924, **18**, 389–404.

Wells, W. R. Expectancy versus performance in hypnosis. *Journal of General Psychology*, 1947, **35**, 99–119.

White, M. M. The physical and mental traits of individuals susceptible to hypnosis. *Journal of Abnormal and Social Psychology*, 1930, **25**, 293–298.

White. R. W. Two types of hypnotic trance and their personality correlates. *Journal of Psychology*, 1937, **3**, 279–289.

White, R. W. A preface to the theory of hypnotism. *Journal of Abnormal and Social Psychology*, 1941, **36**, 477–505.

Whitehorn, J. C.; Lundholm, H.; Fox, E. L.; & Benedict, F. G. The metabolic rate in "hypnotic sleep." *New England Journal of Medicine*, 1932, **206**, 777–781.

Wible, C. L. & Jenness, A. Electrocardiograms during sleep and hypnosis. *Journal of Psychology*, 1936, **1**, 235–245.

Wickramasekera, I. Electromyographic feedback training and tension headache: Preliminary observations. *American Journal of Clinical Hypnosis*, 1972, **15**, 83–85.

Wilder, J. F. *Stimulus and Response: The Law of Initial Value.* Baltimore, Md.: Williams & Wilkins, 1967.

Wittkower, E. Über Affektiv-Somatische Veranderungen. II. Mitteilung: Die Affektleukozytose. *Klinische Wochenschrift*, 1929, **8**, 1082. (Cited in Gorton, 1949.)

Wolberg, L. R. *Medical Hypnosis* (2 vols.). New York: Grune & Stratton, 1948.

Wolff, H. G. *Headache and Other Pain.* (2nd ed.) New York: Oxford University Press, 1963.

Wolpe, J. *Psychotherapy by Reciprocal Inhibition,* Stanford, Calif.: Stanford University Press, 1958.

Wolpe, J. *The Practice of Behavior Therapy.* New York: Pergamon Press, 1969.

Wolpe, J. & Lang, P. J. A fear survey schedule for use in behavior therapy. *Behavior Research and Therapy*, 1964, **2**, 27–30.

Wolpe, J. & Lazarus, A. A. *Behavior Therapy Techniques.* New York: Pergamon Press, 1967.

Wood, A. Contributions towards the study of certain phenomena, which have recently dominated experiments in electro-biology. *Monthly Journal of Mental Science*, 1851, **12**, 407–435.

Zitz, J. L. Evaluation of the relaxation response produced by EMG biofeedback. *Dissertation Abstracts*, 1978 (May), **38 (11-B)**, 5603–5604.

Zynkin, A. M. Krovianoye davleniye v gipnoze (Blood pressure in hypnosis). *Psikhoterapia*, 1930*a*, 123–140. (Cited in Jenness and Wible, 1937.)

Zynkin, A.M. Puls i dikhaniye v sostoyanii i v gipnoticheskom sostoyznii. (Pulse and respiration in waking and hypnotic states). *Psikhoterapia*, 1930*b*, 141–166. (Cited in Jenness and Wible, 1937.)

Index

Psychotherapy: An Eclectic Approach
  by Sol L. Garfield
Handbook of Minimal Brain Dysfunctions
  edited by Herbert E. Rie and Ellen D. Rie
Handbook of Behavioral Interventions: A Clinical Guide
  edited by Alan Goldstein and Edna B. Foa
Art Psychotherapy
  by Harriet Wadeson
Handbook of Adolescent Psychology
  edited by Joseph Adelson
Psychotherapy Supervision: Theory, Research and Practice
  edited by Allen K. Hess
Psychology and Psychiatry in Courts and Corrections: Controversy and Change
  by Ellsworth A. Fersch, Jr.
Restricted Environmental Stimulation: Research and Clinical Applications
  by Peter Suedfeld
Handbook of Clinical Neuropsychology
  edited by Susan B. Filskov and Thomas J. Boll
Personal Construct Psychology: Psychotherapy and Personality
  edited by Alvin W. Landfield and Larry M. Leitner
Handbook of Clinical Behavior Therapy
  edited by Samuel M. Turner, Karen S. Calhoun, and Henry E. Adams
Mothers, Grandmothers, and Daughters: Personality and Child-Care in `
Three-Generation Families
  by Bertram J. Cohler and Henry U. Grunebaum
Further Explorations in Personality
  edited by A. I. Rabin, Joel Aronoff, Andrew M. Barclay, and Robert A. Zucker
Hypnosis and Relaxation: Modern Verification of an Old Equation
  by William E. Edmonston, Jr.